KARMA
and the
DESTINY
of an
INDIAN AMERICAN SURGEON

∽

Navin C. Shah, MD

AMERICAN BAZAAR BOOKS
Germantown, Maryland

Copyright ©2022 Navin C. Shah, MD
All rights reserved.

Cover: Zainul Abid, Dzain
Book Design: Nujumudeen, Dzain

ISBN: 979-888757317-5

Printed and bound in India by Anaswara Offset (P) Ltd., Cochin

AMERICAN BAZAAR BOOKS
Germantown, Maryland

CONTENTS

Foreword 1:	Aziz Haniffa	v
Foreword 2:	Varghese K. George	xii
Preface		xvi
Chapter 1:	Early Life	1
Chapter 2:	A Brave and Scary Journey	53
Chapter 3:	AAPI and the Fight for Equality	96
Chapter 4:	Taking the Best of American Healthcare to India	139
Chapter 5:	Fight for Prostate Cancer Patients	193
Chapter 6:	A Lifelong Love Affair with Indian Coins	206
Chapter 7:	Family	225
Chapter 8:	A Spiritual Odyssey	243
About the Author		273

FOREWORD
— 1 —

When I joined *India Abroad*, the leading Indian/South Asian newspaper in the US in the early 1980s, as its Washington, DC, correspondent, my beat was to cover the Reagan administration and the US Congress vis-a-vis its ties with India, which at the time were still in the throes of the Cold War era. New Delhi was perceived by Washington as a surrogate of the erstwhile Soviet Union, and the relationship was essentially in the doldrums. This malaise was compounded by the fact that the US was solidly behind the military government in Pakistan, India's arch nemesis.

Beyond reporting on this foreign policy phenomenon, an integral part of my reporting mandate was to cover the burgeoning India American community, especially the professional fraternity, then dominated by the first wave of Indian physicians who had immigrated to the US in the late 1960s and 1970s. They essentially constituted the Indian American brand that is widely respected in many facets of the American ethos, be it science, technology, academia, the hospitality industry, politics, arts and culture, journalism, et al.

A few months into my tenure, Dr. Navin Shah, a founder of the American Association of Physicians of Indian Origin some years before, sought to apprise me of his nascent campaign to fight discrimination against foreign medical graduates (FMGs) who, to escape the xenophobia associated with the word 'foreign,' quickly rebranded themselves as international medical graduates (IMGs). He said it was basically a struggle for equality with US medical graduates in the areas of reciprocity in licensing, hospital privileges, residency and fellowship opportunities, promotions, etc., within organized medicine and the medical establishment.

That first meeting, and the scores of meetings, reportage and interviews, and other interactions that followed, metamorphosed into a professional relationship and a deep friendship and that has spanned nearly four decades. During this entire period, what I have found most endearing, inspiring, and motivating about Navin is his impeccable integrity, uncompromising self-discipline (at age eighty-seven, he is still doing five mile jogs at the break of dawn, never ever over-indulging in anything he does), his tangible and purposeful philanthropy (particularly toward the downtrodden in the US and India). He belongs to "the old school" but brings a refreshingly authentic perspective: what you see is what you get. And I could not but admire his scrupulous and unapologetic adherence to the tenants of his faith as a practicing Jain.

Navin has always been honest and candid in our conversations and interviews. The same was true of the IMG physicians he introduced me to, who had been subjected to one form of discrimination or other, as well as the lobbyists and state and national legislators he suggested I speak with, who took up his cause, fighting IMG discrimination. In these tough and probing conversations; I sought facts and required evidence-based claims with regard to their case studies, conducted extensive research, and double and treble-checked. Navin clearly acknowledged and appreciated that I had a job to do if my reports on their struggle were to be credible.

I firmly believe what Navin and his band of activists achieved in terms of equality for IMGs will be his enduring legacy in the US.

Hardly two decades had passed since these international physicians were welcomed with open arms to the US by hospital administrators across the country to alleviate a dire physician shortage (and even promised expeditious permanent residency or green cards on arrival). In addition to an acute need for healthcare in rural and indigent areas and the underserved and the vulnerable in the inner cities, this paucity had been compounded by the thousands of American doctors deployed to the war effort in Vietnam.

The *creme-de-la-creme* of the professional class from India, Pakistan, Sri Lanka, and other parts of South and Southeast Asia, i.e., the Philippines, had been the backbone of healthcare providers in the oft-neglected rural areas in the heartland of American for nearly two decades. Their departure to the US when they left the shores of their native countries in an unprecedented exodus had been bemoaned at the time as "a brain-drain."

To think that these IMGs were suddenly being treated so shabbily by the medical establishment and organized medicine, led by the American Medical Association, was "un-American" at best. IMGs were now considered second-class physicians, unworthy of reciprocity in licensing, promotion, hospital privileges, residency, fellowships, and other options afforded to their US medical counterparts. The veracity of their qualifications and credentials were now questioned. IMGs were subjected to what were clearly civil and economic rights violations.

I was in awe of Navin's chutzpah to take on these "powers that be," whatever the consequences, despite being only a few years into his own practice and with a young family. He faced a flurry of criticism from naysayers in his own physician community and their "why rock the boat" hesitancy to take on a Goliath that could quickly devour them with all the resources and power at their disposal.

Navin's grit, determination, and unrelenting and indefatigable energy to keep going albeit the trials, tribulations, and disappointments (which were many and all too regular) inspired me and triggered my passion about this story. The struggle kept me (day after day, week after week, month after month, and year after year) investigating, and disseminating to our readership an imperative to catalyze a critical mass who would ultimately affect change, using all of the tools and basic fairness that America offers.

Perhaps it could be argued that I stumbled onto a corresponding avatar of advocacy journalism. As both an immigrant and minority, I could easily empathize with the struggle Navin and other international physicians were engaged in; and if it was advocacy journalism, so be it. Sustained reportage of this campaign by a minority specialty group fighting discrimination that had gone largely unnoticed is what finally got the mainstream media to pay attention and take up the issue.

Wall Street Journal reporter, Ken Bacon, who also began covering this issue, later wrote in his foreword to *Fight for Equality: International Medical Graduates in the United*

States by Shawn McMahon in 2005, "Today, Dr. Shah and other leaders of the fight for equality can rightfully claim victory in their crusade for civil and economic rights. Like all civil rights leaders, their achievements have made it easier for the people who follow them. It is important that newly arriving international medical graduates understand the struggle that has made it easier for them to practice medicine in the US.... Finally, it is important for all Americans to see once again that our political system works, but that success requires planning, patience, and persistence."

Success to Navin and his "disparate group of new citizens," the majority of whom where reticent, nay fearful, at the beginning to take on the entrenched establishment and jeopardize their future and seemed resigned and willing to live in a perpetual state of subservience with all the ignominies they were being subjected to, ultimately coalesced. As Bacon wrote, they "learned to use the American political system to win recognition and protection that their own profession refused to grant them."

The Health Professions Reauthorization Act of 1992, signed by President George H. W. Bush, was a first in terms of legislative victory by a specialty Indian American group successfully lobbying US Congress to address their issues and concerns and prevail over the organized medicine arrayed against them with their own powerful team of lobbyists constantly roaming the corridors of Capitol Hill.

Appreciating the early challenges and struggles faced by the pioneering leaders of AAPI, Dr. Ravi Kolli, the president of AAPI as it enters its fortieth year as arguably the largest and most-influential international medical organization in the US, declared, "We are eternally thankful to our senior AAPI leaders who fought hard to end discrimination against IMGs and achieved parity of having the same USMLE (US Medical Licensing Examination) for all medical graduates for state medical licensures as well as for residency training program requirements."

He said, "Our senior AAPI leaders have been a great source of reliable support and encouragement, and every conversation and interaction with them has been educational and inspirational. I pledge to build upon their legacy to keep AAPI relevant and in the forefront in fighting any semblance of discrimination, microaggressions, and inequity across all walks of healthcare and medical education opportunities."

While this fight for equality for IMGs necessarily constitutes the heart of Navin's amazing American journey and legacy, other chapters form the soul of this terrific autobiography that projects that versatility and talents of this multifaceted man. I am so glad that I and my colleague, Asif Ismail, were able to convince him to trace this account that is permeated with such a surfeit of joy, passion, humor, and poignancy.

I would be remiss if I didn't mention how emotional I felt at Navin's moving and touching homage to his wife Leela. I was blessed and privileged to have interacted with Leela for over a decade before she left us all too early at age fifty-four. She was the personification of grace, caring, humility, and simplicity, enhanced by a mischievous albeit refreshing sense of humor that kept us all who interacted with her grounded in reality—sterling qualities that are manifest in their wonderful, multitalented, and erudite children and grandchildren.

Navin has described Leela as his "anchor, friend, partner, and manager for life," and as "a pure and clean soul." She was all of that and then some, and I was witness to much of it in real time. Leela was also the driving force behind Navin and his family's philanthropic endeavors in a plethora of diverse areas in the US and India/South Asia. I remember fondly and nostalgically accompanying the Shahs and their young kids to the Washington, DC, shelters and soup kitchens, including the Community for Creative Non-Violence in conjunction with the Jain celebration of Mahavir Jayanti—a first by a new immigrant family in the Washington metropolitan area.

Every immigrant has a story to tell, and many are unique and serendipitous. This chronicler of the Indian American/South Asian American immigration experience for the past four decades finds Navin Shah's story a beautiful and inspiring contribution to the growing anthology that continues to enhance the mosaic that is America!

Thank you, Navin.

—**Aziz Haniffa** is the cofounder and executive editor of DesiMaxTV.com, a South Asian streaming service; and former executive editor of *India Abroad*.

FOREWORD
— 2 —

Climbing the Faith Mountain

Dr. Navin Shah is always brimming with new ideas and bracing for fresh action. His interests include numismatics to philosophy, and politics to strategy. Being a surgeon of outstanding credentials, Dr. Shah's knowledge of his field is reassuring and mesmerizing for anyone who meets him, patient or friend. Straddling the many worlds that fascinate him, Dr. Shah enriches anyone who comes in touch with him. Dr. Shah inspires, motivates, and lights up the minds that cross his. Having been a recipient of his warmth, hospitality, and kindness over the years that I stayed in the US, I read this memoir with great joy and pride.

At eighty-seven, Dr. Shah is not hanging up his boot, or the white coat for that matter, with this book. It is more of a midterm assessment of a rich life—and I wish him many more of such productive and fulfilling decades. *Karma and the Destiny of an Indian American Surgeon* has an adorable style of storytelling and a breezy prose that might make professional writers jealous, but would amaze all readers. Dr. Shah's sharp mind, harmless wit, and supreme positivity shine through these pages. I have rarely come across an autobiography in which the protagonist sits so softly, with no air of self-importance or hubris, like Dr. Shah's. He is a participant in and a witness to many epochal events; he is also a seeker of new realms, and a believer in many causes, but in all these pursuits, his own footsteps are gentle and calm. He retraces those steps effortlessly here.

Dr. Shah tells us, through his life, that the biggest of the obstacles can be overcome; beginnings do not foreclose the options of varied destinations. But he is also a believer in destiny, a purveyor of the spiritual and the ascetic. His house in Maryland in the suburbs of Washington, DC, where he stays alone, is not a lonely place; it is buzzing with ideas and inescapable energy. Walk in there, through his book, and it welcomes you with the same warmth that Dr. Shah's guests receive.

Though now cliched, there is no better explanation for the relative success of Indian Americans than their ability to synergize Indian and American traits. But Dr. Shah's life is exceptional, though his story too has that universal component of arriving in the US with eight dollars in pocket. Actually a correction—in his case, he left India with eight dollars, but landed in the US with $58, adding $50 along the way! You will read here how.

Dr. Shah welds the spiritual with the material, the scientific with the metaphysical, and the abstract with the precise. Dr. Shah has an inspiring capacity to transcend theses binaries, and more. He would be talking to you one moment about the latest breakthroughs in cancer surgery and Jainism the next; about managing personal finances one moment to being a truly social animal the next. Dr. Shah is not merely Indian and American; he's Gujarati and he's Jain.

In his humility and stoicism, there is no severance from ambition and perseverance. There is always more to be done, not for personal glory, but that is what duty demands. There is more distance to be walked, more barriers to be crossed, more peaks to be climbed and patients to be healed. In his persona, all these contradictory pursuits that would have wrecked normal people, gather well, and nourish his journey.

These pages throw light on the serendipity that lightened his path. The deep awareness that there is something that is beyond planning, though that is no reason to not plan, reflects in this account. Networking and brilliance are all fine, but providence is no less important in Dr. Shah's journey. The abrupt exit of Leela, his wife for three decades, is narrated with such poise and grace that only an elevated mind such as Dr. Shah's can command. Leela's entry into his poverty-stricken home from her own affluent milieu had changed the lives of both. Dr. Shah brings her to life in these pages, laced with anecdotes that sit between self-awareness and social commentary and humor.

Anxiety and trepidation rose as the plane carrying him climbed to cruising heights, Dr. Shah recalls... in his journey to the US from India in 1971. But the vastness and diversity of America welcomed him with open arms. He would go on to build two parallel lives—one in India, around his parents and extended family, and in service of the motherland, a politically very loaded concept these days; the other in his adapted country, where he struggled hard to adapt, and negotiate the contradictory requirements of the US system that wanted more and more professionals from abroad and, at the same time, kept them lower, at the foot of the ladder, through professional barriers and archaic regulations. On the one hand, he was looking back at the challenges in India and what interventions could bring improvement; on the other, he was striving to push back against the blatant discrimination in the governance of the medical profession in the US. His battles that turned out to be decisively successful would make the path less torturous for the generation of doctors that followed him. Dr. Shah's son, the youngest of his three children, is a doctor, an emergency physician. His eldest daughter is a lawyer and the second daughter is a business executives. The success that he could achieve in reforming the restrictive regulatory framework did not repeat when it came to his efforts to bring the medical communities of India and the US closer. Those ideas and his untiring efforts continue to remain entangled in old mindsets.

Success sits lightly on his shoulders. A life of nearly nine decades cannot be devoid of pitfalls, dark moments, and utter frustration. But in these pages you will not see regret, avarice, jealousy, or bitterness. His ability to tell a story with the precision and the level of detail that you will see here may be just an extension of his life as a surgeon. Having read this, and being a witness to this journey albeit shortly, I can assure you that it will be worth your while. And money.

—**Varghese K. George** is the resident editor of *The Hindu* in Delhi, and former Washington correspondent of the paper. He is the author of *Open Embrace: India-US Ties in a Divided World.*

PREFACE

After I was interviewed for *The Trailblazers*, which premiered on Amazon Prime in 2019, hosted by Aziz Haniffa, editor of *India Abroad*, and produced by Asif Ismail, publisher of *The American Bazaar*, both suggested that I pen a book about my life. Not long after that, the COVID-19 pandemic slowed my medical practice almost to a standstill, which gave me time to review almost two-hundred published stories and interviews about me and my multiple initiatives and projects since first coming to the US in 1971.

Coming to America from India was unplanned and serendipitous. On a few occasions I had traveled out of Pune but never out of India. My childhood, education, surgery training and practice, and my marriage, all took place in Poona (After 1978, Poona was called Pune). Before my practice took off, I was offered a residency position and free ticket to travel to America. I accepted my destiny with a fear of an unknown future.

After completing urology residency in 1975, I started a urology practice in the Washington, DC, metro area. Since then, I have lived in the same house in Potomac, and my practice has flourished. I also became an activist of sorts—another unplanned and serendipitous outcome that evolved out of a desire to counter injustices to foreign medical graduates in the US, and to improve the condition of healthcare, medical education, and research in India.

With the willing help of Indian American doctors, American medical institutions, and various collaborations, and after decades of pursuits with federal and state governments, some intermittent and incremental successes were achieved. In that regard, I have been fortunate in receiving the support of presidents, prime ministers, health ministers, health secretaries, officials of the Medical Council of India, and others in India for my health projects to uplift India.

As a urologist, my priority has been on the early diagnosis and treatment of prostate cancer. Since 2012 the number of prostate cancer cases, deaths, and costs are on the rise. I have lobbied strongly to address this issue, published six papers and twelve letters to the editors of US urology journals.

I am grateful to the US lawmakers, senators and representatives, my colleagues and lobbyists fighting for equality for international medical graduates and for appropriate medical care to diagnose and treat early prostate cancer in the US. I cherish and appreciate all positions and awards bestowed upon me over the years.

My thanks to all the journalists in the US and in India for the many interviews and stories about my projects and initiatives. My special thanks to Aziz Haniffa who covered my work over four decades; Asif Ismail who provided his time, encouragement, and interest in this book; and my friend and attorney Donald Seifman for his ongoing guidance since 1975.

My gratitude and love to my family members, especially my daughters, Shefali (Tony) and Sonali; my son Amit, and my nephew Hemant, for helping me in this undertaking.

I have tried my best to accurately record the events described in this book, and I ask you to please forgive me for any inadvertent errors or misrepresentations. I will continue to work on all the unfinished projects as long as my karma and destiny allow!

—**Navin C. Shah**, MD

CHAPTER 1

EARLY LIFE

Throughout my childhood, my little brother's health was a serious concern for my family. Vinod, four years younger than I, fell sick frequently. By the time he turned ten, he had suffered two typhoid infections, a bout of gastrointestinal bleeding, and diphtheria. Whenever Vinod was sick, my father took him to Dr. Vasant Chinchankar, who ran a four-room clinic a block from our home. The doctor knew we were poor; he never charged my father any consultation fee, and any medicines he gave us were also free.

Dr. Chinchankar was the go-to allopathic doctor, and not just for our family. He treated several other poor families in the neighborhood without charging a fee. Only a handful of allopathic doctors practiced in Poona Camp in the 1940s. Many Camp residents also went to practitioners of alternative forms of medicine such as Ayurveda (an ancient holistic Indian system of healing) and Unani (traditional Persian-Arabic medicine) practitioners. But when people were very sick, they almost always preferred to go to allopathic doctors who were able to prescribe medications and sometimes surgery.

Every day, I walked past Dr. Chinchankar's clinic on Center Street at least twice on my way to and from GKH Mandal High School, where I studied from the first to eleventh grades. I always saw patients lined up in front of the clinic waiting to be called in by the physician's assistant. The good doctor had two employees: a compounder named Madhu who mixed the medicines and handed them over to patients, and an assistant who took care of dressings and sterilizations. Madhu also collected fees. He was particularly popular among us children because he did standup comedy for many years as part of the annual *Ganesh Chaturthi*. The festival, which marks the arrival of Ganesh (or Ganpati, the elephant god), was celebrated with great enthusiasm in Poona and across the region.

In many ways, the clinic was my first peek into the medical profession, and Dr. Chinchankar my first role model. My parents always talked about the doctor's generosity and kindness. The doctor often went out of his way to help poor people. On one occasion when I was in tenth grade, Vinod had severe rectal bleeding. Besides referring him to a specialist in Mumbai, a big city nearly 120 miles to the northwest of Poona, Dr. Chinchankar helped my father make arrangements to see the specialist there.

Dr. Chinchankar was a Marathi doctor from a "backward" community. Caste, wealth, and class were defining parts of one's identity in those days. Socially, my father and Dr. Chinchankar were not peers by any definition. Father, a salesman at a clothes store, relentlessly struggled to put food on table; and Dr. Chinchankar was an affluent doctor. But they were friends. One of my father's qualities that impressed me early on was his ability to connect with people despite their very different social status. He easily made friends with rich businessmen and educated people.

Dr. Chinchankar once invited my family to attend the wedding of a close relative in Hyderabad, 350 miles to the east of Poona. The doctor rented a whole train car for us and other guests from Poona to travel to the wedding. He took care of all the expenses. That was one of my first long train journeys.

A heavyset bespectacled man already in his sixties, Dr. Chinchankar was a fine clinician who was deeply committed to the ethics of the medical profession. His kindness and willingness to help others impressed me at a young age. If there is one person who inspired me most to become a physician, it was him—but not by anything he taught me in words. The manner in which he conducted himself and the way he was kind to people in general touched a chord in me. Like Dr. Chinchankar, I wanted to become a doctor and help the poor.

This goal also aligned well with my Jain faith. I was raised as a Jain. A fundamental tenet of the religion, along with practice of nonviolence and truth, is service to others. To be in service to poor people would bring me the gods' blessings. I knew also that, if I become a doctor, I could move upward economically and climb the social ladder, uplifting my family as well in the process.

The idea of becoming a doctor had already germinated in my mind when I was in elementary school and grew on me little by little every time I walked past Dr. Chinchankar's clinic—and every time we took Vinod and/or my sister Aruna (six years younger to me) to him for treatment. Eventually, the dream and desire to become a doctor became integral to my psyche.

When I passed the Secondary School Certificate (SSC) exam, Dr. Chinchankar gave me a unique gift: a membership of the reputed Albert Edward Institute Library in Poona Camp. At that library, I first read international magazines like *Life*, *Look*, and *Time*. Unfortunately, Dr. Chinchankar did not live to see me become a doctor. He died when I was in pre-med, a two-year intermediate degree program offered in college that was required before attending a medical college. A year later, when I got accepted to the B.J. Medical College, one of the first individuals I shared the news with, outside of my immediate family, was his son, Prabhakar Chinchankar, who was working at the Handloom House in Bombay at the time. He congratulated me and said, "My father would be very happy in heaven."

Entry to the World

My grandfather, Chunilal Shah, moved to Poona in 1912 from Umta, a small village in the princely state of Baroda in western India. He brought his wife, Hiraben, and their three children: sons Chimanlal and Shantilal, and daughter Jasudben. Chimanlal, who was born in Jaska, roughly three miles from Umta, was barely five. Generations of Shahs, including Chunilal's father Hakamchand, grandfather Maneklal, and great-grandfather Devchand, all lived in and around Umta. The village, located in the present-day Mehsana district, roughly 60 miles to the north of Ahmadabad, the capital of Gujarat, is known for the historic Jain temple, Rajgadhi Timbo.

However, for Chunilal, a Jain born into a trading family, Umta did not offer much in terms of economic opportunities. At the age of twenty-five, he decided to move with his family to Poona, which at the time was a bustling military town and an industrial and commercial hub. Though predominantly Hindu and Marathi, Poona was very diverse and cosmopolitan in the early twentieth century. A large number of Muslims, Christians, Parsis, and Jews also lived in the region. What attracted Chunilal to the Poona area was the presence of a sizable number of prosperous Gujarati Jains, who mainly engaged in trade and business. The city's main Jain temple was 400 years old. I used to visit that temple on religious occasions, mainly during Paryushan, when all Jains pray and seek forgiveness for eight days.

The Shahs settled in Poona Camp, a military cantonment just outside Poona City. Built by the British in the early nineteenth century as military quarters for the soldiers, the cantonment is a small town in itself. Though initially built for soldiers, civilians have been living and working in Poona Camp from the beginning.

My father Chimanlal and uncle Shantilal started afresh in their new home in Poona Camp. Both boys studied only up to middle school, after which they started working as salespeople at clothing stores. Grandpa Chunilal knew the trustee of the local Jain temple, who was a friend of Keshavlal Shah, a clothing shop owner. He recommended Shah to hire my father. The shop, which mainly sold woolen materials, was one of several clothing stores on Center Street near our home. My father worked in that store for more than two decades, during some of the most productive years of his life.

Uncle Shantilal also started his career as a salesperson. At his first job, he taught himself English, which gave him an opportunity to advance his career. Soon he became an accountant at the Imperial Hosiery Store on Main Street owned by a Jewish businessman. From there, he joined a large construction company as a manager and accountant.

Years later, he landed in London. Jasudben, their sister and my aunt, was married to a rich diamond merchant in Mumbai, and she relocated to the city with him.

My father married my mother, Lilawati Balaram Doshi, in 1932. On their wedding day, my mother was seventeen, and my father was twenty-five. Lilawati was born in 1915, in Kolhapur, 140 miles south of Poona. She had a rough start in life, having lost both parents, Balaram and Muliben, at a young age. She and her two siblings were raised by her grandmother, Jakorma.

Like my paternal grandfather Chunilal, my maternal grandpa Balaram was also a Gujarati Jain. He moved to Kolhapur from Karbatia, roughly 10 miles to the east of Umta. My mother's family was much more affluent than my father's. Grandpa Balaram had an Ayurveda shop, which was taken over by his brother after his death. But his son, my uncle, Hirabhai Doshi, launched his own business, a wholesale and retail grocery store in Kolhapur. He sold rice, wheat, corn, *bajra* (a course-grain), turmeric, chili, and other condiments.

Initially Grandpa Chunilal owned a jewelry shop and employed a goldsmith. Later on, he became a manager of a gold store, Tuljaram and Sons. Chunilal knew members of the Balaram family, which was how the family alliance was crystallized. Despite the wealth gap, my parents got married because both were Jains.

My entry to the world on January 2, 1935, was at my maternal uncle Hirabhai's house in Kolhapur. The age-old tradition was that the first child was delivered in the mother's home. For my parents, who were struggling to make both ends meet with the meager salary of my father, the decision was also financially sound. Both parents and paternal grandparents thought my mother and the baby would be better off under the care of Great-grandma Jakorma.

I remained in Kolhapur for more than two years, though my mother went back to Poona a few months after the delivery. Even now, the southern Maharashtra town, known for leather *chappals* (slippers), holds a special place in my heart. I vividly remember all the annual trips I made to Kolhapur during summer holidays. Great-grandma Jakorma used to give me nice clothes, feed me delicious food, and shower me with love and affection.

When I was two, my parents came to Kolhapur to take me back to Poona Camp. From the inland, hilly terrain of Kolhapur, I relocated to the city I called home for the next thirty-two years. That was, in essence, my first immigrant experience.

Crushing Poverty

My father's job as a salesperson at Keshavlal Shah's clothing store barely kept us fed and sheltered. During the more than a decade he worked at the store, his salary only increased from 70 rupees a month to 135 rupees a month. It kept us above absolute poverty, but only by a nose.

My most enduring childhood memory is living in a *chawl* in one room that was shared with my brother, sister, and parents. A chawl is a typical low-income residential building that has long rows of tiny rooms in living quarters, rising from two to four floors. At the end of the corridor on each floor were common toilets shared by all residents. From age three to fifteen, we lived on a chawl on Kedari Road at a locality called Bhopla Chowk. Our building, 416 Kedari Road, was at the end of Center Street, a commercial hub within Poona

Camp. We were in Room #10 of a two-story building. Besides us, there were nine other families. On the ground floor were five stores. The entire building had only three toilets and two water taps for all the families and stores.

Every household had its own kitchen. Chawls have certain characteristics of a commune. Your life is so open within the premises, and people generally looked after one another. I retain no resentment, or remembrance of any dreadful misfortune there; a slice of that chawl remains in me. Its frenetic energy and the hybrid fragrance of various cuisines still surround me.

By far, I was the poorest student in my class, a feeling that made me a little down from time to time. Even though I was aware of and was very concerned about indigence, the first time I was forced to face it publicly was when I entered the middle school. GKHM School was a private school. Every student had to pay the tuition, which was approximately three rupees a month. Students were required to pay it on the last day of the month.

For my father, even three rupees was a substantial amount. So at the beginning of middle school, he spoke to Bulakhidas Shah, the chairman and trustee of the board of GKHM, and requested tuition assistance for me. Mr. Shah was a rich businessman, who owned a wholesale clothing store in the neighborhood and served as an agent of Madras Cotton Mills, a large textile company. His daughter, Sulochana Shah, was in my class. He and other members of the Mandal management agreed to waive most of my tuition. Instead of three rupees, I was required to pay only half a rupee, or eight *annas* (a currency unit during the British Raj, one-sixteenth of a rupee). Those of us whose fee was reduced were called *maafee* students.

While the cutback in tuition was a big relief for my family, it was a social embarrassment for me. On the last day of the month, the teacher called the name of each student and collected the fee one by one. Once the names of all students who were paying the full fee were called, the teacher would call the maafee students. Most of the time, I was the only one in the category. Nearly everyone else paid full fee, as most students enrolled in the school came from various Gujarati business communities. On the last day of every month, I helplessly got ready to encounter the shame.

But I also knew that it was part of my life and existence as a student from a poor family. From fifth grade to eleventh grade (seven years), my *maafee* status continued. In my heart, I constantly thanked the school authorities for allowing me in the school and providing me an almost-free education. Fortunately, none of my classmates (most of whom were rich) made fun of me for my poverty.

Besides the maafi experience, there was another practice that symbolized and indicated the level of poverty my family was experiencing. All five members of my family used to attend the big *pooja* (worship ritual) that our local Jain temple conducted twice a month. At the end of the pooja, every devotee was given a *prasad*, (gracious gift) which contained sweets, almonds, and coconuts. My mother used one or two coconuts for dishes and desserts, and we routinely sold the remaining ones back to the store that supplied them to the temple for half the price.

My family's destitute status was reflected in most aspects of my school life. From fifth grade onward, I was required to wear the school uniform, which was *khaki* (brownish-yellow) shorts made of cotton, and white shirts. I had only two pairs that I wore on alternate days. My mother washed a pair every day so I could wear a clean pair the next day. Over time, the shorts had multiple holes as a result of constantly scraping against the rough wooden bench I sat on. My mother stitched the holes with patches. The night before special school occasions, I kept the trousers under my pillow so that wrinkles were removed and looked like they were pressed. We had no money to buy an iron box, or pay a laundry man for pressing.

Our one-room chawl on Kedari Road did not have electricity for years. When my family moved to my grandfather's chawl in 1953, while I was in college, we finally got to live in an electrified house. Grandpa's house, also in a chawl, was on Center Street, not far from our first home. Even though we now had electricity, power was available only for a few hours, usually between 7:00 and 11:00 p.m. Nonetheless, with two rooms, an attic and a separate bathroom, Grandpa's home was a huge upgrade from our old one-room home.

My Universe

Until I was about fifteen, Poona Camp was my universe. In fact, it was my complete existence. I was a happy citizen of that little world. Located roughly three miles to the east of downtown Poona, adjacent to the old Poona City, and on the southern banks of the Mula Mutha River, the Camp spanned roughly 3,500 acres (a little over 5 square miles). By 1950, Poona Camp was home to close to 60,000. Poona City at the time had a population of 480,000.

Prior to the Indian Independence in 1947, much of the space within the camp was occupied by British military, but there was still plenty of real estate for me and other children for our activities. My school, temple, *gullies* (small lanes), and grounds where we played cricket and other sports were all within the camp.

During summer vacations, I visited our maternal grandmother's house in Kolhapur. In some summers, I visited another maternal uncle, Rajaram, who was practicing Ayurveda in Vadnagar, near Mehsana. Most Jains routinely undertook *jatras*, the obligatory pilgrimages to holy places, but my family being poor meant we didn't have the resources to go on such jatras.

Nonetheless, I was a happy kid.

Ours was a typical Indian family. Father, who I called Bhai, was the breadwinner. Mother, I called her Bun, was the devoted homemaker. Father's job at Keshavlal Shah's shop was tough. He worked hard, without enjoying any days off or vacations. The shop was on the Center Street, which was popularly known as Kapada Bazaar. (*Kapda* in Hindi means cloth.)

Mother was the axis around which the wheel of my family revolved. Although being from a reasonably rich family, who lived in a big house till marriage, she silently and dutifully adjusted to the pittance my father was earning. We could afford only a one-room home in a chawl.

We spoke Gujarati at home, though Marathi was the more-widely spoken language in the city and the region. In the early years, most of my friends in school and in the neighborhood were Gujaratis, and many were Jains. As I started acquiring Marathi friends and began interacting with the outside world, I learned to speak the Marathi language, which was quite similar to my native tongue.

For centuries, Gujaratis and Marathis have interacted closely. Together, they have been part of many kingdoms and empires, and at times they ruled one another. Many Gujaratis lived in the Maratha land and many Marathis lived in predominantly Gujarati-speaking areas as well. Marathi, as a second language, came naturally to me.

In middle school, I began learning Hindi, which gained prominence nationally after Indian Independence. In the last three years of high school, I also studied Sanskrit, the ancient Indian language.

My neighborhood truly reflected the diverse nature of the India at the time. Most shops on the Center Street, especially on Kapada Bazaar, were owned by Gujaratis. Some of the jewelry shops were owned by Marwaris, who trace their ancestry to the Marwar region of Rajasthan in northwest India. Businesses on East Street were owned mostly by Christians. Almost all communities had representation on the Main Street, including Gujaratis, Bohra Muslims, Christians, Parsis, and Jews. Prior to the creation of the state of Israel, Poona had a thriving Jewish community. Many of its members were businessmen who owned several big stores in and around Poona. Most of them have since migrated to Israel. Ironically, even though the area has been part of various Maratha kingdoms and later part of the state of Maharashtra, Marathis were a minority in my immediate neighborhood. Most of the Marathis that lived and worked there were from society's lower economic strata.

Riches to Rags

Though my mother, having grown up in a relatively affluent family in Kolhapur, losing her parents at an early age, and being raised by her grandmother, she did not feel any financial pinch prior to her wedding because of the family's businesses: Grandpa Balaram's successful Ayurveda clinic and shop, and after his death, Uncle Hirabhai's wholesale and retail grocery store.

Even though she never discussed it with me, the thought has crossed my mind several times that it must not have been easy for Mother to adjust to the hand-to-mouth existence that awaited her after she married my father. Bun never asked for any help from her brother, who inherited much of her family's business. Self-respect and dignity, her own as well as the family's, were at the core of her existence. Aware of our financial situation, Uncle Hirabhai delivered bulk grocery items to our house from time to time.

Like most Indian women, Bun worked hard and never complained about anything. In my more than eight decades of existence, I have not seen anyone who was better at living within means than my mother, or who practiced austerity better than she did. She was extremely good at managing our family's expenses with whatever my father earned from his job, plus what I brought in through multiple odd jobs starting during my high school days. As the eldest son, I felt it was my obligation to contribute to the family's income.

It seemed to me that every single moment that Bun was awake, she was working. She was up most of the time, waking at an insanely early hour. By 5:00 a.m., she woke me up. During year-end exams, we were required to get up at 4:00 a.m. to brush up everything one final time. By sunrise, Bun had finished her morning prayers and a fair amount of work. Then it was time to cook breakfast for the four of us: Vinod, Aruna, Bhai, and myself. For lunch, we ate fresh Gujarati *rotis* (bread), *dal* (lentil soup), *bhaat* (rice), and a small amount of vegetables. As vegetables were expensive, we could not afford much of it. Bun always ate last. As a matter of fact, I rarely saw her eating breakfast because, after I ate, I rushed to school.

Mother managed all our lives efficiently. She made sure we kept on top of schoolwork, went to bed on time, woke up on time, that our clothes were clean, and kept track of dozens of other small things that the other four members of the family did on a daily basis. More than our father, we depended on Bun for everything. Bhai also worked in Keshavlal Shah's shop much of the time.

Bun was a strict disciplinarian who imposed a tight schedule on us. But she never physically punished me or my siblings. At the same time, she was loving and caring, though she never expressed it outwardly. Over the years, I internalized many of her qualities, including self-discipline, self-respect, and even her heroic stoicism.

Father's Struggles

I hardly saw my father at home, as he worked seven days a week. Monday was an official holiday for all the stores on Kapada Bazaar. But Bhai was required to work on that day as well, replenishing the stock and doing various other jobs. Keshavlal was also a Jain, but he never treated Father with respect. A hard-nosed businessman and tough taskmaster, he always found ways to deduct from my father's pay. Bhai dreaded being late. It meant that a few rupees would disappear from his next month's salary, which was a little over 100 rupees.

Bhai had many great qualities. He was an eternal optimist and a staunch believer in the mantra that God helps those who help themselves. He walked the talk, working hard, with commitment and sincerity. Of course, religion played an important role in his life.

Though Bhai worked tirelessly, he was never compensated adequately, as was the case for most salespeople who worked for family-owned businesses. No upward mobility was possible for them. Father's highest monthly pay was 135 rupees, which he received in the early to mid-1950s. That incidentally led to his being fired from his job. By 1955, all five of Keshavlal's sons had grown up and started being involved in the business. So he no longer needed extra help and was ready to cut off the wages to employees outside of the family. Soon, Bhai was fired.

That had been the only job my father had in his entire adult life until then. Now at age forty-eight, after working for the same man for more than two decades, he was suddenly unemployed—a sad day for my whole family. He looked for a similar job at nearby clothing stores in Poona Camp for days, without any luck.

My father had only studied up to middle school, and had not acquired any skills that would land him a good-paying job, and he'd spent the most-productive years of his life working for Keshavlal. Finally realizing he had few choices, Bhai took a job as a gas station attendant, filling up vehicles and cleaning the place. He also maintained its accounts and carried cash to the owner.

Bhai wasn't happy at the new workplace. Employees at gas stations were seldom treated fairly. After two years (in 1957), he quit the job to start a footpath (sidewalk) clothing shop on Center Street, mainly selling cheap clothes. By then I was in Medical College and doing a number of part-time jobs, but I helped him with his business whenever I could.

Five years after he lost the previous job, Bhai found another job at a clothing store. He held onto that position, at the Indo-Foreign Store on Main Street, from 1960 till 1980. After he retired, at age seventy-three, he routinely visited the store in the evening to have tea and meet with his old colleagues.

School days

At age five, I was enrolled at Gujarati Kelvani Hithwardhak Mandal High School (better known as GKH High School) a private institution run by a trust and called a high school because it offered classes from first grade to eleventh grade. With no kindergarten in Poona in the late 1930s, my formal education started in first grade. The school was run by Gujaratis and meant primarily for Gujarati children. In addition to Gujarati Hindu children, Gujarati Jain and Bohra Muslim students studied there. All our textbooks, including math, science, history, and geography, were in the Gujarati language. The English language was only introduced as a second language in fifth grade. The medium of instruction, all the way through the seventh grade, was Gujarati. In grades eight to eleven, algebra, geometry, physics, and chemistry were taught in English.

At age seven, I started attending a Jain *pathshala* (seat of learning) for religious lessons. The pathshala was across from the Jain temple. The classes were in the evening, from 7:00 to 8:00 p.m. Religious lessons were also in Gujarati. Jain scriptures were originally written in Ardhamagadhi (similar to Sanskrit), and later translated into Gujarati to some extent.

Elementary, or primary school as it was called in India, was uneventful but with a sense of routine. In the morning before school, we all sang a common prayer, followed by an announcement by the headmaster. The last period of the day was devoted to physical education classes and sports. Most of my classmates were from the neighborhood in Poona Camp. After fourth grade, we moved to a new building, adjacent to the old primary school. Back in the days, school education consisted of three phases: four-year primary (elementary) school, three-year upper primary (middle school) and a four-year high school. Until the tenth grade, school exams were conducted by respective schools that promoted students based on grades. A matriculation exam (SSC, or Secondary School Certificate Examination) was administered at the end of eleventh grade by a statewide school board.

My mother was in charge of the overall education of all three of us. In elementary school, Bun helped with lessons. Whenever I had questions, she answered them, and she clarified doubts from time to time. But she had completed only middle school-level education at a Marathi language school. She could not help much once I was in middle school.

Bun had a disciplined routine. She wanted me to study at the sunrise, which was considered the best time to memorize lessons. She believed, like most Indian mothers, that passing the examinations with good grades is the key to success in life. She woke me at 5:00 a.m. for two hours of study, then a brief visit to the temple and breakfast. I got to school at 8:30 a.m. At 1:00 p.m. I was back home for a quick lunch. School lasted until 4:00 p.m. Evenings were devoted to temple, religious studies, and school assignments. Most observant Jains went to the temple twice daily, morning and evening. I typically studied until 9:00 p.m.

Doing classwork in the evening was a challenge, as we had no electricity in the house. Reading kerosene-powered lanterns was quite stressful on the eyes, and the fumes were equally suffocating. But I found a creative solution to the problem. Just outside the chawl, across the street, was a mosque, and the block had a powerful streetlight. For years, I studied under that streetlight, braving an army of mosquitoes. The weather in Poona was nice even during winters, enabling me to study outside. At 9:00 p.m., I hit the bed. Our home was electrified by the time I was in middle school. Though the power distribution was spotty, we had uninterrupted supply from 7:00 to 11:00 p.m., enabling me to study during the evenings.

Occasionally, starting in fifth grade, I visited classmates' homes for joint study sessions. A classmate, Navnit Shah, invited me to his house. He had a third-floor room and a terrace for himself, which became my favorite study place till the matriculation exam. The fact that I was a good student worked in my favor, as some of my classmates treated me well and did homework with me.

I mostly breezed through elementary and middle schools, earning good grades all the way. In high school, things were quite different, with the workload increasing drastically. Although I was a studious and hardworking student who literally burned the midnight oil, I was never the best student in my class. Most of the time, I finished third behind my good friends, Sevantilal Shah and Arun Patel. Sevantilal was related to Keshavlal, my father's boss.

Throughout middle school and high school, I was among the top three, earning "merit cards," for scoring more than 70 percent marks. My favorite subjects were history and geography. I was good in physics and chemistry as well, but not in math. Both Arun and Sevantilal were good in math.

The final year of high school, eleventh grade, was the most critical year of my school life. Unlike previous years, the final exams were conducted by a statewide Secondary School Certificate board. The minimum qualification for attending a medical college in India those days was passing the two-year, pre-degree program offered by regular colleges. For admission to a medical college, I had to do my pre-degree from a decent college. To get into a decent college, I must have good marks, meaning pass with at least a "first class," which is 60 percent marks. That whole year, my goal was to pass the matriculation with a first class.

In the runup to the exams, I studied hard, staying up later than usual and waking up earlier than my normal time. My mother stood like a solid rock behind me, taking care of all my needs. We had no clock in the house, but the next-door neighbor had a clock and a radio, which we found useful.

The exams lasted a number of days and we had to wait for several more weeks for the results. Finally, they came. And I passed with a first class. With 60 percent marks, to be precise. As was the case with my whole high school life, I finished third behind Sevantilal and Arun.

Life in College

Within a month of my matriculation result, I enrolled for pre-degree at the Nowrosjee Wadia College, which was founded two decades earlier. The college, named after a prominent local Parsi businessman, Nowrosjee N. Wadia, was initially funded by his two sons, Cusrow and Ness. The primary reason I chose Wadia College was because it offered me an annual scholarship of 50 rupees. I took the three subjects, biology, physics, and chemistry, required for medical college admission.

The fee at Wadia College was 100 rupees per year. Since my scholarship covered half the tuition, the first six months of education was virtually free. Besides the fee, I also needed to pay for books and other expenses. For those, I received assistance from two other sources. One was a 400-rupee grant from the Mahavir Jain Vidyalaya, a local Jain charity; and the other a 100-rupee donation from a wealthy lady.

The college was roughly two miles from home, walking distance. But to save time, my family and I decided to buy a bicycle. By bike, it was a twenty-minute ride. Bhai knew an accountant in a bike store owned by a Parsi gentleman. The store sold us a bicycle for 120 rupees. They gave us a special deal: we could pay the amount in twenty-four monthly installments.

In college, I began meeting people from different cultures and regions, which vastly expanded my social and intellectual horizons. I acquired friends from diverse backgrounds. During high school, most of my friends were Gujaratis. Now my best friends were two Muslims, Basheer Sheikh and Abid Baheranwala, a Bohra Muslim. Abid's brother-in-law was a businessman who owned a big store in Poona Camp. Basheer's father, Nizamuddeen Sheikh, was a superintendent of police who received the president's medal after independence. I also had Marathi, Gujarati, Christian, Parsi, and Jain friends. Most of my friends back then were richer than me. But they never looked down upon me, and all treated me well.

As in high school, I never stood first in my class during the two-year pre-degree program. But again, I made sure that my marks were good enough for me to be accepted to medical college. Admissions to the medical schools in India are now based on entrance tests. But in the 1950s and '60s, the only criterion for admission was the marks a student received in the pre-degree exams. Since my single-minded goal was to study medicine, I had to cover all the bases. In order to improve my odds of acceptance, I joined Wadia College's National Cadet Corps (NCC).

NCC cadets serve as a voluntary student wing of the Indian armed forces. As a cadet, I learned basic military training and wore its uniform. But I was never into fighting and had little appetite to become a soldier. NCC cadets were granted 1.5 percent additional marks in final exams, which was my specific objective behind joining NCC. Similarly, I enrolled for another activity that would pad my marks by another 1.5 percent. I played *kho kho*, a traditional tag team game, popular in western India. I was never a starter for the college team. Nonetheless, it got me the additional 1.5 percent marks that proved to be priceless during the medical college admission process.

The two-year college passed fairly quickly. I studied zoology, botany, physics, and chemistry. In zoology class, I dissected frogs. College assignments, NCC, and nearly half a dozen part-time jobs kept me really busy. In the summer of 1955, I passed college with an overall first class—a huge relief. I was the first member from my family to pass pre-degree. My parents were overjoyed.

But the celebrations did not last long. I had a job at hand: applying to medical college. Within days, I delivered in person my application to B.J. Medical College, the only medical school in Poona at the time. I had to wait for another six weeks to know whether I was accepted—six long weeks of anxiety, stress, optimism, and pessimism, among other feelings and emotions. Since I knew I had done everything I could, the only thing I could do additionally was pray, which I did more than usual.

Finally on the day of the admission result, I biked to B.J. Medical College. The mile-and-half ride seemed never ending. Upon arriving there, I was disappointed to learn that my name was not on the first list of students who got admission. The admission office told me that a second list would be released the next day. When I went back some twenty-four hours later, there I was! Navin C. Shah was the thirty-fifth student selected on the merit list out of a total of ninety.

I was euphoric and wanted to break the news to Bhai and Bun right away. I biked faster than ever. On the way, I didn't forget to stop by at the Jain temple to pray. At home, for the first time, my parents could not hide their emotions. Bhai distributed sweets to our neighbors and friends.

But the jubilation lasted only a few hours; then the reality hit us. All along I knew that I wanted to attend medical college and become a doctor. But I had not thought about the means to finance it. My thinking was *I will cross that bridge when I get there*. Now I was there. Somehow I needed to cross it.

Good Samaritan

In eighth grade, a new student joined my class, a Gujarati boy who recently moved to Poona. Arun Patel grew up in Kampala, Uganda, and did all his schooling until then in that East African country, where his father, C.M. Patel, had a thriving business. After Arun finished seventh grade, his father moved some members of the family from Uganda back to Poona. Mr. Patel split his time between Kampala and Poona. While he was in India, the business in East Africa was managed by his two older sons. His wife, Chandanben, stayed in Poona with Arun and two other sons. One of Arun's older brothers was studying law, and another was in engineering college.

Arun and I hit it off immediately, becoming great friends. Arun lived in a spacious, two-story bungalow, in Koregaon Park, a posh and elegant part of Poona Camp, where rich businessmen and prominent people lived. During weekends,

Arun often invited me to his bungalow, just two miles away from my home, and I walked there. Thus I spent a lot of time, especially during weekends, at Arun's home, chatting and playing cricket on the terrace with him, his brother, and other friends.

During those visits, I got to know Arun's parents well. I called them Papaji and Momiji. That's what Arun and his older brothers called them. Momiji was always interested in my studies. Whenever I met her, she asked me how I was doing in school. Momiji was an epitome of hospitality. She fed me delicious vegetarian food and always treated me well.

Arun had a nice motorbike, and he often came to high school on that bike. The family also had a big Ford car. The driver Sammy and the family's cook stayed in an outer house of the bungalow compound.

After our matriculation, Arun also joined Wadia College. While I was in the science division, he was in engineering, as he was planning and training to join Papaji's business.

When I got admission to B.J. Medical College, Arun was among the first few friends I shared the news with. During our two years at Wadia College, he knew it was my dream to become a doctor. Momiji also knew that I wanted to be a doctor.

When the medical college admission results were announced, Papaji was in town. He had recently returned by ship from Kampala. That weekend, I visited Arun's house to share the news of my admission with his parents and seek possible financial assistance from them. They had already learned from Arun that I was accepted at B.J. Medical College.

I did not know how to ask for money from Papaji; I was scared to do that. Despite struggling mightily, my parents had never asked for financial help from anyone. Asking even for a loan was considered beneath one's dignity. But now, I had hit the wall. Without help, my education would come to a halt. Here I was, in front of a man who could potentially make my dream a reality. I was looking for the right words to broach the subject.

However, Papaji, knew my situation and the purpose of my visit. I had explored with Arun the possibility of a loan from his dad, and Arun had already discussed it with him. Papaji readily agreed to finance my medical education through an interest-free loan from a foundation that he established.

The C.M. Foundation was set up by Mr. Patel to help needy and talented students from the community to complete higher education. The annual fee at B.J. Medical College was 600 rupees. Five years of medical education cost 3,000 rupees in tuition alone. The foundation paid the fee in installments, with the first 300 rupees taking care of the first six months' fees. Then the money kept coming, whenever I needed it. By the end of five years, the loan totaled 3,000 rupees.

Papaji's generosity did not end with his support for my education. In 1963, my father found a groom for my sister Aruna. Youngest of the three Shah children, she was twenty-two at the time, six years younger to me. For some reason, Aruna had not completed matriculation. The groom, Subashchandra, had a bachelor's degree in commerce from a college in Poona. He was working in Sangli, 150 miles to the south of the city.

Marriages in India, always accompanied by festivities, color, and dance, have a huge bill attached to them, and it is mostly the bride's family that picks them up. For an average family, a daughter's wedding can be a huge financial setback. As the eldest son in the family, I was in part responsible along with my father for underwriting the expenses of Aruna's wedding. Again the only person who we could count on for financial assistance was Papaji. He gave us a loan of 3,500 rupees. Both Papaji and Momiji attended the wedding of Aruna and Subashchandra, held in February 1964.

Helping Every Which Way I Can

The Gujarati Jain community has been known for its business acumen for centuries. For that reason, it is among the more affluent ethnic, religious, and linguistic groups in India. While there are many poor Gujarati Jain families like mine was; on average, members of my community are more affluent than a typical Indian family. Growing up poor as a Gujarati Jain, I was forced to confront and reckon constantly with that reality. But how would we get out of the rut? By the time I was in middle school, I decided I would become a doctor. I was certain that was a path to prosperity for me and my family. But to become a doctor would take years. And to become a successful one would take a decade of medical practice. Short of discontinuing my education, I was willing to do anything to help my family stay afloat as I pursued my bigger goal of becoming a doctor.

With that in mind, I broached the idea of doing some part-time work with my father. Being a salesperson, Bhai knew many businessmen in the locality. I knew that, through his connection, I could land some small jobs. It turned out Dad had already found a job for me even before I volunteered to work. A friend of his who worked for the Poona Soap Factory, which manufactured detergent soap bars, told him that I could collect piles of soap clumps (called *choora* in Gujarati) from the factory on a particular day of the week.

These clumps are essentially scraps formed when soap bars are cut by machines. My father suggested I collect and sell the choora to those who could not afford to buy soaps from the market. I collected between four and six pounds of choora a week and sold them for 2 rupees per pound, much lower than the price of a regular soap bar. I went to the Poona Soap Factory on my bicycle, collected all the scraps, and sold them. Eventually I developed a regular clientele. Nearly all customers were poor women who lived in the Poona Camp area. The entire job took me no more than a few hours a week.

Selling the choora, which I did for three years, was my entry to Poona Camp's unorganized job market. Over the next seven years, I did at least four other part-time jobs. They all allowed me to help my struggling family by supplementing my father's income, chipping in with whatever I could. I continued doing these jobs till I graduated from the medical college. Studying medicine and doing odd jobs became an integral part of my routine, and I did both with great enthusiasm and sincerity.

The second part-time job was much more intellectual and interesting. As soon as I joined Wadia College for my two-year pre-degree program, I got to know that an old Parsi lady, Miss Amy Poonawalla, was looking for someone to read the bilingual Gujarati-English newspaper, *Jam-e-Jamshed*. The paper, in publication since 1832, covered the Parsi community. Parsis, who fled the present-day Iran between the eighth and tenth centuries to escape religious persecution, found a safe home in western India where local rulers welcomed them. The minuscule community still retains its highly distinctive religious identity. Some of India's prominent industrialists, such as Tata Sons' chairman emeritus, Ratan Tata, and textile mogul, Nusli Wadia, are Parsis. Since most of their original settlements in India were in southern Gujarat, the community mostly speaks Gujarati language even now.

Miss Poonawalla, who wore thick glasses, taught French at Poona's prestigious St. Helena's School. Because of her poor eye sight and unfamiliarity with written Gujarati, she could not read the paper. She employed me as a reader. Miss Poonawalla's home was about a half- mile from my chawl. I went there in the evening around 7:00 p.m. and finished reading the entire newspaper. She paid me 30 rupees a month. I explained difficult Gujarati words and complex sentences to her. Miss Poonawalla's sister and mother also listened to my reading.

In addition to the much-needed money, the job had another benefit. On certain days, *Jam-e-Jamshed* was bilingual. Besides Gujarati, on those days, the paper also published news and columns in English. My communication skill in English was not good, as I had studied in a Gujarati middle school. Miss Poonawalla spoke excellent English, and my conversation with her helped me improve my English tremendously. She corrected me every time I mispronounced a word or messed up my grammar. I enjoyed her company and continued the job till I became a doctor.

Thanks to Miss Poonawalla, I landed another reading job while at medical college. The good-hearted French teacher was friends with Dr. Taraporwala, a retired surgeon and renowned leprosy specialist and also a Parsi. Like Miss Poonawalla, the doctor had poor vision and wanted someone to read articles from *The British Medical Journal (The BMJ)* and other publications. Though he was retired, Dr. Taraporwala wanted to keep in touch with developments in the world of medicine, and there was no better way to do that than meticulously reading one of the best-known medical journals in the world. Every weekend I went to his house, about a mile away from my home, and spent a couple of hours reading the medical journal to him. He paid me 25 rupees per month.

Dr. Taraporwala wanted me to read at a slow pace. He sat silently, eating his food, and listening to my reading. Occasionally, he commented or explained certain diseases and medical conditions. That made the time I spent with him fruitful.

Not all odd jobs I did in those days were intellectually stimulating. Some part-time jobs were purely for the money. For instance, one job was helping local banker and insurance agent, Adil Frenchman, with calculating rent for safe deposits in his bank's vaults.

I also landed a tutoring job when I started medical college. My friend Arun Patel's nephew, Manish Patel, was starting middle school and Momiji asked me if I could tutor Manish. I was deeply grateful to Papaji for a loan he gave me, so of course I agreed. I was paid 30 rupees a month. Every day, I went to their house from 7:00 to 8:00 a.m., and this job had an added perk. Each morning, before I left their home for college, Momiji served me a hot breakfast.

The most-glamorous and best-paid part-time job I did was working as a ticket collector and door keeper at the Poona Race Course during racing season (July to October). The prestigious Poona horse races attracted elite horses from western India and around the country, not to mention rich fans, especially from Bombay where the racing season starts in November. I earned 14 rupees a day, a big amount for me—more than a tenth of what my father earned a month, working twelve hours a day, seven days a week.

I got the job through a professor of mine at medical college, Dr. G.S. Mutalik, a professor of medicine and an avid racing fan. His friend Dr. M.S.H. Modi, a London-trained cardiologist, was well-known in Poona's racing circles. Both doctors helped me land the job. Initially I worked as a doorkeeper in the third class, where the general public watched races. I was quickly promoted to first class, and eventually to the member's stand. My job was to collect tickets from members and let them go in.

Regulars at the course included some of the biggest names in the Bombay film industry, including Raj Kapoor, billed as the greatest showman of Indian cinema. He knew I was the doorkeeper of the member stand and always greeted me with a "Hi" as I let him in. In person, I found the actor and director even more handsome and impressive than on screen. My friends at medical school were impressed that I was able to share space with Raj Kapoor. However, I never had a conversation with him, despite running into him dozens of times during the four years I worked at Poona Race Course. I was required to act in a professional manner, which meant I could not invade the privacy of members.

Other racing fans who attended the races included Dev Anand, another great actor, popular actresses such as Nargis, and other leading heroines of the day. But they were not "regulars" like Raj Kapoor. Those who came from Bombay usually traveled by car, reaching Poona by 1:00 p.m. in time for the races, and they returned to the big city in the evening.

I gave all my earnings to my mother, keeping only one rupee for myself. It was quite a struggle to keep up with twelve hours of medical school while also doing these jobs, but I managed it. And it gave me some satisfaction that I was able to lessen my father's burden a little bit.

Life in Medical College

Byramjee Jeejeebhoy Medical College had been in existence since 1879, named after Sir Byramjee Jeejeebhoy, a wealthy Parsi businessman who founded and supported a number of educational institutions in western India. The only medical college in town at the time, it was better known as B.J. Medical College. Attached to Sassoon General Hospital, the 1,000-bed government teaching hospital was affiliated with the University of Poona.

When my classes began in late summer 1955, wearing the white coat for the first time was an exciting experience. Medical school was different from every educational institution I attended in the previous thirteen years where, except for a few science classes at Wadia College, nearly every class was theoretical. Now it was real practical training. I was dealing with cadavers and organs, feeling the pulse of live patients, and shadowing surgeons while they conducted complex surgeries. However, there were also plenty of theories to be learned. We were taught anatomy and physiology in the first two years; hospital training started the third year. On average, I spent more than ten hours a day on campus.

The interest-free loan from C.M. Patel was a tremendous relief for me, as it took care of the annual tuition. Still I needed to buy books and help my family (being the eldest son). That was why I had to do as many as five different part-time jobs.

One of the biggest expenses was buying medical textbooks. Some were imported from Britain and the United States. A few kindhearted individuals came to my rescue. One was Dr. Jamshed Frenchman, father of Adil, a local banker and insurance agent for whom I worked part-time. Dr. Frenchman, a general practitioner running an independent practice, was introduced to me by Dr. M.S.H. Modi, a cardiologist at Sassoon General Hospital. Dr. Modi told my father that Dr. Frenchman was a generous person and might be able to help me. I went to meet Dr. Frenchman, who had a clinic a couple of blocks from home. I could sense that he liked me.

Over the next four years, he routinely gave me money to buy textbooks. *Grey's Anatomy* was a book I purchased with his money. Another person who helped me with textbooks was P.A. Tarachand, who owned a bookstore near the vegetable market behind Center Street. The store bought used textbooks from students at the end of semesters and sold them for almost half the cost of new books. Mr. Tarachand, a Jain, knew my father well, and gave me further discounts. He wanted to see me succeed in life. At the time, most Jain men went into business, and very few were in the medical profession. In fact, I was the first Gujarati Jain to get admission to medical college from Poona Camp.

Another wonderful gift I received while in medical college, that I treasured, was a watch from Papaji. Besides helping me keep my tight schedule, it allowed me to count the pulse rates of patients. Initially used by Papaji, I wore it with great pride.

In 1960 I finally completed my MBBS (bachelor of medicine, bachelor of surgery). Now I was officially a doctor. The feeling was inexplicable. But the person most elated was my father. He knew that at long last, after decades of toil, our family's fate was now going to change for the better. A doctor was considered an elite professional in India. Many doctors lived in bungalows. They owned cars and had helpers to manage household chores. My father thought eventually I would have all those perks. And of course, being a practicing Jain, he also wanted me to help the poor.

But the upward mobility that my Bhai dreamt of was still years away. Before I started my practice, I had to do a MS (master's degree in surgery). Even before I completed MBBS, I knew I wanted to be a surgeon. Being a surgeon was a big deal, but getting into the required four-year residency was not that easy. At the time, Sassoon General was the only teaching hospital in Poona. The competition was statewide, as every MBBS holder from Maharashtra could apply. I was a little nervous about my chances, but I was accepted and began my residency right away. Though my preferred choice for residency was surgery, I was initially allotted orthopedics. Thankfully, a year later, I was able to switch to surgery.

During residency, my workload was huge. I decided to quit all my part-time jobs and focus on training. Luckily I was also allotted a room in the Sassoon Hospital Doctors' Quarters and received a monthly stipend. The 70 rupees was not a lot of money, as I was used to earning as much as a hundred rupees from my various part-time jobs. But by now, Bhai had landed his second sales job at a clothing store; and my brother Vinod, after earning a diploma in automobile engineering from Bhavnagar in Gujarat, was now working for the state transport company in Poona.

As a house surgeon (resident), I visited my parents at home on weekends for a few hours. Once each weekday, Bun sent food in a *tiffin* (a lunch box). I worked hard throughout the four-year residency; that was the nature of the training. I had no complaints; I was young and wanted to do well. A lot of days, I worked as many as twelve to fourteen hours. Being a junior guy, I was always on call.

The Sassoon General campus was quite large, spread across about ten acres. Each department was in a separate building with several-minute walks from one to another. I was often posted at the Burn Unit, where the death rate was really high. Many of the patients I attended were severely burned over more than 50 percent of the total body surface area (TBSA). Their survival chances were low.

My workload was especially high in my second year, when a major dam, Panshet, burst, flooding the surrounding areas. Panshet, on the Ambi River (a tributary of Mutha), was a brand-new dam built a few years earlier. When it burst on July 12, 1961, the water even reached Poona, 30 miles to the northeast. More than a thousand people died in the incident. In the next three to four months, the hospital rescheduled all surgeries. The only work that was going on was in the intensive care unit and the emergency department.

As a doctor, I was quite desensitized to death, having been trained to handle it since my third year at medical college, but this was the first time I witnessed mass deaths. I was not prepared for it.

I was living at the Sassoon Hospital with other house surgeons. The senior surgeon, Yashwant G. Bodhe, could not travel to the hospital, as his home and private clinic (both in the same building) were submerged up to the first floor. Dr. Bodhe and his wife, Dr. Lilatai Bodhe (a gynecologist and general practitioner) ran a hospital on the first floor of the three-story building with a general ward for about eight patients, two private rooms, an operation theater, and a consulting room. The dispensary was on the ground floor, and they lived on the top floor.

I walked through high grounds and mud to reach Dr. Bodhe's home, where he was happy to see me.

Becoming a Surgeon

In 1964, I completed my residency, obtaining my Master of Surgery degree. Now my goal was to become an assistant professor at the Sassoon Hospital. But the application and selection process was time consuming, taking possibly months or perhaps a year. In the meantime, I needed to find a job. During the nine years of my MBBS and MS, I had come into contact with a number of physicians in Poona Camp, and some of them had become my mentors, such as Dr. Jamshed Frenchman, who helped me buy medical books.

Dr. Frenchman ran a clinic two blocks away from my home, out of a small, old building. He was in his seventies and not in good health. After I obtained my MS, he had asked me to attend to his patients when he was sick, and I did. By now, Dr. Frenchman's health had deteriorated further. When I visited him a few days after I completed residency, he asked if I was interested in running his clinic. Dr. Frenchman died in only a few months.

After consulting with his wife and son Adil, I took over the dispensary and did surgical consultations. Initially I found the arrangement eminently workable. Dr. Frenchman had a steady number of patients he had been treating for years. Most were poor people from Poona Camp. No surgery was involved, as there was no room or facilities for doing even simple surgeries. I did only general practice. Each patient paid no more than 5 rupees per visit, which was good enough for me. After paying employees (mainly a compounder), rent, the electricity bill, and a small amount to Mrs. Frenchman, I was making 200 to 300 rupees a month. That was enough to meet my expenses and support the family.

After completing the MS, I had moved back to my parents' home. But I still had the loans from C.M. Patel to pay back. So I considered this job as a temporary one till I could get a job as an assistant honorary surgeon at Sassoon Hospital.

When I learned there was an opening for that position at Sassoon Hospital, I applied. Over the next several months, I appeared for a series of interviews. I thought they went well. The hiring committee included Dr. V.G. Ganla, my physiology professor and dean of the B.J. Medical College, and Dr. Bodhe. I knew both men well.

Marriage

At first it was a gentle suggestion. Then it became a modest push, especially by my father. Soon it was a demand. My marriage was a topic of concern for my family once I completed my MBBS degree in 1960. But Bhai and Bun both knew I was focused on completing my MS, and they did not exert any pressure on me to tie the knot while I was doing my residency. But that changed when I moved back home. A stream of suitors had approached Bhai, and he had been stonewalling them all along.

In India of the 1960s, marriages were mostly arranged by the family. Now I was thirty, really old for marriage by Gujarati standards. Those days, men from community got married as early as age twenty-one. More than three decades earlier, Bhai had got married at twenty-five. I knew why my father was agitated.

My mother sided with me till I finished my studies. But once I completed the MS, she joined hands with Bhai and forced me to look at the various proposals coming in, and get married soon.

Dr. Bodhe, my mentor in surgery, was a family doctor of the Sanghvis, well-known industrialists in the city. Like us, the Sanghvis were also Jains. But unlike us, they were rich. The four Sanghvi brothers ran a number of businesses, including their flagship steel factory that manufactured lunch boxes (tiffins) and stainless-steel utensils.

Soorajmal Sanghvi, the eldest brother and patriarch of the family, came to Bombay at a young age. He also had a humble beginning, having started by selling utensils in Poona. Once that business flourished, he enlisted his three younger brothers and started a factory to manufacture the utensils. The Sanghvis soon became one of Poona's richest and most-influential businessmen.

Soorajmal Sanghvi was also a leader in the Congress Party in Poona. He led social, medical, and charitable organizations in the city. The elder Sanghvi told Dr. Bodhe that he was looking for a bridegroom for his niece Leela, daughter of his younger brother Rikhabchand, and they were looking for a doctor.

"If you know one, please introduce him to us," he said.

Dr. Bodhe said he knew a young doctor trained under him, whose medical education was financed by C.M Patel. Soorajmal immediately met Papaji to inquire about me.

Leela Rikhabchand Sanghvi was of a different nature. The twenty-four-year-old had suitors from rich Jain families across western India; but she wanted to marry a highly educated man who was "down to earth" and not into business.

Papaji and I thought such an alliance was not a workable proposition. I believed that it wasn't a good idea to marry a girl from such a rich family because of the enormous mismatch in the social statuses of our two families. We both thought of rejecting the proposal as it would be difficult for a rich girl to live in a chawl. Given the overall skepticism about the match, actually the mismatch, in my household, we asked Papaji to dissuade the Sanghvis. I was convinced the marriage would be disastrous and Leela would not be happy with me. But as

Leela and the Sanghvis, persisted, Papaji invited Soorajmal to come and see our home. He thought that, if the Sanghvis see our living conditions, they will question the wisdom of the alliance and withdraw from it.

So a meeting between Leela and I was arranged at Papaji's bungalow. Leela wore a green sari, and she looked beautiful. She was around four-foot-ten. I asked her if she had any questions for me; she answered in the negative. I felt as though she had already decided she would marry me. My parents liked Leela instantly, as did Momiji. Mrs. Chandanben Patel respected my education and did not think much one way or the other about my family's financial situation. Eventually, Papaji was also in favor of the wedding.

A week later, I met with Leela's father, Rikhabchand Sanghvi. He was in charge of the family's sales office in Bombay and lived there most of the time. He traveled to Poona on weekends by car. Like his siblings, Rikhabchand also had great business acumen. A smart salesman, he handled sales of factory products. He always had a smile on his face and the telephone number of the "who's who" of Bombay. Rikhabchand thanked me and my parents for our willingness to accept Leela into our family.

After our engagement, I started feeling even poorer than before, constantly comparing my family's poverty with her affluence, my deprivation with her privilege. How would an immensely rich girl live with my family, which did not even have a proper bathroom?

Leela was born in Takhatgarh, in Rajasthan, on January 1, 1942. Takhatgarh, a small town, is roughly 135 miles to the north of Umta, my ancestral village. The Sanghvis were originally from the Marwar region of Rajasthan. The Marwari community was highly successful in business. Leela grew up in Bombay and lived in the city till age seventeen. After completing high school, she and her siblings moved to Poona, along with their mother Ujiben, to enroll for a bachelor's degree program in economics at Fergusson College, the most reputed college in Poona at the time. After graduation, she worked for the family business in the Accounts Department under Uncle Phoolchand Sanghvi. Phoolchand, a finance wizard, was the youngest of the Sanghvi brothers. The third Sanghvi brother, Bhabhulmal, was a technical person who looked after all the factories.

Our wedding took place at the estate of the Sanghvis over two days. The three brothers lived in different homes in one compound called Juna Bungalow, or Old Bungalow. Soorajmal Sanghvi, the patriarch, lived in Nava Bungalow, or New Bungalow, a block away from Juna Bungalow and the main Sanghvi factory.

The *muhoorath* (ritual) was on the first day. The next day, at the reception, more than 2,000 people were treated to a feast at a wedding *pandal* (a makeshift hall) on the Sanghvi Factory campus, next to the Sanghvi bungalows. As was the custom, Leela's family paid for the wedding expenses. Most of the guests were from her side. From my side, besides my family, the guest list included my childhood friends; colleagues from B.J. Medical College and Sassoon General; Aruna, her husband, and his family; and Uncle Hirabhai Doshi, my mother's brother, and his family from Kolhapur.

After the rituals, Leela's brother dropped the two of us at our new home in Poona City. A two-bedroom apartment was rented for us by the family. A couple of days after the wedding, Leela and I went on our honeymoon to the nearby resort of Mahabaleshwar, a popular hill station in the Western Ghats, 75 miles southwest of Poona. The travel and stay were arranged by my father-in-law. We were provided a car and a driver, who remained with us during our stay in Mahabaleshwar.

My parents did not like my living arrangement. They thought Leela should have lived with my family at least for a while, the tradition among Gujarati Jain families. My father felt it was demeaning for me to have accepted it. The first year's rent for the apartment was paid by my father-in-law. Additionally, he gave us a car that was used by Leela and other members of the family prior to the wedding. My father in-law thought that, being a doctor, I should live in a decent place and have a car to move around.

The reason I agreed to move to the apartment was because I thought Leela was used to a certain level of luxury, and I did not want her to struggle on Day One of our marriage. On our wedding night, there were twelve people staying in our two-room chawl, all relatives who came to attend the wedding. Some people slept in the attic and others in the kitchen.

Bhai remained opposed to my move to the apartment and continued to express his displeasure for a long time. Both my parents never visited our Poona apartment in the one and a half years we lived there. But I visited them every other day, as my clinic was a couple of blocks away from their home. I felt bad and was pained to see my parents being unhappy. They wanted all of us, the whole family, to stay together in the chawl till I could afford to buy an apartment. I told my parents that, in a year or two, I would be able to have an apartment for all of us to live together. All four Sanghvi brothers were sure that fairly soon I would earn enough money to be able to move into a nice apartment along with my parents.

To move from a chawl to a 1,000 square feet apartment was a big upgrade for me. So was swapping a bike for a car. Leela drove the car till I became comfortable driving it. She had been using the same four-seat 1950's Fiat for several years prior to our marriage.

Soon I realized that having a place of our own, our little universe, was critical to the growth of the relationship. Even though she grew up in a very rich family, Leela was not enamored by money or luxury. In fact it was that attitude of hers that helped our marriage to be so warm and undemanding. It was her adamant decision that she would marry only an educated man that brought us together.

However, even after the marriage, it was difficult for me to get used to the fact that two people with such a disparity in wealth could live together as husband and wife. I wondered whether Mr. Sanghvi really loved his daughter and, if he did, would he have got her married off to someone like me, who was so poor. Then I reasoned to myself that they have money, plenty of it, and wanting an educated match was understandable.

Eventually I overcame self-doubts largely because of Leela's down-to-earth character. She was a soft-spoken person, at the same time, optimistic that everything would work out. She managed the household within the money I earned. She prayed daily for my success and my family's peace and happiness.

My father-in-law, mother-in-law, and other members of the Sanghvi family accepted me wholeheartedly. Leela's parents never spoke of their wealth, and they treated my family with respect. Rikhabchand Sanghvi stood by me and Leela throughout. His sense of humor, pragmatism, and honesty were admirable. After knowing them, I could sense how Leela became the person she was.

Leela also got along well with Papaji, Momiji, Arun, and other members of the Patel family who treated her as a member of their family. Arun's wife, Yasuben, and Leela became close friends.

Brand-New Hospital

I continued my practice at Dr. Frenchman's clinic. But I was also anxiously waiting for my appointment as an assistant professor, for which I had applied more than a year and a half earlier. Finally, six months after the marriage, the letter came: I was appointed as an assistant (honorary) surgeon and honorary assistant professor of Surgery at Sassoon General Hospital and B.J. Medical College.

The unpaid position required me to work from 8:00 a.m. to 1:00 p.m. I opted for an honorary position because I would not be eligible to continue my private practice if I took a full-time faculty job. Because of my family's financial situation (we still had to pay back more than 7,000 rupees to C.M. Patel), I wanted to continue the practice.

I was delighted by the appointment. It was a nice feeling to have the title of assistant professor after my name. For the first time in my life, I felt that I had some standing in the society. I was one of the very few Gujaratis to be named as an assistant professor at B.J. Medical College and assistant honorary surgeon at Sassoon Hospital. I was the only Gujarati Jain to serve in that position at the time. Additionally, I felt that, at age thirty-one, I finally acquired *gravitas*, which I thought I didn't have until then.

However, doing two jobs meant working longer hours and spending less time with Leela, who would soon become pregnant with our first daughter. At about 2:00 p.m., I headed directly from the Sassoon Hospital to my clinic and remained there until 7:00 p.m. Nevertheless, I was not averse to working longer hours. I had done that throughout the nine years of my medical college and residency.

However, the initial excitement about becoming a surgeon faded after seeing almost no growth in my practice. Nearly all the patients were poor people who could not afford to pay more than 5 rupees for consultation. A specialist with experience charged as much as 30 rupees from rich patients. But I was a junior doctor, and not many rich or upper middle-class people came to me. Even those who came wanted my help in getting referrals to experienced specialists with bigger practices.

A surgeon's job is to operate. But here I was, with no facility, unable to operate upon patients. So the practice was limited to consulting. I was becoming despondent as the practice plateaued. Money was not coming in as I expected. After the marriage, our expenses were growing. After the first year of my marriage, where our rent had been paid by my father-in-law, I now had to pay the rent, and several other expenses as well. Being a surgeon, I had to dress up in suit. Then I had to maintain the car. On top of that, the fact that I married into a wealthy family and was unable to give my wife a decent living bothered me a lot. I started feeling inferior.

My father-in-law knew why my practice was not picking up, and he had a solution to that as well. He suggested that I convert the clinic into a full-fledged hospital. In other words, I tear down the clinic and build a hospital, a more-modern and spacious one. Having run several successful ventures, he knew how to scale a business. He pointed out that my growth prospects are limited by the lack of space and facilities at Dr. Frenchman's dispensary. It was a six-room building with a toilet outside. There was no space for X-ray machines, operating tables, and other instruments. Mr. Sanghvi said if I built a proper hospital, my practice would grow manifold.

The idea was appealing. After giving it a little thought, I concluded that building a hospital was the right thing to do. Leela was also on board. But I was a hesitant about borrowing money from her dad, who offered to finance the construction of the building.

One person I consulted before making every big decision since my Wadia College days was C.M. Patel. Papaji, also being a businessperson, was on the same page as my father-in-law. For both of them, it was about scaling up my practice. Papaji volunteered to pay half the construction cost in loan. He pointed out that, if I take all the money from my father-in-law, it would be a poor reflection on me.

Thus I decided to tear down the building and construct a brand-new hospital, with two private rooms, four general beds, an operating room, an X-ray room, an exam room, a consulting room, and a waiting area. The building would cost more than 100,000 rupees. Mr. Sanghvi and Mr. Patel would split the cost. A civil engineer from the Sanghvis' company oversaw the construction. While the work was on, my clinic was moved to a small room I rented at the edge of Poona Camp. A year later, my hospital, or nursing home (small-size hospitals in India are known as nursing homes) was ready.

Chandan Nursing Home was named after Chandanben Patel. Momiji was there for me every step of the way, ever since I knew her. She treated me like a son. She had given the blessing and the stamp of approval for my alliance with

Leela before anybody else. Even though she was rich, Momiji was pragmatic and a great judge of people she came across.

The hospital was inaugurated by N.B. Parulekar, a reputed journalist and editor of the Marathi-language *Sakal*, the largest newspaper in Maharashtra. Soorajmal Sanghvi was friends with Mr. Parulekar. Bhai, Bun, and Aruna (who came with her one-year-old son Hemant) were present at the opening ceremony of Chandan Nursing Home.

With the opening of Chandan Nursing Home, my practice improved a little bit. Most of my patients were poor, with hernia, prostate, and gastrointestinal problems. Some days I saw six or seven patients. Now I was making 800 to 1,000 rupees a month. But expenses were also much higher. I had to pay the rent as well as salary to employees. Because it was a bigger place, I had to pay lab workers and other technicians.

After a year and a half, Leela and I moved to an apartment near the nursing home in Poona Camp, a two-bedroom apartment in a new building. The rent was in fact higher than the previous one, but I could be in the nursing home within a few minutes. And now we are nearer to my parents. Bun was happy that we were nearby, but Bhai was still upset.

Though the practice was growing, it did not register the growth I was expecting. I was just a junior surgeon. Experienced surgeons, and Poona had a number of them, and had more patients. For complex surgeries, upper-middle class and rich patients always went to older and experienced surgeons, preferably foreign-trained ones. Those who had a fellowship from England's Royal College of Surgeons (FRCS) were in demand. So without having a foreign degree or seniority, it was not easy to expand the practice.

At Sassoon Hospital, I operated once a week, from 8:00 a.m. to 2:00 p.m. Daily at 8:00 a.m., I made rounds of about thirty to forty inpatients with the house surgeons (residents). At about 10:00 a.m., Chief Surgeon Dr. Bodhe made rounds with all of us and students. He would teach for about thirty minutes. Then we would examine X-rays with the radiologist and go through surgical slides with the pathologist. Dr. Bodhe was a skillful clinician with conservative surgical approach to treatment. We had one day of the week as off day, but being a junior surgeon, I visited the hospital all five days of the week.

I also routinely did voluntary consultations, especially for nonprofits that the Sanghvis were supporting. Soorajmal was the chairman of the Mahatma Gandhi Eye Hospital, and Babhutmal was the president of the local Lions Club. I helped them run medical camps of both these organizations.

Birth of Shefali

By late 1967, we were expecting our first child. Closer to the delivery, Leela moved in with her parents, as was customary for daughters to go to her parents' home for the delivery of their first-born. In our case, it was also convenient. As the Sanghvis were rich, Leela got better care at their house than my family and I could have provided her during the critical late stage of the pregnancy and delivery.

Shefali was born on July 23, 1968, at the hospital run by Dr. Lilatai Bodhe. Leela was scheduled to undergo the cesarean, but before the surgery, she delivered normally. Dr. Bodhe took care of the delivery and the follow-up care.

Shefali was a bundle of joy for all of us. As a baby, she was the favorite of all of our relatives. We called her Tony, which is her nickname even to this day. Leela moved back with me after a few months. Having my mother-in-law Ujiben nearby was a big help, especially as Tony began developing from an infant to a toddler. Even though I was not making a lot of money, I was spending a lot of time at work, especially at Sassoon Hospital, where I routinely got emergency calls. Being a junior surgeon, they called me first. Senior surgeons were called only when I could not handle a case. So I could not spend a lot of time with Leela and Tony.

While marriage can change you, the birth of a child can change you and your priorities even more. And in my case, it happened in more ways than one. Being married to a woman whose family was way richer than mine, and who moved around in circles that were more elite than I had ever done, was an added pressure to do better in life. Even though I was no longer living in an apartment paid for by Leela's parents, we still relied on them for many things. I did not like that; I did not want to be dependent on them rest of my life. So I wanted to get out of the city as soon as possible and make more money.

Until now, my goal in life was to first become a doctor and then a surgeon. Now I started thinking about professional development. How do I grow in my chosen field? Is Poona the right place for me to practice my craft and raise the family? An obvious thought that came to my mind was to obtain a fellowship from the Royal College of Surgeons.

The Royal College of Surgeons, which has been in existence in some form since the late fourteenth century, was the gold standard when it came to surgery, especially in India and other countries that were once part of the British empire. Many of my professors and colleagues at Sassoon General Hospital had fellowships from there.

I began exploring various ways to go to England for higher studies. I consulted mentors, friends, acquaintances, and even friends of friends. The basic findings were these:

studying in London or any other part of Britain was expensive; and if I managed to go there, finding a job there after completing the studies, which would allow me to recoup the money spent on training, was not easy.

I thought about asking for a loan from my father-in-law. But I did not have the courage to do that because my father was still angry with me for accepting a car and an apartment from Leela's father after our wedding. In fact, he constantly reminded me that I had sold myself to the Sanghvis. Another option was taking one more loan from C.M. Patel. I was already saddled with two big loans from Papaji and owed him unpaid debt. So both were nonstarters.

Serendipities

Lachchu Pherwani was my classmate at B.J. Medical College. While most of us were enamored by the British medical education and that country's healthcare system (because of India's historical ties to Britain), Lachchu, a bright student, had a different dream. He wanted to do residency in the United States and work there. To get a residency status in the US, foreign medical graduates needed to pass a test conducted by the US Educational Commission for Foreign Medical Graduates (ECFMG). Additionally, they had to clear an English language test.

The ECFMG test was offered in only a few major cities in India. The nearest center for those of us in Poona was in Bombay. Lachchu, who was a Sindhi, a prosperous business community, persuaded me to take the test along with him. He suggested that we travel to Bombay together. Out of curiosity and because the test was free, I agreed. Even though I could not prepare much, on the day of the test Lachchu and I boarded a local train to Bombay for ECFMG.

The test format was different from any examination I had taken before then. I had to choose the correct answer from multiple choices to each question. I was used to the Indian education system where students had to provide short answers or lengthy essays. Nonetheless, I enjoyed taking the test. I had no pressure to perform. Months later, I received a letter from the US Education Commission stating that I passed the ECFMG and English language tests—a pleasant surprise. However, I was disappointed that Lachchu did not pass.

The next challenge was finding out how to apply to US hospitals for residency programs. As luck would have it, a friend of my father-in-law who was working as a psychiatrist in Philadelphia visited India in early 1970. While he was in Poona, I met Dr. Mohan Jain at Juna Bungalow, Rikhabchand Sanghvi's residence. When Dr. Jain inquired about my practice, I told him my practice was not prospering, and I was considering doing an FRCS. I added that all the well-known surgeons in Poona had Royal College of Surgeons fellowships.

His response intrigued me. "Why do you want to go to England? We have a better system in America and more job opportunities and more money," he said. "I am a psychiatrist, and I make good money in America. If you go to England, even if you do FRCS, you wait for six months for a job, and if you don't get a job, then you have to come back to Poona. Why don't you come to America, since you have already passed the ECFMG. The US now needs more doctors."

I was swayed by Dr. Jain's pitch. I learned from him that 80 percent of all residency positions in the US back then were for US medical graduates and the rest was open for medical graduates from all over the world. The United States always had a dearth of doctors; so they try and fill the training positions by bringing in doctors from other countries, who have passed the ECFMG and an English language test.

A month later, I received an application package from the St. Thomas Hospital, in Akron, Ohio. More than a decade earlier, Dr. Jain had done his residency in Akron. Upon his return to the United States, he got in touch with a senior attending physician he knew there and asked him to mail an application to me. I was excited to fill in the application, even though not sure what to expect.

Right around the time, Leela and I welcomed our second daughter, Sonali, born November 3, 1970. Like Tony's arrival, Sonali's birth also brought great joy to all of us, the Shahs as well as the Sanghvis.

Akron-Bound

In March 1971, I received a telegram from St. Thomas Hospital, while I was at my parents' house in Poona Camp. The message was concise: "Accepted for residency. Contracts and ticket to come via mail." I had to wait for a few more weeks for the papers to arrive for the details: a one-year residency in general surgery, from July 1971 to June 1972.

I was ecstatic that I could go to the United States, make more money, and pay back the loans. Dr. Mohan Jain had already given me an idea about the money surgeons in the US were making. Leela, who was still recovering after the delivery, was supportive and excited. However, my father was against the idea of me moving out of Poona, to even another region of Maharashtra, not to mention the US, a whole world away. "Surgeons do so well here. Why do you want to leave Poona?" he reasoned.

When he learned that I would have to undergo another year of general surgery and three years of specialty training to be able to practice in the US, he was even more upset. Bhai had seen so much poverty in his life. After I became a surgeon, he hoped I would lift the family out of the misery that followed us all our lives.

Bhai was particularly against the idea of me going abroad because he was getting old, and my younger brother, an automobile engineer, was not earning much. He thought my nursing home would eventually become profitable. He was still working as a salesman to run the family.

Bun agreed with Bhai. She hated to see her eldest son leave the country for a long time. I had never left Poona for more than a few weeks at a time. However, Bun was also a big believer in destiny: if it had to happen, it will happen.

On the other hand, my father-in-law encouraged me to accept the residency. The Sanghvis inhabited a world that was very different from the one my in which Bhai and Bun lived. In their world, people traveled to faraway places and lived abroad for long periods. Fortune always favored the ones who moved across boundaries and oceans. Leela's older brother, my brother-in-law Sushil, had already moved to Geneva, Switzerland, after his marriage, and he was running a business there. So they looked at my going to America as part of the natural course of life.

Two other people I needed to get the blessings before I made the decisions were Mr. and Mrs. Patel (Papaji and Momiji) who supported me in everything I did since high school. They both thought a big door of opportunity was opening for me and were delighted about it. They gave me their blessings to undertake the trip.

Despite the opposition from my father, I decided to accept the offer from St. Thomas Hospital. I sent the signed papers back within days, applied for the visa at the US Consulate General in Bombay, and contacted the Air India office to book the ticket. The fare had already been paid for by the hospital.

I had a few important things to take care of. One was getting permission and a one-year leave from the Government of Maharashtra. The Sassoon General Hospital and B.J. Medical College, where I worked, were both public institutions. Approvals for the leave took more than a month. It would have taken even more time, but the intervention of Surajmal Sanghvi, head of the Congress Party in Poona, expedited the process.

A second key decision to be made was on what to do with my hospital. Only a couple of years earlier, I built Chandan Nursing Home with a loan from my father-in-law and Papaji. After consulting with the two of them, I decided to rent the building to a bank with the landlord's permission. The money received was enough to return the construction loan. My father-in-law sold all equipment and furniture to a surgeon. The amount was not enough to cover the remaining loan owed to C.M. Patel, but I would pay that back years later, during my first visit to Poona from the US.

I left Poona for Akron in the last week of June. Before arriving in New York, my entry point in the United States, I had a stopover in Geneva, and spent a couple of days with Leela's brother Sushil and his wife Daksha. Leela and our two girls, Bhai and Bun, father-in-law and mother-in-law, and Papaji and Momiji, were all at the Bombay airport to see me off. My eyes welled up, bidding good-bye to Shefali, barely three at the time, and Sonali, who was less than ten months old.

With just eight dollars, the maximum amount the government of India allowed to take out of India, in my wallet, I was both nervous and excited about the journey to the unknown land—a risky adventure for me, but one I had to undertake since my practice was not going anywhere. I also felt considerable relief to be free from surroundings that had always made me feel inadequate and inferior.

CHAPTER 2

A BRAVE AND SCARY JOURNEY

The Air India Boeing 707 took off into the Bombay skies right around midnight. As the aircraft started its steep climb in the northwest direction, my heart began to pound harder and harder. It was the anxiety and fear of someone taking the first flight of his life and venturing into a new territory. Everything that happened since leaving Poona Camp on that morning was new to me: the good-byes, the check-in, the customs clearance, the boarding, and now the takeoff. Once the jet was at the cruising height, more than thirty thousand feet above the Arabian Sea, I was overcome by a sense of melancholy and loneliness. The thought of leaving my two young daughters (one an infant and the other a toddler), my wife, Bhai, Bun, my siblings, and Poona Camp made me miserable.

Soon I was overcome by trepidation. *Was the whole enterprise of going to the US for training worth the separation and the pain? Was I doing the right thing? Was my father right in his insistence that I should not have left Poona and that I could very well have succeeded there?*

Then another thought struck me like a lightning. *What if I fail?* The thought that bothered me the most was my failure as a surgeon. In addition to my unpaid debts, now I have burdened my father-in-law, Rikhabchand Sanghvi, to settle the outstanding debts of my newly built Chandan Nursing Home. I was really afraid of the thought of letting everyone down: Bhai, Bun, Leela, Shefali, Sonali, Momiji and Papaji to whom and I was indebted literally, and the Sanghvi family. If I failed, I would be in that proverbial no-man's-land, neither in India nor America.

I did not want my mind to wander too far into that direction. So I reminded myself of my *plan*, which was to spend about five to six years in the United States, get the specialty, and come back to Poona and practice. By then I would have made enough money in America to pay off the debt. With that comforting thought in mind, somewhere above the Middle East, perhaps Iran or Turkey, I dozed off.

When I woke up hours later, hearing the pilot's public announcement, it was early morning in Geneva, and the plane was already descending. My brother-in-law was at the airport to pick me up. Sushil Sanghvi, younger brother of Leela, had moved to Geneva after his marriage to the daughter of a prominent Jain businessman who emigrated to Switzerland in the 1950s. With a nice four-hour sleep, I had overcome the whirlwind of emotions and the sadness that had overwhelmed me during the first half of the flight. Now I was happy to spend a couple of days with Sushil, his wife Daksha, and their family. I felt even nicer after calling Leela and her father. As usual, Leela's tone was assuring and optimistic, which I found comforting.

The two-day transit, proposed by my father-in-law, gave me a peek into life in the western world. I liked what I saw there. The West had an order and structure to life that I'd never experienced until then. Before I boarded the New York flight, Sushil handed me fifty dollars. His father had asked him to give me dollar bills. Knowing I could take only eight dollars abroad with me, my father-in-law knew I might require some cash in the initial days in the United States. That was also part of the reason he suggested I have a stopover in Geneva.

The flight took off late morning and touched down at the John F. Kennedy International Airport in the early afternoon. JFK being the port of entry, I had to go through the immigration and customs clearance at the airport. The process was surprisingly seamless, and didn't take much time.

At JFK, I got my first glance of America. Two things impressed me right away: its vastness and breathtaking diversity. The airport itself was bigger than anything I had seen before. Bombay's Sahar International Airport was big, much bigger than the Poona airport. But JFK was in a different league in terms of both size and traffic handled. However, more than the hugeness and enormity of the airport was the diverse nature of the travelers who flew in and out of JFK that amazed me—people of all races, ethnicities, color, and languages: Europeans, Africans, South Americans, and Asians, including some Indians and Chinese.

In India, I'd mainly seen Indians and Britons, who were in large numbers in the country until 1947. I was reminded of the memorable words of Miranda in Shakespeare's *Tempest*, "O brave new world, that has such people in 't!"

Upon collecting my bags, I realized I was very hungry. I had not eaten much during the nearly eight-hour flight.

Being a vegetarian, I was careful about what I eat. Before going to the domestic terminal to board the connecting flight to Akron, I decided to have a quick lunch. After surveying multiple restaurants inside the international terminal, I chose an eatery that had grilled cheese sandwich and salad on the menu. My first bite of American food was rather disappointing. It was as bland as one could get. Truth be told, I was not accustomed to the western cheese. We grew up eating its Indian counterpart, *paneer*, or Amul (the company that produced it). However, that sandwich and salad gave me an indication about what was in store for me when it came to food.

The flight to Akron left 5:00 p.m. The aircraft was a much smaller one than the two wide-bodied jets that carried me from Bombay to Geneva, and from there to New York. The flying time was only a little over an hour. At the Akron-Canton Airport, I was received by Marjorie Clark, a friend of Dr. Mohan Jain. Mrs. Clarke (Marjie) was instrumental in me getting the residency, a fact that I did not learn until much later.

Marjie was in the healthcare industry, working as a secretary at a hospital in Canton, a small city roughly twenty miles south of Akron. She dropped me at the apartment that served as my first home in America—a sort of dorm for doctors doing internships and residencies at St. Thomas Hospital. I had a room for myself. After a quick shower, I went straight to bed. My body clock was still tuned to Indian Standard Time (nine-and-a-half hours ahead).

The next morning, I awoke early and prayed before heading to the hospital, a block from the apartment. The first few hours were spent on administrative matters and meeting the teachers and attending surgeons. The hospital gave me an advance payment for my expenses, which was a huge relief, considering that I arrived in the United States with only $58.

I called Leela from a phone booth and told her I reached Akron safely. I was excited to hear her voice. She was equally happy. However, the call was expensive.

St. Thomas Hospital

Akron is a typical Midwestern city, located roughly forty miles south of Cleveland, and once known as the Rubber Capital of the World with its four industry behemoths' headquarters: Goodrich, Goodyear, Firestone, and General Tire. In 1971, it had all the moorings of an industrial hub, with factories all around.

On the first day of my residency, I attended orientation in a large teaching room with eight or nine new interns and residents. The instructor gave a quick walking tour of the hospital through various departments and gave us a sense of what to expect in the next twelve months.

The first thing that struck me was the cleanliness of the hospital. I noticed how it functioned in a systematic and organized manner with a protocol for everything. Multiple staffers, including nurses, head nurses, attending physicians, and the education director, coordinated seamlessly.

At Sassoon Hospital, I was used to multitudes of people (patients and their relatives) whether in the emergency room or in the wards, which was more or less the same in every hospital in India I had visited. But here it was more streamlined. Hospital staff and patients were much more disciplined in the way they went about their daily business. Fewer people accompanied patients. Relatives came to see patients only during visiting hours.

The next thing I noticed was the number of specialties the hospital offered, each segregated and separated from the other. In India, Sassoon Hospital had only a limited number of specialties: a general surgery, pediatrics, internal medicine, gynecology, and orthopedics. St. Thomas had all those and many more, such as oncology, hematology, nephrology, and cardiology. The Intensive Care Unit was well equipped and always busy. A research department at the hospital was where experiments, including dog surgeries, were done. Another novelty for me was computers. By 1971 St. Thomas had started using computers to do billings, but in those days, computers were huge, requiring a large room.

Most patients at the hospital were White, even though Akron had a significant African American population. Similarly, nearly all nurses at the hospital were White. This was before the United States started inviting foreign-trained nurses.

Getting a Paper Published

US medical school graduates typically start their career as interns at a hospital, followed by residencies (postgraduate training in their chosen fields before becoming attending physicians and practicing their specialties). All doctors go through a year of internship, during which they get to spend time in departments of their choosing. St. Thomas Hospital allowed me to bypass the internship and start as a first-year resident in general surgery.

In India, I was already an assistant professor of surgery and an assistant surgeon, with years of experience. When I came to the US, I was a fully trained surgeon, with an MS degree. I had done roughly a thousand surgeries, both minor and major, from suturing up small wounds to major abdominal surgeries.

What prompted the hospital to make the exception was a paper of mine about to be published in a major US journal, *Archives of Surgery*. During my stint as an assistant honorary surgeon at Sassoon General in Poona, I had begun developing some academic and research interests. I was conducting a number of hernia and prostate surgeries, which provided me with real-time data on hernia and prostate enlargement. Over a period of thirty-three months between April 1968 and December 1970, I treated thirty-seven patients who had a combination of bilateral inguinofemoral hernia (a hernia that is in femoral and/or inguinal regions) and a prostatic obstruction by a midline extraperitoneal route. All the patients were followed from three to thirty months.

The results were encouraging. None of the patients had a recurrence of hernia or the signs and symptoms of prostatic obstruction during the follow-up period. Summarizing the findings of the treatment, I wrote a paper titled "Midline Extraperitoneal Approach for Bilateral Inguinofemoral Hernias and Prostatic Obstruction" about treating patients with hernia and prostate enlargement with one incision. Those days we performed open surgery, unlike robotic surgery, which is common now. After consulting with my teacher and senior surgeon, Dr. Y.G. Bodhe, and colleagues, the paper was submitted to the *Indian Journal of Surgery*, one of the most reputed academic publications in the country. However, it was rejected.

By the time the rejection letter came, I had already received the job offer from St. Thomas Hospital. So I ventured to submit it to the US journal, *Archives of Surgery* (now *JAMA Surgery*). Within weeks, I received the acceptance letter, and my paper was published in 1972 as the lead article, with an editorial on my work by Prof. Lloyd Nyhus, a well-known name in the profession. The article received some significant attention among US academics.

I had promptly written to the education director of St. Thomas Hospital, stating that my paper was accepted by *Archives of Surgery*, a peer-reviewed journal, and requested they allow me to start as a resident, rather than an intern. To my delight, the request was granted. I only later learned that such exceptions were rare and doctors had to go through internships regardless of experience.

The training period was hectic. I was required to spend at least twelve hours a day at the hospital. Usually, I was at the hospital at 7:00 a.m. Every third day, I was on-call, when I spent eighteen hours or more at the hospital. On call days, residents slept in the hospital Call Room. I had no complaints about the work hours. I was used to long hours in Poona. I wanted to get trained and trained well. On most days, I stayed longer at the hospital than scheduled and did more work than required because, like every immigrant, I wanted to show my mettle and prove I belonged here. I preferred spending less time in my room, as worries about the future engulfed me when I was alone.

My typical day consisted of following patients, making rounds, and writing the history and physical (H&P) for the benefit of attending surgeons, detailing each patient's condition. We also worked some weekends, making rounds and taking care of patients. I worked well with attending surgeons, looking after their patients and calling them for instructions when needed. Some attending surgeons were impressed with me. They knew I had years of experience in India. But there were a few senior surgery residents who seemed not to like the attention I was getting.

Most of the nurses treated me with respect. Some nurses, it appeared to me, were not used to working with doctors who spoke with accents. We were called foreign medical graduates (FMGs).

Forlorn in Akron

The first three months in Akron were extremely miserable. The emotions that besieged me during the plane ride constantly revisited me. I was haunted relentlessly by the fear of failure and the pain of leaving Leela and my two daughters. The thought that I came to America despite strong objections from my father was messing with my mind. *Was I right in not listening to him? What if I become an abject failure as a surgeon and end up going back to India? How will I face Bhai? How will I face Leela's dad, who has backed me to the hilt?* I had no answers to these questions.

The kind of work I was doing at the hospital was not helping. Even though the hospital went an extra mile in admitting me as a resident, my work in the initial weeks was similar to what I'd done as a resident at Sassoon General. Here I was an assistant professor of Surgery, mainly assisting attending surgeons and performing small surgeries, "punching way below my weight." I felt as though I were downsized professionally. Before signing up for the residency, I knew and accepted that I had to do all those things and more. But now I was sad and somewhat resigned to my fate.

At the hospital, I put on a brave face, immersed in my work, and tried my best to be a good resident. But back in my apartment, alone and gloomy, I cried in the evenings. I knew I would miss Shefali, Sonali, and Leela, but I never I thought that it would be so torturous. I tried to be in touch with Leela and my parents as much as possible. I called Leela every two weeks, mostly during weekends. Sometimes, my father-in-law called me. I had a telephone in my room, but international calls were costly. The time difference also made it difficult for me to call regularly. I had to book international calls and wait for the telephone exchange to connect the parties at both ends. At times, the wait was long. Voice quality was also a problem; sometimes I had to shout so they could hear me in India.

Leela wrote frequently. Bhai's and Bun's letters were mostly succinct and to the point. Leela's, on the other hand, were descriptive and reflective, containing a lot of positive energy. She constantly reassured me that things would get better. She knew I was restless inside. A letter used to take from three to four weeks to arrive, but it was worth the wait. Letters and calls from home were comforting, a balm for my soul and mind.

On those forlorn and tormenting evenings and nights, I had another survival tool. I had brought with me cassettes of several Bollywood film songs. My first purchase was a tape player. I found refuge in the mellifluous voice of Mohammed Rafi and Lata Mangeshkar. Apart from songs by the legendary duo, I had cassettes of Kishore Kumar and Asha Bhosle, two other singers I liked. I also had some songs from hit movies of Dilip Kumar, my favorite actor then.

Food was another major challenge in the first few months in Akron. Among the very few things predictable about life in India was the quality of food. Whether it was Poona, Bombay, or any part of the country, one was assured to get a variety of vegetarian cuisines. But Akron was a whole different world. I was not expecting *bhel puri* (a popular snack), *chapati* (a traditional Indian flat bread), *dal* (lentils), and *pulao* (a type of rice) for every meal. But the blandness of the city's vegetarian cuisine was beyond what I was prepared for. For someone used to mouth-watering dishes three times a day all my life, I was on a different gastronomic planet.

My typical culinary day included a donut, or bread and tea for breakfast; and soup, salad, and bread for lunch; both meals from the hospital cafeteria. In the evenings, three South Asian residents (two Sri Lankans and an Indian from Punjab) on my floor cooked dinner: mainly rice, dal, and a side dish. The side dish, on most days, was chicken curry. So I ended up consuming a lot of rice, bread, vegetables, and fruits. Occasionally, we went out and ate pizza from a nearby restaurant. But I was not a huge fan of pizza, as it contained a lot of cheese.

On a few weekends in the initial months, the Clarks, Marjie and John, took me to their home in Canton, a thirty-minute drive from the apartment, where they fed me nice vegetarian food. They picked me up from the apartment and dropped me back after dinner. After I bought a car, I visited them almost every other weekend when I was not on call or traveling out of Akron. Marjie cooked excellent Indian vegetarian food. Years earlier, Dr. Mohan Jain, his wife Mohini, and their five sons had lived with the Clarks for two years when Dr. Jain was doing his residency in Akron. Marjie had learned recipes for a number of vegetarian dishes, including dal, roti, vegetables and pulao, from Mohini.

Besides eating to my heart's content, routine visits to the Clark household helped me in two other ways: combating my loneliness and learning the American way of life. More than any other person, Marjie helped me get over the Akron blues. I often shared my concerns with her and talked about my plights over dinner. Her words were always reassuring.

Spending time with her and John was like being with family—a home away from home for me. Both exuded such genuine warmth that I could understand how the two got along so well with Dr. and Mrs. Mohini Jain, who were also noble souls.

When Marjie first picked me up at the airport, I did not know she was instrumental in me doing residency at the St. Thomas Hospital. After meeting me at Leela's house, Dr. Jain had called Marjie and asked her to explore whether I could get a residency in surgery at St. Thomas. As a secretary in a Canton hospital, she knew someone at St. Thomas and asked that person to send my application. She had similarly helped many other Indians.

Marjie and John both had great respect and appreciation for Indian culture and tradition. I learned another important detail that may have played a role in them taking good care of me: they knew my father-in-law and other Sanghvi brothers. The couple had even visited the Sanghvi factory in Poona. In the mid-1960s, upon completing his residency in psychiatry in Akron, Dr. Jain had gone back to India for a few years. On his invitation, the Clarks visited India and traveled to different parts of the country. Hearing this, I assumed that their special affinity to me was because they accepted the hospitality of the Sanghvis. Of course, my father-in-law was happy that I was well treated by both the Jains and the Clarks.

Marjie and John were each in their fifties. Marjie was affable and motherly. John had a great sense of humor. He told me many stories about the Jains, his and Marjie's India trip, their meetings with the Sanghvis and the visit to their factory. He always kept a jar of roasted peanuts. I enjoyed John's stories and nuts.

Years later, after Leela and my daughters joined me in Washington, DC, the four of us visited Marjie and John in Canton. Both were delighted to see my family and the progress I made in my career.

Back on My Feet

Without question, the Clarks were instrumental in me getting back on my feet. It probably took me roughly three months to acclimatize, settle in, and get a hang of America. By then I got to know most of my fellow residents in the Residents' Quarters. Nearly all foreign residents lived in the two-floor building, a block from the hospital. I was one of eight residents on the first floor; a similar number lived on the ground floor.

In my room was a table and chair beside the bed—more like a dorm than an apartment. The toilet and shower were outside, shared by all residents of the floor. Two kitchens were on the top floor. International residents included four Filipinos, two Sri Lankans, and three from India (including me). The two other Indians, one Gujarati and one Punjabi, and the Sri Lankans were all doing residencies in internal medicine. There were also residents from South America and England. The chief resident in surgery was Cuban.

Soon I befriended two attending physicians from India. Those with the privilege to practice in the hospital and had private practices were called attending physicians. One was married to a Filipina. The other was a Bengali, who spoke with little or no accent, and was married to an American. I gathered that he had been in the country a long time.

Around the same time, my initiation into a great American ritual took place. I accompanied a few senior residents to a bar. I did not drink alcohol, and only took a few sips of a soda and ate nuts. The bar, which was noisy with people talking in loud voices and television screens broadcasting multiple games live, was a new experience for me. I could have enjoyed the experience, if not for the thick blanket of cigarette smoke and, to a lesser extent, the intense smell of alcohol.

At thirty-five, I was the oldest among the residents. Others were between twenty-five and thirty years old. Even those from India were younger than me. But because of my paper, I was respected by everybody. Most knew that my internship was waived by the hospital. But unlike in Poona Camp, resentment of some neighbors was never outwardly expressed, or manifested publicly.

When I was in the first year at B.J. Medical College, the tires of my bike were intentionally flattened by some people in the chawl who resented the fact that I (born into a poor family) was attending a medical college. I was used to people making snide remarks about my background and family status. But in Akron, resentment was never verbalized or resulted in any action. Here in a busy hospital environment, no resident had time to pay more than a cursory attention to another person's life. Everyone went on with his or her own life. I also had such a tunnel vision, focused only on my training. The only people whose words I really cared about were those close to me, members of my family and Leela's family, and my attendings and colleagues at St. Thomas Hospital.

I realized that it was impossible to live and move around the vast expanse of the United States without a car. So after three months, I bought a brand-new Torino. The dark green car cost me $3,000, but I got a nice financing deal that allowed me to pay in installments. Though I drove in Poona for four years, I had to start all over again. India was one of the few countries that followed a left-hand traffic system. The vehicles were all configured for right-hand driving. In the US, I had to get acquainted with right-hand traffic. I also had to learn parallel parking, which was compulsory in Ohio back then.

I took driving lessons before obtaining my license. Initially, driving on Ohio's highways was a scary experience, because I was not used to such high speeds. I was also not familiar with side and rear-view mirrors. I drove on the wrong side on a few occasions by mistake.

Having a car gave me great mobility and helped improve my food situation, as I now began visiting Marjie and John regularly. I visited Cleveland, the nearest big city on Lake Erie, roughly an hour's drive. One such trip was to attend a seminar on breast cancer at the Cleveland Clinic. On another occasion, I visited the Cleveland Clinic to see Dr. Mohan Jain, who was recuperating after a brain surgery. During the trip, I was introduced to Dr. Mohan Bafna, a cardiologist at the Cleveland Clinic and friend of Dr. Jain. Dr. Bafna was also a Jain. Later during another visit, I spent a weekend with Dr. Bafna and his wife. The Bafnas fed me well and made me feel like a family member.

After I became comfortable with the car, I had my first road trip, another American ritual. Along with a few residents, I drove to Niagara Falls, a four-hour, 240-mile trip from Akron. Until then, my longest drive was to Marjie's home in Canton, twenty miles away.

The highlight of the trip was a helicopter ride over the majestic Niagara Falls. From 300 feet above, the falls looked even more spectacular. But the helicopter ride was cut short when the pilot encountered technical problems. Plan B was a boat ride, which took me insanely close to the falling waters. A few years later, I would make another trip to Niagara with my family.

In 1972, a gallon of gas cost roughly thirty-five cents. I could fill up the whole tank for less than four dollars. Gas stations encouraged motorists to fill up the tanks, with prizes such as drinking glasses. In order to get those prizes, I almost always filled up the tank.

Another major purchase that I made in my first few months in the United States was life insurance. Having grown up in a poor family, in a community known for wealth generation, I have always been insecure about my future. Now with a wife, who was born into riches, and two young daughters, I was even more concerned about the future. How will they survive if something happened to me? Who will look after them?

So when an insurance agent came to my apartment to sell a policy, it did not take long to convince me to sign up. The policy was for $100,000. It cost me twelve dollars a month, not a small amount for me at the time, but brought a lot of peace and security to my life.

The American Way

A few weeks into my residency, I got to see American egalitarianism in action. On a Monday morning, the chief surgeon and a few of us residents were scrubbing in preparation for a surgery. A janitor was in the room, restocking cleaning materials. The surgeon and the assistants were required to scrub in order to decontaminate hands and forearms before wearing surgical gloves and gown. The process was thorough and lasted several minutes.

During scrubbing, one of the most senior surgeons at the hospital and the janitor got into an argument. The subject: a supposedly blown call by a referee in an NFL game the previous day. The surgeon insisted that the call was correct. But the janitor strongly and vehemently objected to it. Even though the topic was football, about which I had little understanding, I followed it curiously. The conversation went on for a while, even as both men were doing their jobs: the surgeon scrubbing and the janitor cleaning the floor.

What amazed me about the incident was the fact that a janitor was not only talking to the chief surgeon, but he was also arguing fiercely on an equal footing. From the way they spoke and their body language, it was clear that the two men had several football-related conversations before as well. I could not help but compare and contrast how rich people and those in power treated lower-level employees in Poona and Akron. It occurred to me that in India, most surgeons and assistant surgeons hardly spoke to lower-level employees about any subject other than the work. In stark contrast to our hospitals back home, physicians here treated their subordinates well. In my early years, even I as a doctor was not supposed to speak to senior surgeons. We only listened. Whenever, we had a point to make, we did it speaking softly, with great respect.

Outside of the hospital ecosystem in the Indian society at large, I had noticed even more discriminatory attitudes while growing up. Once I had tears in my eyes seeing a few men from what was then called scheduled caste communities, or *Achhoot* (now Dalits) carrying human excreta in a pot on his head from the area's private and public toilets.

Having come from such a society, witnessing the debate between the chief surgeon and the janitor, which was seemingly won by the latter, was an eye-opener for me. Till then, I had routinely encountered strangers on the street greeting me and exchanging pleasantries. In India, I never talked to strangers except when I lost my way. Later I realized the thought behind starting a conversation with people you run into on the street and the positivity it triggers. It was one of the many incidents that taught me to respect everyone, irrespective of their professions and backgrounds.

In those early days, I landed myself in a few embarrassing situations, mainly because of my over-eagerness to sound American. At the hospital and outside, I heard men addressing women as "honey." One day, I was working with a nurse, who was in her fifties. I wanted her to get a catheter for the patient from another room. So I said, "Honey, can you..." Even before, I finished the sentence, she interrupted me. "I am not your honey," she said rather brusquely, in a commanding voice.

Taken aback, I apologized to her. I was under the impression that it was a term of endearment with no other connotation. But that was the last time I addressed any woman other than my wife as "honey."

Deciding to Stay in America

By December 1971, my fifth month in Akron, I had become quite familiar with the hospital environment. I learned how America's behemoth healthcare system functioned and the precise role of various elements within its supply chain, including doctors, hospitals, laboratories, and insurance companies. I knew who sat where, and how they all interacted with each other. I knew the great divide between the private and public healthcare systems. I marveled at the amount of money American taxpayers spent on healthcare, especially on Medicaid and Medicare, the multibillion-dollar federal government programs that pay for the healthcare of poor people, disabled people, and senior citizens.

Each day I spent at the St. Thomas Hospital, my admiration for this country's healthcare system grew exponentially. In the initial months in Akron, I constantly compared the medical and hospital systems in India and the US. I am sure people in other professions made similar comparisons. It was part and parcel of the immigrant experience. I finally stopped doing that when I realized it was not an apple-to-apple comparison.

Now all my energy was focused on figuring out what was best for me. When I came to Akron, my goal was to specialize in an area, make some money, and go back to Poona, where I would build a practice. My plan was to stay for at least five to six years in this country. That's the time it takes to complete the residency program, be fully trained and ready to practice.

I could continue in Akron, complete the residency in another three-and-a-half years, appear for a board exam, and land a job at a hospital. But the residency I was doing at the St. Thomas Hospital was in general surgery. The hospital did not have a residency in specialties that I was interested in: urology and gastroenterology (GI). I had already done the residency in general surgery in Poona, and worked as an honorary assistant professor of surgery and honorary assistant surgeon for another four years. But doing the same thing over and over again was not in my best professional interest. Instead, I wanted to specialize in an area. That meant I needed to find another hospital to get into specialty residency.

So halfway through the first year of residency, I had to make a decision: whether to continue with the residency program in general surgery at the St. Thomas Hospital or go to some other hospital and train to be a specialist.

In the meantime, I had made another consequential decision: that I would not go back to India after the residency. The decision was arrived after conversations with a number of senior residents and attending physicians. One Indian doctor told me that it would be stupid of me to go back to India. He said, "It is much better here, the training, the knowledge, the practice, the opportunity, the research, and of course the money."

He was right about everything. As a first-year resident, I was making more money than I ever made in India. At St. Thomas, I drew a stipend of $580 a month. I was saving most of the stipend, as the apartment was free.

Another person I consulted with on whether to go back to India was Dr. Jain. He echoed the sentiments of other Indian physicians. Dr. Jain's opinion was important for me. He was a father figure responsible for bringing me to the United States. Additionally, Dr. Jain was someone who was trained in the US and went back to India before returning to this country. He told me, "Don't go back. Take the residency. Stay here and practice."

Those words sealed the deal for me. The fact that I was already more than thirty-five years old, with a wife and family to support weighed on me heavily. I was cognizant of my responsibility to my family and my parents. I concluded that staying in the United States was in the best interest of all of us.

By now, I decided that I would move out of St. Thomas and do a specialty elsewhere. Where I would go was dependent on the specialty itself. The two options I considered were urology and gastroenterology. By January 1972, I started looking for hospitals with these two specializations in mind. I was keen on remaining on the East Coast, as I was getting used to the region. But I was prepared to go to any hospital in the country that offered me a residency. The first place I explored was the Cleveland Clinic, the most reputed hospital in the state of Ohio and in the Midwest region. I had been to the hospital a few times. But it did not have any opportunity in either urology or gastroenterology.

A position in gastroenterology was available at Lahey Clinic, a well-known hospital just outside of Boston (now Lahey Hospital & Medical Center, affiliated with Tufts University). I had heard a lot about the hospital while in India. In February, I flew to Boston for an interview. But what Lahey offered me was a fellowship in gastroenterology, not a residency. After the interview, I consulted with a few friends at St. Thomas about whether to accept the fellowship. Most advised me against it for two reasons. A fellowship in GI was not going to help me in the US, as it would not get me a license in the country. Secondly, gastroenterology specialists were not allowed to perform surgeries here. A urology specialist is trained to do surgery. That left me with one specialization option: urology.

As a surgeon, prospects were better in urology. Even if I did go back to India, a specialization in urology would be more advantageous than GI or general surgery. Urology was not as developed in India, and was rare as a specialty, and procedures such as cystoscopy and cystoscopic surgery to examine and treat the ailment of urethra, bladder, and prostate.

In March, I learned from a senior resident at St. Thomas of a position in urology at the Washington Hospital Center, in the nation's capital. The Washington Hospital Center was a relatively new hospital, started just fourteen years earlier. The public hospital was established by US Congress after the Hospital Center Act, signed into law by President Harry Truman in 1946. By early 1972, it was one of the largest hospitals in the country, with about 1,000 beds.

I applied for the residency in urology and was invited for an interview. The hospital's urology department was headed by Dr. Dabney Jarman, a giant in the field. In late spring, I drove down to Washington, DC, in my Torino, a six-hour, 350-mile drive. On my first visit to Washington, I fell in love with the place right away.

The interview was conducted by Dr. Jarman and other senior urologists of the hospital. They asked me about my paper on prostate surgery that was published in the *Archives of Surgery*. I was also asked about my surgery experience in India and the training in Akron. Overall, I was able to make a good impression, especially on Dr. Jarman, who was at the time the president of the American Board of Urology.

A few nail-biting weeks, I received the offer letter. The hospital had to overcome a technical and procedural hurdle to admit me: I had not done an internship in the United States. Dr. Jarman approached the American Board of Urology and received a special permission for me to be admitted into the residency program. I was lucky that, the second time in a year, a mandatory standard requirement was waived for me.

I was delighted to have the opportunity to pursue the residency in urology. I could not help but wonder what would have happened if I had not sent my paper on prostate surgery to the *Archives of Surgery* after it was rejected by the *Indian Journal of Surgery*. At the time, it was a "Hail Mary pass," to borrow an expression from football. Something you try, having exhausted all other options. But it worked out well for me.

Moving to the Nation's Capital

On a Saturday morning in late June, I packed all my belongings in a few bags and headed to Washington, DC. I was relocating from the Midwest to the Mid-Atlantic; from the manufacturing and Corn Belt to the Beltway, the seat of power of the US government. I had bid good-bye to Marjie and John the night before and thanked them for all the assistance and love they offered me during the previous twelve months. Marjie cooked me a sumptuous dinner one last time.

Throughout the six-hour ride on Interstate 76 and 70, I was excited about the next chapter in my life. My dream of becoming a specialist was finally going to be realized. Now I was also in a position to bring Leela, Tony, and Sonali, whom I had not seen for a year, to the US. My salary as a resident at the Washington Hospital Center was $9,500 a year, which was more than the annual salary of $6,969 I received in Akron. However, Washington being a big metropolitan area, the cost of living was more. In high spirits throughout the road trip, I did not feel any fatigue, either mental of physical.

In the first few weeks, I stayed at an apartment near the Washington Hospital Center, provided by the hospital and similar to the one in Akron. But I was eager to have my own apartment soon because I had already started making arrangements to bring Leela and the girls. My father-in-law had already initiated the consular process.

As was the case in almost every stage of my life, two guardian angels were waiting for me in my new hometown as well. During my medical college days, it was C.M. Patel and Chandanben Patel; in Akron, it was Marjie and John Clark; and in Washington, it was the Fowlers, Joseph and Muriel. At St. Thomas Hospital, I had a patient, a top-level executive who worked for Hecht's, a department store chain that later became part of Macy's. When I told this patient, during a consultation, that I was moving to Washington, she told me about her two relatives in the city. "Joseph and Muriel are great people; you should meet them. They could be of help," she said.

I did not know anyone in Washington, DC. The only time I had been there was for the interview. I knew that there was a substantial Indian population in the area because the Embassy of India was located there. But I did not know anyone. So I took the phone number of the Fowlers and called them a few days before leaving Akron. The lady had already called the Fowlers. On the phone, the Fowlers were extremely courteous and friendly. They promised to help me find an apartment once I arrived in the city.

Muriel and Joseph lived just outside the city, in Hyattsville, Maryland, a small suburb of Washington. Within a few weeks, they helped me find an apartment near their home. The rent for the two-bedroom apartment, with a den, in a nice building was $100. The apartment was roughly five miles away from the hospital but took anywhere from twenty-five to thirty minutes to get there because of high traffic on Washington roads.

My schedule at the hospital was hectic. So the Fowlers graciously agreed to purchase the furniture, including beds and mattresses, dining table, chairs and a sofa set, as well as essential kitchen gadgets. Having lived in the area for a long time, they were familiar with furniture shops and department stores. As a man of modest means, utility was more of concern for me than luxury. They knew where to get the right things at the right price.

Now I was ready to welcome Leela, Tony, and Sonali.

Leela and the Children Arrive

US visas for Leela, Tony, and Sonali were processed fairly quickly. Rikhabchand Sanghvi, who spent a lot of time in Bombay for business, knew how to navigate the process. In early September, my wife and children arrived at the JFK Airport in New York, which was also where I landed fourteen months earlier. It was a Monday and I could not excuse myself from the hospital to go and receive them in New York. Dr. Mohan Jain and Mohini Jain, who lived in Allentown, Pennsylvania, offered to pick them up from the airport. From their home, JFK was just a little over two hours.

Dr. Jain was a childhood friend of the youngest of Sanghvi brothers, Phoolchand. They were classmates in Rajasthan. My father-in-law became good friends with him after Dr. Jain returned to Bombay, following his residency in Akron in the late 1950s. Rikhabchand was running the Sanghvi family's business in the city, where the US-returned psychiatrist launched his practice. My mother-in-law, Ujiben, also got to know Mohini Jain well during the period. The Jains had known Leela since her elementary school days. So during Leela's brief transit at their home, they took care of her like their own daughter.

I was busy at the hospital that whole time and could only drive up to Allentown over the weekend. But we spoke over the phone several times. I could hear the joy and relief in Leela's voice. Her parents were happy that Leela and the girls spent a few days under the care of the Jains. They had raised their daughter in a very protective environment, and she had never traveled alone anywhere until then. For Leela, the stay with the Jains was like a boot camp where she was initiated into the American life.

On Friday evening after my hospital work, I left for Allentown, roughly 180 miles to the northeast of Washington, DC. So eager to see my wife and daughters, I drove faster than usual and covered the distance in three hours. I was thrilled to see Leela and the children. Sonali had grown quite a bit. She was nearly two now, and had learned to walk and speak. At four, Tony had grown a few inches taller. Physically, she was beginning to look a lot like her mother.

Both girls were excited to see their dad. Leela was equally delighted to see me. Reuniting with the girls and Leela was one of the happiest moments of my life. The Jains insisted that we spend a couple of more days with them, and I agreed. On Sunday morning, after a sumptuous breakfast prepared by Mrs. Mohini Jain, we drove back to Hyattsville to begin a new life as a family in America.

Leela and the girls quickly settled in our new apartment in Hyattsville on the ground floor of a two-floor building of some twenty units. The apartment was quite modern, with an excellent heating and cooling system. Muriel Fowler took Leela under her wing right away. A motherly figure, she accompanied Leela and the girls for grocery and shopping. Luckily, the 600,000 square-foot Prince Georges Plaza (now The Mall at Prince George's) was right across the street from our apartment building. Eventually, Leela began driving. Having driven in India for nearly a decade, she needed only a few lessons from Muriel to get a Maryland driver's license and venture out on the road on her own. As a result of her newfound mobility, Leela was able to go to the lone Indian grocery in the area more frequently and get authentic Indian grains, spices, and condiments that were imported from India. On weekends, we went out and ate pizza, which fast became the favorite food of Tony and Sonali. At a nearby pizzeria, bands played on weekends.

Leela got acclimated to Washington and adjusted to the American way of life fairly quickly. I would say she did so in a shorter timeframe than I did a year before. Already she spoke English well, having spent her childhood in Bombay, the most cosmopolitan of India's cities, and attended some of the best schools in the country. In Poona, she graduated from Fergusson College, an elite liberal arts institution. She quickly figured out how to navigate life in a new town and country. Of course, the Fowlers, especially Muriel, were there for her, to hold her hand, whenever required. Leela was free to call both of them for any help. Mrs. Fowler even took Leela and children to their church's Sunday school. The Fowlers were both very religious people. Joseph, a senior government official, was an elder in Lutheran Church. Muriel had worked as a telephone operator during World War II, a quarter century earlier. She was a retiree now.

Dr. Mohan Jain and Mohini Jain visited us many times, with their five sons. We also visited them multiple times. The drive up north on Interstate 83 and eastward through central Pennsylvania was scenic. During every visit, Mrs. Jain fed us various homemade Indian delicacies. The couple also took us around to different places, as we were new in America.

Within a few months of Leela's arrival, we got to know some Indian families in the area. Fortunately, a Gujarati couple lived in our apartment complex: the Dhokais and their daughter, Palu, who was Tony's age and who remains one of her closest friends today. In 2022 the Greater Washington, DC, metropolitan region is home to more than 150,000 Indian Americans. But back in the mid-1970s, only a few hundred Indians were in the area—before the influx of healthcare, engineering, or information technology professionals.

At the hospital were two other Indian residents, one in anesthesia, the other in internal medicine. We ran into a few compatriots at the Indian grocery store in Silver Spring, five miles west, which we visited every few weeks.

To my knowledge, there was only one Indian restaurant in town, Siddhartha, run by a Gujarati, Saurabh Ponda. Initially located in downtown Washington, it was moved to Silver Spring, five miles north. Siddhartha was a modest restaurant, so modest that years later a *Washington Post* reviewer wrote that the restaurant's "somewhat dismal environment is worth putting up with for the food" and its price. The review went like this: "Siddhartha, understand that it's a modest place, almost excruciatingly so. You'll carry your own tray from the order counter to a bare Formica table, eat with plastic utensils, drink from a Styrofoam cup, all under the merciless white glare of overbright light bulbs."

There were no temples or *mandirs* in the area. A gentleman from Gujarat ran a weekly class during weekends where he talked about Hinduism and Jainism.

A few weeks after arriving here, we enrolled Tony in preschool at a public school run by the Prince George's County. Tony enjoyed the school, where she made a few friends. We regularly visited the Fowlers, roughly eight blocks away. Tony and Sonali loved playing in their backyard with Muriel and Joseph's son Mark.

Training in Urology

Reunited with my family and accustomed to life in the US, I was now in a peaceful space, personally and professionally. Coming from the relatively small St. Thomas Hospital to a large public hospital like the Washington Hospital Center was a big jump for me. Most of the patients I treated in Akron were White and middle class. In Washington, a Black-majority city, a lot of patients were African Americans.

Washington being the seat of power, the hospital also counted a number of high-profile patients as well. Patients of Dr. Jarman and a dozen other attending urologists included US government leaders, such as senators, members of the House of Representatives and their staffers, and officials who worked for the administration. The top floor of the hospital was reserved exclusively for the so-called private patients and dignitaries. From these patients, I learned a lot about American life and society.

On average, I spent eleven to twelve hours a day at the hospital, reaching there at 7:30 a.m. and working till 7:00 p.m. On a call day, which was every third day, I slept in the hospital's call room. There were six residents, two at each level, first, second and third years. Since urology was new to me, I had to work hard to become good at it.

Working along Dr. Jarman (my mentor) and a dozen other attending urologists was a valuable experience. Being a large hospital in a diverse city, physicians at the Washington Hospital Center were dealing with an incredibly complicated pathology. During rounds with Dr. Jarman and other urologists on the staff, we visited radiology and pathology departments. I learned to interpret X-rays and pathology slides during such visits. Dr. Jarman also taught me to pay attention to comorbidities of the patient in understanding the whole patient. He was systematic in his approach to examination of patients, diagnosis, treatment, and plans for follow-up.

In the first year, I mainly assisted attending urologists with surgeries and learned to perform cystoscopy, an examination of the urethra, bladder, and prostate by a scope. One of the main tasks I was entrusted with was writing patients' H&Ps. With the hospital admitting as many as seven or eight urology patients each day, writing H&Ps was time-consuming.

By my second year, I attended clinics cases and conducted minor surgeries, besides helping doctors with major surgeries. During the second year of residency in 1974, I appeared for the licensing examination and passed in the first attempt. I was granted a license to practice in the state of Maryland and in the District of Columbia. In the second year, I spent two months at the Armed Forces Institute of Pathology under the renowned pathologist Dr. F.K. Mostofi. There I learned to read pathology slides of all different common and rare urological diseases. Dr. Mostofi received slides from all over the world for his opinion. The same year, I spent months at Children's Hospital studying pediatric urology. The stint gave me an opportunity to study and treat common and rare urological diseases.

Under Dr. Jarman, I began improving my research skills. A consummate urologist who was extremely good in both the clinical and research side, he guided my research activities. Dr. Jarman knew I was interested in prostate cancer, as I had done research and published a few papers on the subject during residency; he sent me to Sloan Kettering Memorial Hospital in New York for a weeklong urology cancer training program. Dr. Jarman also encouraged me to go to different residency programs at the Washington Hospital Center and provide lectures in urology subjects. The research skills I honed back then have helped going forward. Even over the most recent seven years, I have published six papers and twelve letters to the editor in various reputed US urology journals on prostate cancer. I credit Dr. Jarman's methodical training and sound judgment for helping me build a solid foundation in the field.

In the third year, I was named the chief resident. With that came a salary increase as well. Now I was receiving an annual salary of $14,156. An important milestone I crossed during the period was passing Part 1 of the urology board exam, a written test. That allowed me to appear for the second and final part. Now I was performing major surgeries and cystoscopic surgery of prostate and bladder diseases. With the help of attending urologists on call, I took care of urology trauma and other urological emergencies. I also taught the hospital's junior residents. During that busy third year, I wrote three papers on urological diseases. One won a prize at the Washington, DC, urology residents' annual meeting. Though one of the busiest periods of my life, I began enjoying success. Now with the DC and Maryland licenses, I started moonlighting to earn and save more money.

Birth of Amit

In the second half of 1974, we were in for a pleasant surprise: Leela became pregnant with our third child. Tony and Sonali were excited that we were going to have a baby. Like everything else that happened in the previous two years, the pregnancy was also a new experience for the family. When the girls were born, Leela and I had the support and help of our two families. During both pregnancies, Leela stayed with her parents, where Ujiben and her domestic support staff took care of every need. In Washington, our support system consisted of two people: Joseph and Muriel. Since the moment I arrived in Washington in the summer of 1972, I had been relying on the couple for all kinds of help. Now with Leela's pregnancy, their role in our family increased even more.

Being the chief resident, my workload and responsibilities had increased significantly, making it impossible for me to stay away from the hospital during work hours. But there was one benefit that came with my job at Washington Hospital Center. I was able to choose a gynecologist affiliated with it, which meant Leela could have the delivery at the hospital.

Once Leela was in her third trimester, I was beginning to get a little nervous. My schedule was not getting any easier, as I had started performing major surgeries. I was worried that I would not be able to take Leela to the hospital if she developed labor pains during my hospital hours. But Muriel and Joseph reassured us that they would accompany her if I was not there.

Around 11:00 a.m. on June 11, I got a call from Leela saying that the contractions had started, and she might need to rush to the hospital. I had a surgery that day, and there was no way I could go home and bring her to the hospital. Immediately, I called Joseph, who said that Muriel and he would drive Leela to the hospital. Unfortunately, on the way their car had a flat tire, forcing them to take a cab to the hospital. Since I was in the middle of the surgery, I could not meet Leela. Instead, I told an assistant nurse to take care of my wife. By the time I finished the surgery Amit had already arrived.

The day Amit was born, Tony and Sonali were recovering from chicken pox. So I asked the hospital to keep Leela and Amit for three more days, even though both were in good health. In Leela's absence, Muriel cared for the two girls.

After three days, Leela and the baby came home—a joyous occasion for all of us. Amit was a cute baby, who was doted on by his big sisters. Even though Tony and Sonali wanted a baby sister, they were thrilled to have a baby brother.

Looking for a Job

Six months before the end of residency, I started looking for a job. With the family already well-settled in the United States and a newborn son having just arrived, there was no question of returning to India. I had already made the decision to make this country my home. One of the first things I did after moving to Washington was to apply for the permanent resident status, or Green Card, which was the first step in obtaining the US citizenship. Once I got the Green Card, a visa was not required. I could work anywhere in the US, provided I had the license to practice. I already had licenses in Maryland and the District of Columbia and had been moonlighting for a while. Now I needed to find a full-time job.

In the medical profession, the time-tested method of job-hunting is via word of mouth. So I let as many senior colleagues and hospital administrators who were known to me that I was on the job market. I soon landed my first job interview, which came through my network of physicians. The job was in a mining town in West Virginia. The employer was a solo urologist nearing retirement who was looking for a younger urologist.

Leela and I drove with the children for the interview. The three-hour drive gave me a fascinating view of the Appalachian America, where poverty was rampant. The physician, an elderly southern gentleman, had lined up an

Indian doctor in order to woo me. I learned from him that, besides him, there was only a couple more Indian families in the entire town.

I did well in the interview and was offered the job. With bonuses, the starting salary was in the vicinity of a hundred thousand dollars. It was a real dilemma for me. I was not sure Leela and the children would be comfortable living in the region. Should I relocate my family to Appalachia? It was a tough decision because the money was more than I could imagine at that point. It was roughly five times the stipend I was earning as a resident at the Washington Hospital Center. I had never seen the kind of money in my life. After consulting with Leela, I turned down the offer and decided to look for a job in the Washington area, where we had built a nice comfort zone fairly quickly. Over three years, we had made quite a few Indian friends in Washington. Being a very cosmopolitan city, it was also easier for my wife to adjust to the region. The Fowlers were always there.

Another incentive for remaining in the city was the Embassy of India. For us culturally, it was the closest we could get to India. The area had small Gujarati and Jain communities, as well as a significant number of people from India's Hindi belt. For my children, the metropolitan area offered many Indian cultural activities.

Meanwhile, I had another offer from West Virginia—this time from a group of practitioners. They were looking for a urologist to join them. After the interview, they offered me a private practice with the group. Whatever I made, I could keep. That was the offer. Again I rejected it. Like the previous West Virginia town, this one also had only three Indian families. By now I had already made up my mind that, for my family's sake I should have a job in the Washington area.

A few weeks later, I ran into a familiar face at the Washington Hospital Center. I had first met Dr. Ronald Kretkowski at the Armed Forces Institute of Pathology, where I did a two-month training in genitourinary pathology. Dr. Kretkowski was a urologist running his own practice based out of the Leland Memorial Hospital, a 100-bed hospital in Riverdale Park, Maryland. He was also the chief urologist at the hospital. After exchanging pleasantries, he said somewhat casually, "Since you are finishing residency, why don't you join me?"

Intrigued by that idea, I said I would surely consider it. That conversation resulted in a more-than-two-decade partnership between Ron and me. In the next few days, the two of us discussed the details of the job. Ron offered me a position as a urologist, with an annual salary of $35,000, with the promise of increasing salary every year and making me a full partner in three years. His wife Vicky, a registered nurse, had two roles at the practice, as a nurse and as a manager.

In the initial years, money-wise, it was roughly a third of what I was offered by the West Virginia practitioner. But being in Washington and not uprooting my family for a second time in three years were important considerations to me.

In late 1975, I joined Dr. Kretkowski's private practice at Leland Hospital. Among many perks of the new job was the proximity of the hospital to home, which enabled me to spend more time with the family.

I found the practice at Leland, a midsize hospital, very exciting. We were the only two urologists there, which meant we were running the whole show. In addition to Leland, we had patients at the Prince George's General Hospital in Cheverly, Adventist Hospital in Tacoma Park, Doctors Community Hospital in Lanham, and Laurel Hospital, all within twenty-five-minute drive from my apartment, and all in Maryland. The travel time was important, as I took emergency room call at all these hospitals. We had privileges at all four hospitals and kept patients at all of them. Our office was within Leland in one wing of the hospital.

I became a partner of the practice in 1979, and by 1981 I was making $100,000. Later on, I was made the chief of Urology at Leland. Ron and I continued our association till 1998, when he retired due to chronic backache. I bought his half of the practice share and went solo. After Ron's retirement, Vicky continued to work with us at our Leland office until her retirement in 2012.

In 2006 I closed my solo practice and joined with nine other urologists to form a group practice, Mid-Atlantic Urology Associates. In 2012 we moved into a new office in Greenbelt, Maryland, and I served as the director of Medical Education in the group.

The American healthcare landscape had changed drastically in the last few decades, with the advent of health maintenance organizations (HMOs). These large groups offer their members an array of basic healthcare and supplemental services through a network of physicians. When it became impossible for solo practitioners and tiny practices to operate in such an environment, with the help of my accountant and attorney, we formed the group. By doing so, all the partners managed to cut their costs by having a group billing and collection system.

Buying Father a House

Having completed the residency and landed a job, my next goal was to buy a home for my parents and continue to repair my relationship with Bhai. Though his disappointment with me had diminished over time, it had not totally vanished. Our relationship soured immediately after my marriage due to the two decisions of mine that he disapproved of completely: my move to an apartment whose rent was initially paid by Leela's parents and my acceptance of a car from the Sanghvis. In his world, it was tantamount to deserting my parents and an egregious violation of the honor code he lived by. Bhai was also unhappy with my decision to come to the United States, which he interpreted as abandoning the family and running away from responsibilities.

After I came to the US, he continued to air grievances through angry letters. "You married a rich lady and didn't stay with us. You sold yourself," he wrote once.

I constantly tried to mend the relations with him. I knew he grew up in a different culture and milieu. I understood where he was coming from, and I never said anything to escalate the tension. I kept letting him know that I sincerely cared for him and the family. After starting my practice, I called Bhai and Bun every week. I realized I could not wave a magic wand and make my father's anger disappear; I had to work on thawing it drop by drop.

The first step was buying a new home for Bhai and Bun. With that in mind, I had been moonlighting during my residency several nights a month. Each night, I was getting $130, and I had been saving most of that money from the second job. When I joined Dr. Kretkowski's practice, I finally had the resources to buy parents a new home. Bhai and Bun did not want to move out of Poona Camp, where they lived their entire life together. I did not want to uproot them from there and plant them elsewhere.

I called my father-in-law and requested him to help me find an apartment in Poona Camp. Ever so resourceful, Rikhabchand Sanghvi found an apartment in a brand-new building being built in the Camp. The Maher Apartment building, on Sachapir Street, was next to Chandan Nursing Home that I'd built a few years earlier. It was just two blocks away from the chawl that we moved in after my grandparents' death, as was the clothing store where Bhai worked. The Jain temple was a block away.

I paid about 200,000 rupees for the apartment. In dollars, it came to roughly $25,000. Bhai and Bun moved into the third floor flat in late 1975. By the standards of Poona's apartments of the day, it was a modern building. It was one of the few apartment buildings in the area with an elevator. With Bhai and Bun ageing, having an elevator was one of my requirements. The 1,200-square-foot apartment had two bedrooms with toilets, a sitting and dining room, and a balcony. After living in different chawls for more than four decades, it was a big move for my parents.

After his marriage in 1974, my brother Vinod and his wife had moved in with Bhai and Bun to their chawl. When our parents moved to the apartment, Vinod and his wife took over the lease of the chawl.

I was grateful that the purchase of the apartment considerably improved my relationship with Bhai. But having experienced poverty throughout his life, deep inside he was still insecure. He was not sure whether his newfound status was for real. Bhai wanted to continue to work at the clothing store. He was apprehensive that, living far away, I might not always subsidize his mounting living expenses. After seeing his stress level, I paid him the expenses for a whole year and advance for another year. I wanted him to be happy and feel secure. My brother Vinod and nephew Hemant, who stayed with my parents, took good care of Bhai and Bun.

My father still had some reservations about me. An unfortunate accident involving my brother Vinod was required to completely mend ties with him. Vinod, an automobile engineer, was working at a dealership of Ashok Leyland, India's leading truck-maker, in Poona City.

On March 29, 1978, the day of Rang Panchami, the festival of colors celebrated in Maharashtra, Vinod got under the hood of a vehicle to make sure that all parts were in good shape. Accidentally, somebody lit a matchstick and threw it his way. The resulting fire burned Vinod badly. Initially, he was admitted to the Sassoon General Hospital.

When I learned about the mishap, I immediately called Dr. Keki Byramjee Grant and Dr. Wadia, my teachers at B.J. Medical College, who were now at Ruby Hall Clinic, a well-known private hospital in Poona. I made arrangements to shift Vinod to Ruby Hall the same night. There he was under the care of specialists for a few months in a special isolation room. Subsequently, he underwent skin grafting and plastic surgeries.

I paid for the entire treatment. My caring for Vinod finally convinced Bhai that I had not abandoned my family, and that the family actually benefited from the life choices I had made until then. It felt as though, his son had lived up to his expectations at long last. I was happy. Hemant, who was in school at the time, took over all responsibilities of the household. My sister Aruna, who lived in Sangli, roughly 150 miles to the south of my parents, visited Bhai and Bun regularly.

Going to India

After finding a new abode for Bhai and Bun, I felt a big load was off my shoulders. Since my middle school days, I felt that it was incumbent upon me to give my parents a better life—a big obligation as a son, a duty I had to perform. With every milestone I crossed over the years, that sense of duty had become stronger. I was the first member of my family to go to medical school. In fact, at the time, I was the only boy from our chawl in Poona Camp studying to become a doctor. I was hoping to lift all around me out of penury as soon as I became a doctor. It was a rude shock to me that I could not do that when I became one. As a matter of fact, it was that realization which led me to come to the United States. Once I was in this country, I could not have thought of going back to India, even for a visit, before improving the quality of life of my parents. Now that I was able to give Bhai and Bun a comfortable living, I was ready for my visit back home.

I had not been to India since leaving its shore in 1971. Until 1975, I was not in a position to take time off, as I was in the middle of my residency. Upon completing residency, I had to meet my twin goals: find a good job and buy a home for my parents. Now I had met both of them, but we had to wait till next summer to visit India, as Tony and Sonali were in school, and holidays did not start until June.

We booked the tickets to Bombay via London, where we had a stopover for a couple of days to spend time with Uncle Shantilal, my father's younger brother who had moved to England a few years earlier. We bought plenty of gifts for all members of our families, Leela's and mine. Everyone was excited to see the children, especially Amit, whom they had not seen before.

When I met Bhai, I could feel clear signs of a thaw in our relationship. He showed some respect for me and communicated with me more than he had in the past decade. I could spend only three weeks in Poona, as being relatively new to my job, taking a long vacation was not possible.

The entire time I was in Poona, I stayed with Bhai and Bun and visited Sanghvis frequently. In between, a number of relatives, old friends, and former classmates and colleagues dropped by to see me. One was Dr. Lacchu Pherwani, with whom I had traveled to Bombay to take the ECFMG examination. He was pleased that I had completed urology residency and was in practice.

While in India, I had to meet another obligation: meeting Papaji and Momiji. C.M. Patel and Chandanben Patel had relocated from Poona Camp to Baroda after I left for the US. They had started a new factory there, Chandan Metal Works, which manufactured steel furniture. We took an overnight train from Poona to Baroda. Papaji and Momiji were excited to see my family.

During the visit, I carried with me 10,000 rupees for Papaji. He had given me an interest-free loan of 3,000 rupees while I was in medical school and another 3,500 for my sister's wedding. Additionally, he also financed the construction of my clinic in Poona Camp. The last two loans had been repaid, but the student loan had remained in the books for nearly two decades. When I gave Papaji wads of 100-rupee bills totaling 10,000 rupees, he was pleasantly surprised. I asked him to accept the amount, even though the remaining loan amount was only 3,000 rupees. It would make me feel happy if he did that, I told him.

Papaji took the money for the foundation and said he was proud of me. "In my experience, it was the first time someone is paying me back three times the amount that he took," he told me.

I returned to Washington in early August. But Leela and the three children stayed in India for one more month. She enrolled the girls for crash courses in Hindi and Jainism. The four of them also visited Rajasthan, the ancestral home of Sanghvis.

When I got back, I was a much-relieved person. My mind was more at peace than it had been in decades. I finally felt that I accomplished something.

Moving to a New Home

Leela and the children returned to the US in late August, in time for Tony and Sonali to start their next school year. Now with a couple of obligations out of the way, I began thinking about buying a new home for my family. After Amit's birth, we had thought about moving to a bigger home. Each of us now needed our own little private spaces. Additionally, there was another important consideration. Tony and Sonali were both in elementary school. Their current school was good, but not great. Even though I was earning a decent paycheck, it was not good enough to send the children to private schools.

A colleague at the hospital, a general surgeon, suggested that we move to the neighboring Montgomery County where the standard of public school education is much better. In fact, his wife was a teacher at the Lake Normandy Elementary School in a neighborhood named Potomac, and that school was rated among the best in the region, the surgeon told me.

In the fall of 1977, Leela and I started our house-hunting in earnest. On the advice of my colleague, we decided to buy a house near Lake Normandy. Since I could not afford to take time off from the hospital, we did our search during the evenings and weekends. In the first few days, with the help of our realtor, we visited more than a half-dozen homes that were on the market. But Leela liked none. I trusted my wife's instincts much better than mine when it came to properties and living space, as she had lived in much better homes and neighborhoods than I did. Finally, one evening, we found the home that met our specifications. It was owned by a German American admiral in the U.S. Navy. Leela liked it the moment she saw it. The asking price was $135,000. The same night we signed the contract. I did not want to wait and be outbid by someone else.

We moved into the new house in early 1978. We enrolled both girls at Lake Normandy Elementary School, which was a few hundred yards away. A middle school, Herbert Hoover Junior High, was nearby. The Winston Churchill High School, considered to be one of the best schools in the county, was also close to our home. All our three children would go on to graduate from Churchill.

The most difficult part of moving out of the Hyattsville area was in communicating with Muriel and Joseph. For years, they had been our closest friends. They were the ones who introduced us to the Washington area. From apartment hunting to childbirth both of them were there. Without their support, life would have been a lot more difficult for both Leela and me in the initial years of our lives together in the United States.

CHAPTER 3

AAPI AND THE FIGHT FOR EQUALITY

I had some much-needed order and stability to my life by 1977. My job was rewarding and came with a good salary. I was able to finally crawl out of the hand-to-mouth existence that felt like the story of my life until I was well into my forties. I had managed to tick off most of the important items on my checklist: I brought Leela, Tony, and Sonali to the United States; made my first visit to India since leaving; paid off my debts; purchased a home for my parents; and bought a home for my family in a nice neighborhood. I was in a good space mentally and emotionally.

I began socializing with the small but growing Indian community in the Washington, DC, area, and attending events organized by the Embassy of India, such as Indian Republic Day (January 26) and Independence Day (August 15) celebrations. From time to time, I received invitations to receptions at the embassy for Indian officials visiting Washington.

Once President Harry Truman signed the US Information and Educational Exchange Act (Smith-Mundt Act) in 1948, the country attracted physicians from different parts of the world in large numbers. The legislation allowed doctors who earned their degree from overseas medical schools to do residency (training program) in the US and remain here up to seven years. In the initial years, most foreign medical graduates who came under the provisions of the law were European. That changed when President Lyndon Johnson signed into law the Immigration and Nationality Act of 1965, which removed discrimination against Asians and non-Western European immigrants. By 1975, foreign medical graduates (FMGs) accounted for more than 28 percent of the medical resident population in the US.[1]

A good number of FMGs from various countries practiced medicine in the DC area. And most of my interactions were with other Indian physicians. Many of us met for meals on weekends, usually hosted by one of the physicians. During celebrations such as Diwali and Holi (festival of colors), the size of the gathering was bigger. To interact and identify with others from our common culture and heritage reflected a shared desire to keep our culture and traditions alive for our next generation.

We socialized, compared notes, and our families benefited from the support system. Conversations in these gatherings ranged from family matters and politics to our respective practices. The condition of the medical profession and patient care in India came up in almost every discussion. Like me, most physicians in our circle came from India in the '70s and maintained strong bonds to our old medical

---

[1] *Fight for Equality: International Medical Graduates in the US*, by Shawn McMahon, Potomac Publishing, 2005.

colleges and teaching hospitals. While studying and practicing medicine in India, we were intimately aware of drawbacks and deficiencies of medical education and healthcare in India, especially patient care. When we came to the US and started practicing here, we learned firsthand how much more advanced the US medical profession was; and we genuinely wanted to contribute somehow to improving healthcare delivery in India. Many of us felt a sense of obligation to give back to our country of origin for all that Indian taxpayers had made possible for us.

The more I participated in those informal discussions, the more I was convinced that India-born physicians should organize ourselves under a single umbrella. We were all aware of some issues needing to be addressed in the US medical system as well. We practiced state-of-the-art medicine in this country, but our hands were somewhat tied because the US medical establishment continued to label us "foreign" medical graduates (FMGs) with the implication that we were "second-rate" doctors. As I interacted with other FMGs, I found some who faced various forms of discrimination.

AAPI Precursors

After weeks of discussions in 1976 about creating an umbrella organization for Indian American physicians, a few of us met to finalize the contours of a new organization: Indian Medical Association of America, Inc. (IMAAI). Those present at the meeting, held at a Ramada Inn in Lanham, Maryland, included three physicians who had been practicing in the US for a long time: Dr. Gurbux Nachnani, Dr. Raj Sidhu, and Dr. K. Joseph Mathew. Nachnani, a cardiologist and a senior physician in the area, was elected president. I was named secretary.

Initially, most IMAAI activities were networking, social events with celebrations, and annual meetings, which were attended by spouses and other family members. Though the meetings were primarily meant for socialization, we discussed a number of issues relevant to our respective careers, the medical profession in general, healthcare delivery in India, and discrimination that FMGs faced in the US. I learned that similar organizations existed in other parts of the US: Michigan Association of Physicians of Indian Origin, in Detroit; the India Medical Association of Illinois, in Chicago; and the Indian Medical Association of New England. In addition, physicians organized themselves on the basis of their medical and surgical specialties, such as the Association of Indian Urologists in North America.

By 1980, I was president of IMAAI, and the young organization's primary focus in the DC area was to increase membership. We had about 130 members when I floated the idea of having an organization to represent *all* Indian physicians working in the US. A substantial number (17,000) of Indian physicians were practicing in the US. Among foreign medical graduates, Indians were the largest group. If we could unite, we could use our voices to fight against the discrimination we faced here and also help India. Having groups like IMAAI in different parts of the country was good, but having a similar organization at a national level would be empowering.

My IMAAI colleagues agreed that a country-wide, central organization would be a strong force for advocacy, with more members and greater resources. After our brainstorming, I discussed the idea with leaders of a dozen other organizations in different parts of the US. One was practicing psychiatrist, Dr. Ujamlal Kothari, president of Michigan Association of Physicians of Indian Origin in Detroit. He had been in the US since the 1950s and was a close friend of Dr. Mohan Jain, my mentor.

The Embassy of India published a magazine, *India News*. with major news items from and about India, information on events the embassy hosted, and visits of top officials from India, along with news about the Indian American community. *India News* was mailed to thousands of Indians living in the US, and many physicians read the publication. I concluded that *India News* was a prime medium to reach these physicians and organizations.

As a government publication, *India News* did not carry paid advertisements. So I contacted the embassy official in charge of the publication and asked him to carry an appeal from me. He agreed. This was posted in the December 1980 and January 1981 editions of *India News*:

> The Indian Medical Association of America, Inc. (IMAAI), Washington, DC, has issued the following appeal to Indian medical doctors in this country:
> Across the US, physicians of Indian origin have expressed a strong desire for a centralized federation. We in Washington, DC, have formed an Indian Medical Association of America, Washington, DC, chapter, since the last four years. This association has to unite and progress toward goals of mutual interest. We request that you in all in different cities and counties all over America form a similar association. In the month of October 1981, we plan to host a convention of leaders of such associations toward the formation of a central body. Many other foreign medical groups have benefited from similar organizations. Sincere effort by all Indian

> physicians in this endeavor will be extremely helpful. For further information and details, please call Navin Shah, MD, president, IMAAI, Washington, DC.

Meanwhile I contacted the American Medical Association (AMA), the trade group that represents physicians and medical students in the US, and obtained a list of all physicians of Indian origin working in US hospitals and medical schools. I wrote letters to every physician on the list, inviting them to join with us to form a national organization. I was in touch with leaders of Indian physicians' organizations in New England, Ohio, Iowa, Michigan, Alabama, Kentucky, Cleveland, and Illinois, as well as groups representing Indian physicians in different specialties such as psychiatry, radiology, urology, and general surgery.

This multipronged campaign had the desired effect. Leaders of more than a dozen associations, and many physicians called or wrote back. They agreed enthusiastically that a national association of Indian physicians was an idea whose time has come, and such an organization would provide a platform for all Indian American physicians to address common concerns and assist India in the healthcare arena. I kept IMAAI members informed of the progress, and they strongly supported my efforts.

Since most organizations and individual physicians I contacted were in favor of a national organization, I proposed convening a meeting to form the body. Dr. Kothari suggested that we meet in Detroit because his organization had already scheduled their meeting there, and Detroit was a more centralized location for physicians across the country.

AAPI Is Born

Nearly fifty physicians representing about a dozen organizations convened at Hyatt Regency Hotel in Dearborn, a suburb of Detroit, in August 1982. In my welcome address, I cited multiple advantages of having such a national organization and highlighted two areas where having such a group would be a game-changer: fighting discrimination against FMGs, and augmenting medical education and healthcare in India.

Participants agreed unanimously to form the American Association of Physicians of Indian origin. Thus AAPI was born.

As a founder, I proposed Dr. Kothari, the meeting host and an elder statesman among us, as president. Kothari proposed my name for vice president. We were both elected unanimously. Kothari suggested another Detroit-based physician, Dr. Jagan Kakarala, for secretary and treasurer. Kothari felt he could run the organization more efficiently if the secretary and treasurer were near his base in Detroit. His was a fair demand in that coordinating and working across states and cities was not so seamless in those days.

I wrote the first AAPI report in September 1982 to all associations involved in its formation. In October, Kothari and I issued an appeal in *India News* to all organizations that were not already part of it to join the newly minted association. Even though Kothari strongly believed AAPI should focus on issues related to Indian physicians in the US (starting with discrimination of FMGs), he allowed me to pursue activities in India as long as I did not ask for any funds for such activities. AAPI had limited resources in the beginning.

Fighting Discrimination

Though I was lucky enough not to face overt discrimination, I knew that many FMG colleagues did. While serving as vice president of AAPI from 1982 to 1985, I received a number of telephone calls and letters from members in different parts of the country, complaining of the types of discrimination they faced in several areas of medical practice. I got in touch with each physician who contacted AAPI to learn about their individual cases.

These interactions opened my eyes to the unequal world of American medicine of the time, which was divided into three strata. US medical graduates (USMGs) were at the top. US citizens who obtained their medical degrees from international schools were in the middle. And on the bottom rung of the ladder were FMGs, those of us who completed medical education in our non-US countries of origin.

In the early 1980s, roughly 120,000 FMGs were practicing in the US. Projections were that the US would have a huge surplus of physicians in the US by 2000, which had translated into hostility toward FMGs and widespread discrimination. Hospital authorities, county and state medical societies, and even the AMA, whose mandate was to represent the interests of *all* doctors, took no significant steps to assure that FMGs were treated fairly. An intense lobbying campaign to pressure Congress to cut the cost of Medicare, the government-funded healthcare program, which also provided funds for residency training, affected FMGs adversely.

FMGs coming to the US were required to pass a medical examination administered by the Educational Commission for Foreign Medical Graduates (ECFMG) and an English language test in order to get into a US residency training program for three-to five years, then pass US exams to become licensed. In some states, FMGs were required to pass an additional English test to obtain licenses. But even after meeting all extra qualifications, FMGs were not treated equally. Some hospitals made a policy to only employ US medical graduates. A few openly advertised that FMGs were not allowed to apply for positions. Federal agencies including the CIA and the military branches denied jobs to FMGs. Even when FMGs had superior qualifications, their applications were not looked at or responded to by employers.

FMGs had a harder time earning a residency position. For decades, FMGs with ECFMG certificates sent out as many as 100 applications for a residency. For a time, some who were not accepted into a residency offered to work for free to gain experience and a possibility for a future residency. This practice was later stopped, thankfully. But some people even paid hospitals to intern there. Others trained and worked as medical technicians.

Medical licensing requirements for FMGs were more stringent as well. Done independently by each state's medical board, licensure in every state had different endorsement requirements. A US medical graduate had automatic reciprocity in other states; not so for FMGs who could not move their practice from one state to another. Their applications were treated with dissimilar and unfair requirements. FMGs were required to score higher on the licensing exam and were often asked irrelevant questions by staff and licensing board members who were frequently openly hostile toward them. Their licensure was sometimes revoked on flimsy grounds without due process.

As hard as it was to get a job, being promoted once you had one was even harder. Fully qualified FMGs were denied promotions, as less-qualified USMGs were granted higher positions. Some FMGs were given restricted hospital privileges, or terminated without objective evidence or due process. They were required to provide fresh documents even after being in practice with a medical license for many years especially if they wanted to practice in another state. Providing fresh documents from their country of origin was not easily done, and the original documents were sometimes not available. For USMGs, these documents can be obtained directly from medical schools.

The US did not recognize any graduate medical education training done outside the US, and FMGs were still considered second rate because their medical schools were "inferior" compared to US medical schools.

AMA Hostility

I had learned about the critical role the American Medical Association played in organized medicine as soon as I completed my urology residency. When it came to policy matters related to medicine and medical practice, the AMA was and still is the most influential group in the US. Every fourth physician and medical student in the country is an AMA member. The mission of the venerable organization, founded in 1847, is to promote "the art and science of medicine and the betterment of public health." Upon receiving my license to practice in 1975, I became a member of the organization right away, and I still am.

When we took up the cause of FMGs, the AMA was one of the first organizations we approached for support. For our group to be successful in addressing discrimination, we needed AMA backing. FMGs were 22 percent of the country's physician force, so how could the AMA not listen to our complaints? The AMA already had many subsections, including ones for African Americans and military doctors. I thought the organization needed a section to support Indian Americans in our fight against discrimination.

However, despite being aware of discrimination cases, the AMA did not officially act on any. In fact, far from being sympathetic to us, the organization seemed hostile. In 1982, the AMA introduced a new requirement that put responsibility on qualified FMGs to "prove" that the medical schools they graduated from were as good as American medical schools.

In my meetings with top AMA officials, I detailed and discussed the problems faced by the FMGs time and again. I told them that the discrimination was mainly due to the existence of a dual standard: one for the US medical graduates and another for the FMGs. Our position and principal demand remained the insistence that once an FMG completed US residency training and obtained a medical license, which demonstrated the same qualifications to practice as USMGs, they should be treated on par with USMGs.

Though repeatedly stating being "against all discrimination," the AMA refused to address the blatant bias against FMGs.

Bringing FMGs Under One Umbrella

In 1984, while still AAPI vice president, I asked other FMG organizations to join us to form a coalition to coordinate advocacy efforts on behalf of all FMGs. Those who responded positively included the American College of International Physicians (ACIP), Association of Philippine Practicing Physicians in America (APPPA), Association of Pakistani Physicians of North America (APPNA), Islamic Medical Association of North America (IMANA), etc. We formed the Alliance of FMGs to push back on the various anti-FMG bills being moved in Congress. But many FMGs still sat on the sidelines. Fewer than 10 percent of the estimated 30,000 Indian American physicians had joined AAPI. I told my fellow Indian American physician immigrants, "We pay on average $15,000 in malpractice insurance every year; is giving $100 per year for your own professional survival asking too much?"

The Wake-up

By 1985, Medicare, America's federally funded healthcare insurer for the elderly and the disabled, was in a crisis. The energy crisis in the late 1970s had been followed by the worst recession since World War II. Double-digit unemployment was accompanied by severe inflation. Many Americans were deeply concerned about increasing budget deficits. Medicare reimbursements per enrollee had increased 13.6 percent a year between 1975 and 1985, and the supplementary medical insurance programs' physician reimbursements had grown 15.5 percent per year. For Congress, alarmed at the rising cost, FMGs were a convenient target.

On March 19, 1985, Florida Congressman Claude Pepper and sixteen cosponsors introduced a bill in the US House of Representatives, proposing that American students studying in foreign medical schools would be ineligible for federal loans or loan guarantees unless the school met certain US-set accreditation standards. The primary goal of H.R.1582, to restrict physician reimbursements, would give a negative incentive to provide maximum care to patients. In addition, Medicare funding of intern and resident training was to be slashed. One study projected the Medicare Hospital Trust Fund to be bankrupt by 1990. If the graduate medical education (GME) payment (4 to 5 percent of the Medicare budget) was eliminated, the program would presumably save $40 billion by 1995.

Considered a federal government investment in medical education, GME payments typically covered the costs of approved medical residency programs of a hospital: resident salaries, faculty, administration, and other personnel. Why use Medicare money to train FMGs, when a glut in physician supply was being projected? This argument combined the anti-immigration sentiment and the decreasing tolerance for budget deficits.

A typical FMG was focused on trying to take care of their family and earning enough money through their practice, and wasn't paying much attention to congressional bills or other regulatory moves unless it directly affected them. But as vice-president of AAPI, I found the inherent discriminatory practices in H.R.1582 unnerving and humiliating.

The shocks of 1985 woke up FMGs to some extent. Though replacing FMGs was projected as a cost-cutting measure, the reality was more complex. To replace a hospital resident working about one hundred hours a week for $25,000 per year in 1985, a hospital would have to hire two full-time physicians, costing $60,000 to $75,000 each. We were determined to bring this argument to the forefront in our defense. We also had a civil rights claim: over the years, FMGs had helped to increase racial diversity in US medicine, and a deliberate legislative action against them would also result in a *reduction* in diversity.

ACIP (based in Washington, DC) represented FMGs of all nationalities and was the oldest international medical graduates group. As a collection of individual professionals, ACIP was effective in articulating the challenges faced by the FMG community, but the organization lacked enthusiasm and resources to launch a successful lobbying campaign. Nor did it have the money or strategy to battle against special-interest groups out to undermine FMGs.

My Presidency

I became president of AAPI at its third national convention, held in Chicago in May 1985. AAPI had grown from an upstart coalition of a dozen or so groups to a national organization recognized by, among others, the AMA. We brought seventeen different organizations of Indian physicians from various US cities, states, and specialties under the AAPI umbrella. About 500 physicians from different parts of the US attended the event, up from the fifty delegates at the first meeting when AAPI was formed.

For the annual convention, Dr. Harrison L. Rogers, Jr., AMA president, accepted my invitation to be our chief guest, a significant achievement, considering the AMA's long-standing exclusionary policy toward foreign medical graduates!

Taking over the AAPI presidency was a proud moment for me. I never planned to be a community leader or an activist, or head a professional association. When I first started organizing Indian physicians in the US, uppermost in my mind was socialization and a strong desire to help India. I never imagined that it would lead to a leadership role in a trailblazing Indian American group in the US. But I am a big believer in destiny. So wherever it led me, I followed.

As president, my workload increased further. Often I came home from the hospital around 10:00 p.m., after attending emergency room and other practice-related activities. My weekends were completely devoted to AAPI. Fortunately I had a partner in Leela, who was a true trooper. She managed the household and children's education without complaint.

AAPI initiated a series of concrete actions on our two areas of focus: the fight for equality for FMGs and some targeted initiatives in India. In late May 1985, I was shocked to see photos in an Indian American newspaper of an Indian physician and a dentist shaking hands with Senator Dan Quayle (who was pushing an anti-FMG bill) during a fundraising event held at the physician's home. Even when lawmakers were bent on harming the prospects of immigrant physicians, a large number of FMGs were still not ready to fight for our rights. Many FMGs, who themselves did not face discrimination, were either skeptical or outright dismissive of our efforts. Some physicians did not want to rock the boat: they were already in this country, earning good money, and providing a good lifestyle for their families. They thought that taking on the establishment might jeopardize their status. Some even stopped referring their patients to me!

FMG leaders in our struggle for fair treatment were alarmed by the absence of sympathy for their plight among state boards, the AMA, and lawmakers in general. The ACIP model had success, but also had limits. Ethnicity and nationality-based associations that had been monitoring the looming threats against FMGs needed to find a way to group together and consolidate efforts to stall the tide.

As AAPI president, I was studying how various interest groups were using lobbying to get things done in Washington, DC. The AMA itself was a case in point.

Flurry of Bills

The central theme of four bills introduced in Congress that same year was eliminating Medicare funding to medical residency programs, of which FMGs made up more than 25 percent. Just a week from when Quayle introduced his bill, Utah Senator Orin Hatch, a Republican, introduced another anti-FMG bill, S.1210, which put a limit on the number of GME positions a hospital could fill with FMGs. A few days prior to that bill, two GOP senators, Robert Dole and Dave Durenberger, introduced a bill that would have made FMGs ineligible for federal training funds, eliminating them from residency training.

The fact that US medical graduates were spared from these restrictions meant FMGs were being specifically targeted. In October, Ohio Republican, Representative Ralph Regula, proposed that no training program that hosted FMG residents graduating after 1987 would receive payment for those residents' training costs unless they passed the Foreign Medical Graduate Examinations in Medical Sciences. The mood in Congress was becoming increasingly xenophobic.

We were increasingly concerned that legislative measures being introduced to manage the Medicare budget would lead to harassment of FMGs, and the harsh scrutiny proposed by several bills would tar legitimate FMG talent. I held several meetings with officials of the AMA including the president, Dr. Harrison Rogers, and the US Department of Health and Human Services to voice our strong concerns about the legislative moves that institutionalized discrimination against FMGs, which affected residency positions, jobs, promotions, hospital privileges, licensing, reciprocities, and a number of other areas related to medical practice. But even after repeated presentations to hospital authorities, county and state medical regulators, and the AMA, no significant steps were taken to ensure that FMGs were treated justly.

In February 1986, the Reagan Administration proposed new measures to cut Medicare. Unlike earlier proposals, this did not target FMGs directly, but its impact on them would still be significant.

By now I'd been living and working in suburban Washington for more than a decade. I had learned more about the phenomenon of lobbying, one of the most-lucrative professions in the nation's capital. It was no secret that many members of Congress become lobbyists once they left public service. With the Alliance of FMGs, we were ready and confident to employ the two widely prevalent practices in American politics: paid lobbying and knocking at the doors of lawmakers.

We would have to lobby Congress to enact legislation that guarantees equality and justice for US physicians who earned their medical degrees from schools outside the US. To accomplish this, two actions were required: join forces with FMGs from other countries who were now practicing in the US; and mobilize our resources, which included raising money.

The first hurdle was convincing the AAPI board to launch a political action committee (PAC) to legalize our lobbying efforts. I told the board that if AAPI was to be a force in US politics, we had to play the American way. PACs have a huge role, raising money to support or oppose candidates running for offices.

The AAPI PAC we formed in 1986 was the first known occasion of an Indian American group launching a PAC. As PAC chairman, and AAPI president, I visited many cities, mostly on weekends, to persuade members to make contributions to AAPI PAC and be in touch with their own lawmakers in Congress.

After months of searching, which included brainstorming with some of my patients who were Washington insiders, I found a lobbying firm, The Keefe Company. The lobbyist assigned to the Alliance, William A. Signer, had worked previously with the House Ways and Means Committee and a couple of congressmen. The tasks assigned to Signer were to turn around the AMA and to push back against proposals to cut Medicare that would harm FMGs. In the next several months, Signer and I visited a number of congressmen, senators, and their staff to educate them about the plight of FMGs. However by April 1986, basic anti-FMG proposals proposed in 1985 had become law.

The other tangible action was forming a coalition of national bodies representing physicians from other countries (Philippines, Pakistan, Iran, and several South American and African nations) and join hands with ACIP. The ACIP mission to fight for "non-discriminatory public policy development legislation" aligned with AAPI goals. While Indian physicians were the single-largest group of FMGs, about 112,000 physicians from 100 different countries practiced across the US.

To build a coalition and work as one group, we had to navigate the egos of various leaders, as well as the cultural differences, biases, and prejudices existing among them—not easy, but all FMGs had the same goal. After several meetings with ACIP and other FMG groups, we formed the umbrella organization, Alliance of FMGs, in 1986. I served initially as chair.

AAPI also urged members to be actively involved in AMA activities and their subspecialty groups, as well as hospital, county, and state-level bodies. Only through participation could we gain a seat at the table and have our complaints heard and acted upon. (As the adage goes, if you don't have a seat at the table, you will be on the menu.) With that in mind, I wrote letters to 18,000 physicians of Indian origin who were not part of AAPI and AMA, inviting them to join the organizations and be active participants.

FMGs in greater numbers were paying attention. By the end of my tenure as president of AAPI, we had welcomed another nine organizations, totaling twenty-six member associations. In cities and states where local groups did not exist, we admitted 350 physicians directly as individual members. The annual membership fee for associations was $50 plus $2 per member.

I stepped down as president at AAPI's third convention, held at Omni Shoreham in Washington, DC, during the July Fourth weekend in 1986. More than 500 delegates attended, many from the DC metro area. The delegation included leaders representing almost half of all FMGs in the US. Leaders of all coalition groups within the Alliance of FMGs were present, including Dr. Robert Braun of the American College of International Physicians, Dr. Romeo Perez of the Association of Philippine Physicians in America, Dr. Hossan Fadul of the Islamic Medical Association of North America, and Ikramulla Khan of the Association of Pakistani Physicians. The convention was addressed by the new AMA president, Dr. John J. Coury, Jr. This was the first opportunity for a majority of FMG group leaders from different countries to meet in one place and hear from an AMA president.

On the sidelines of the convention, representing the Alliance of FMGs, we presented Dr. Coury with a list of grievances and injustices institutionalized against FMGs. But in the face of our protest against AMA support for cutting Medicare residency training funding, the AMA position was firm: Medicare should not be used to finance FMGs. This disappointed me, as I had aggressively campaigned AAPI members to join the AMA.

I was thoroughly exhausted as the convention came to a close on Sunday. Organizing a three-day event for 500-plus people had required a lot of planning and coordination. I was ably helped by a host committee, led by Dr. Krishna Rao, a physician at the Prince George's County Hospital & Medical Center, where I was an attending urologist. Ending my tenure, I handed over the baton to Dr. Roshan Lal, who would lead AAPI over the next twelve months.

Once the convention ended, I dashed home for some much-needed rest before going back to work the next day. I felt quite relieved at the thought that I'd be able to spend a bit more time with Leela and the children, now that I was no longer AAPI president. I had missed the *bharatanatyam* (dancing) and painting classes of Tony and Sonali, and Amit's tabla classes.

After a year of near nonstop activities to promote AAPI and fight discrimination, plus kickstarting two initiatives aimed at helping India (CME training and donations of medical equipment from the US), I was more than ready for some down time. However, I soon learned that the work was by no means over. It was just beginning.

The potential of AAPI was now being recognized by high-ranking Indian officials. Minister of Health and Family Welfare Mohsina Kidwai, and the Minister of State for External Affairs, K.R. Narayanan, had sent messages to AAPI members attending the Washington convention. Kidwai wrote, "I have no doubt that the deliberations at this convention would further extend the areas of cooperation between medical institutions in India and the professional institutions in the United States." Citing AAPI's attempts to take continuing medical education to India, she added: "The efforts made by the association to mobilize the doctors of Indian origin working in the United States and generating an increased interest among them towards their motherland are really laudable."

In his message, Narayanan wrote that he was acquainted with the work of AAPI during his time as the Indian ambassador in Washington: "I am glad to learn that the association has worked out some important projects which are now under the active consideration of the Government of India. I would particularly like to commend the recent decision of the association to donate medical equipment to hospitals in India."

Another top Indian official, S.S. Dhanoa, Secretary of Health at the Ministry of Health and Family Welfare, sent a message to the convention from New Delhi, saying he was proud of the contributions of Indian physicians to US healthcare.

Though I was no longer AAPI president, I remained active in the battle again FMG discrimination for the next four years in different capacities. We replaced the word "foreign" with "international" by 1987, and FMGs were rebranded as IMGs: international medical graduates. At the same time, I served as the medical education director for AAPI for the initiatives in India.

The AAPI PAC had made some efforts in lobbying, but without a big impact. With an already unfavorable climate for IMGs turning hostile, something more dramatic needed to be done.

Along with other IMG leaders, I testified in the AMA House of Delegates, arguing strongly in favor of forming a section in the AMA to address IMG issues. The House, modeled upon Congress, is the main policymaking panel of the organization. State and national medical groups, specialty societies, and different AMA sections are represented. In my testimony before the AMA House Reference Committee on June 22, 1987, I reminded the panel of the benefits the AMA would receive by creating an IMG section. Potentially, as many as 80,000 new members would join the organization; and such a contingent (just like already-existing ones) would strengthen the AMA financially and politically. I submitted a stack of documented cases of discrimination before the panel and pleaded for the members to review them.

The House of Delegates rejected our plea for the creation of a separate section to take up our concerns despite repeated representations. The AMA still didn't come around. They just set up another ad-hoc committee, as it had several times earlier, to address our grievances. Despite the repeated setbacks, I did not give up on the AMA. We continued our efforts to sensitize them to our plight.

Hiring a Lobbying Powerhouse

When practicing medicine in the world's political capital, a slew of influential patients come with the territory. Respecting client privacy, I normally don't ask my patients about their professional backgrounds unless it might be relevant to their treatment. I had never asked Kern Smith about his day job—until we had a casual conversation about healthcare issues. Turned out, Smith was an alumnus of the Kennedy administration, and now worked as lobbyist dealing with a number of healthcare issues. He told me he had connections to former Senator Vance Hartke, a Democrat who represented Indiana from 1959 to 1977. The next day, Smith brought Hartke to my office, and we had a long conversation about FMGs on the issue of discrimination and the various bills in Congress. Both Hartke and Smith were shocked by the treatment meted out to FMGs and were keen and eager to represent IMGs. That casual exchange with Smith led me to recommend that the Alliance of FMGs hire him and Hartke as our lobbyists as of July 1987.

Initially, the former senator believed we could achieve our goal of getting a pro-FMG bill passed by educating members of Congress about challenges faced by US-trained immigrant physicians. But once he went to work, Hartke realized the difficulties involved in overcoming the strong opposition to such bills from the organized medicine. He came up with a plan that included a grassroots effort to create a voter block and donor group to influence elected leaders, along with a well-planned media campaign.

Another point was becoming increasingly clear. While our efforts had been mostly directed at the AMA, the real high-stakes game was in Congress! Despite a lull, there was no indication that an even more-dangerous law wouldn't be forthcoming. American lawmaking is often a compromise of multiple interest groups who manage to reach out to impress legislators. Various interest groups came together and argued their positions, but Congress controlled the money for Medicare. Rather than pleading with the AMA to change its stance, the Alliance of FMGs had to make a shift and direct its attention to convincing Congress about the concerns of its members.

Hartke was straightforward in his assessment of the situation. "When we came into the position of representing the foreign medical graduates, we were immediately faced with an already-established congressional impression of foreign medical graduates. To put it bluntly, the attitude was unfavorable. We have been using our best efforts to turn this attitude around. We are making progress. It is not an attitude that can be easily changed." He added, "FMGs are not a high priority for most senators or congressmen. There is not a big constituency."

This was more proof that we had to focus our attention on Capitol Hill, the seat of US lawmaking. Visits to the Hill became a part of my routine. I developed a great working relationship with Hartke and Smith, the lobbying duo. Every Wednesday, I finished my rounds early. I asked my partner to take my calls between 11:00 a.m. and 5:00 p.m. Smith arrived at 11:00 a.m., and we headed to Capitol Hill in his car. I could never find a parking place on the Hill; and even if I did, parking in the narrow lanes was a Herculean challenge for me. But Smith knew where to find a parking place and always deftly parked his big Studebaker without difficulty.

We met Hartke at the Democratic Club for a coffee and snack after Smith and I made rounds in House and Senate offices. Having served in the Senate for eighteen years, Hartke knew most staffers and cafeteria employees, not to mention senators who were his former colleagues. Smith focused more on the House side, working on congressmen and their staffers.

One of Hartke's favorite meeting places was the Senate dining room where he met senators and their staff. He introduced me to several doyens in the Senate, including senators Daniel Patrick Moynihan of New York, Ted Kennedy of Massachusetts, and Joe Liebermann of Connecticut, among others. Hartke was a well-respected figure among his former colleagues. By the end of the decade, I met with nearly eighty members of the Senate and the House; most were introduced by either Hartke or Smith.

While representing the Alliance of FMGs during these interactions with lawmakers, we realized that the word "foreign" had a damaging effect on our campaign. When some lawmakers wondered why they should bother about "foreigners," we had to explain that we were all US citizens or permanent residents, and we had been referred to as "foreign" medical graduates (FMGs) because we initially attended a medical school in another country. So in 1988, we changed the name of the organization to the International Association of American Physicians (IAAP). I was elected as the first chairman of IAAP. From 1988 onward, we only used the term IMG instead of FMG.

Tide Begins to Turn

Initially our strategy was to play defense to stop all legislation and regulations detrimental to IMGs. Buoyed by small successes, we decided to throw out our old playbook. From a position of desperately trying to prevent further damaging measures, we now sought to gather support for laws that ended discrimination and unfair practices. We went all out to end discrimination, and it was another long battle.

Thanks to our lobbying efforts, the tide slowly began to turn in 1987. In September, two Democratic congressmen, Jim Bates of California and Stephen J. Solarz of New York (both sensitive to the plight of IMGs in our meetings), introduced two bills that allowed IMGs to practice in any state of the US without having to get a new license on relocation from one state to another. More specifically, Bates' bill, H.R.3241, "The Equal Opportunity for Medical Licensure and Reciprocity Act," proposed to alter Title XIX of the Social Security

Act "to promote nondiscrimination in state medical licensure and medical reciprocity standards."

H.R.3273, "Fair Physician Licensure Reciprocity Standards Act of 1987," introduced by Solarz, also proposed to amend the same law to "prohibit states as a condition of Medicaid funding, from discriminating among licensed physicians in its medical reciprocity standards on the basis of the location of the medical school from which they graduated."

Toward the end of the year, we started seeing more pro-IMG bills from politicians we'd met with many times. Prominent among them was the Senate companion to Bates' H.R.3241, introduced by Moynihan (former ambassador to India), which prohibited discrimination against IMGs in licensing, reciprocities, jobs, promotions, residencies, hospital privileges, and others aspects of medical practice. Introduced in November, S.1868, "Equal Opportunity for Medical Licensure and Reciprocity Act of 1987," had two cosponsors, senators Quentin N. Burdick, a Democrat from North Dakota, and Republican Mitch McConnell of Kentucky.

These legislative efforts contained built-in penalties against states and institutions that supported discrimination. The bills proposed ending prejudice against IMGs for obtaining their medical degrees from schools located outside the US, and guaranteeing equality to IMGs by ending the existing two-tier system.

Most pro-IMG bills in the House and the Senate were written primarily by me, with the help of Hartke and the legislative aides of concerned lawmakers. After multiple meetings and discussions with Bates, Solarz, Moynihan, and their legislative aides, on March 11, 1988, as IAAP chair, I testified before the subcommittee on Health and the Environment in support of the Bates and Solarz bills. In the testimony, I highlighted the following facts:

- IMGs make up 22 percent (123,000) of all US doctors; they graduated from approximately a thousand medical schools based in roughly eighty countries.
- Approximately 20 percent of US medical faculty members and 50 percent of NIH doctors were IMGs.
- Six IMGs had won the Nobel Prizes in Physiology and Medicine.

I submitted thirty-four cases of discrimination in residency, job, promotion, privileges, reciprocity, and other areas of medical practice. I pleaded for total equality for IMGs and USMGs once IMGs completed residency in the US and obtained licenses to practice in this country.

The chair of the committee, Representative Henry A. Waxman, lauded me, saying that the testimony was clearly first rate. The committee was mainly focused on reciprocity in physician licensure, and the question of whether federal intervention would be desirable in regulating medical education.

The Federation of State Medical Boards and the AMA were the principal opponents of the proposed legislation. The AMA boycotted the hearing (as they opposed all pro-IMG bills). No surprise. But what was not fathomable to me was the absence of my Indian IMG colleagues at the hearing to support us. Dr. Virendra Bisla, chairman of the AAPI political action committee, who also testified, was the only other Indian physician present to testify on behalf of our colleagues and leaders. (Later I realized that my AAPI colleagues were probably worried that the bills might invite backlash against IMGs.)

Fortunately, as always was the case with any India-related event in Washington, the man present to document the hearing for the world and for posterity was Aziz Haniffa of *India Abroad*, who covered the hearing and wrote a detailed report on it.

Though the hundredth Congress did not pass a single pro-IMG bill, we saw some encouraging signals. In July 1988, yet another endorsement of our position came from a newly created official body: the Commission on Graduate Medical Education (COGME) said in its first report that "a single medical knowledge examination for all GME candidates should be implemented as soon as possible." I had previously detailed to COGME the achievements of IMGs and the role they played in enhancing medical education and healthcare in the US.

In December 1988, Bates introduced a bill to have the Government Accountability Office (GAO), an agency that serves as a research wing of Congress, study the issue. That bill was passed, leading to a GAO study. A major breakthrough for our campaign! We had catalogued seventy-seven cases of discrimination by then, and I provided GAO with all cases involving complaints.

As a result of our persistent efforts, more members of Congress were now sensitive to our demand for justice and began to openly state their support for IMGs and for prohibiting discrimination against IMGs. In the next Congress (1989), we had four pro-IMG bills: two each in the House and the Senate. H.R.614, introduced by Solarz, had twenty-three cosponsors, and Bates' bill, H.R.1134, had sixty cosponsors. Their companion bills in the Senate, Lieberman's S.8790 and Moynihan's S.304, each had eight cosponsors. I had many meetings with the four lawmakers and their staffs in preparation of the bills. IAAP leaders had held a Capitol Hill rally and, along with Hartke, met later with several lawmakers, seeking their support. Finally a total of ninety-one lawmakers from both chambers came on board as sponsors or cosponsors of bills to end the prevailing discrimination against IMGs. That they included Democrats (who controlled Congress) and Republicans (who had the presidency) was a victory of sorts for us.

Smith and Hartke each played a major role in the introduction of pro-IMG bills and more were introduced in 1990. The International Medical Graduate Anti-Discrimination Act was sponsored by Illinois Democrat Senator Paul Simon. Fellow Democrats, Lieberman and Moynihan, introduced similar legislation to prohibit discrimination against IMGs.

Even as we began seeing our support increasing on Capitol Hill, prejudice against IMGs continued unabated. A case in point was an article published in the May 1988 issue of *Medical Economics*. The article, essentially a list compiled by a physician, Dr. Robert S. Brittain, mentioned various ways for patients to figure out if their doctor would put them at possible risk. On top of the list was the term we all dreaded: "a foreign medical graduate."

IAAP promptly sued the publication for $170 million in damages for defaming the IMG community. The magazine tendered a public apology for publishing the piece.

GAO Weighs In

After the passage of Bates' bill mandating the Government Accountability Office to study the IMG discrimination issue, the GAO began to work on its report. I met with GAO officials weekly and provided them with dozens of cases of discrimination. On April 29, 1989, I was invited as the sole spokesperson for IMGs to attend a roundtable conference chaired by a GAO official. Among others invited to speak were representatives of HHS, AMA, Federation of State Medical Boards, American Association of Medical Colleges, National Board of Medical Examiners, and Educational Commission for Foreign Medical Graduates. Hartke and Smith accompanied me to the roundtable. I used the term IMG instead of FMG throughout the conference.

This was the first opportunity IMGs had to actually meet with leaders of organized medicine. During the day-long deliberations, education, examination, and experiences of IMGs were discussed. Many participants went to great lengths, mostly under the guise of "safety of Americans," to belittle IMGs' initial medical education. They conveniently ignored the fact that IMGs had passed American exams, successfully completed their residency training in the US, and passed all required licensing and board exams.

I pointed out that all physicians in the US, including IMGs, must have continuing medical education certificates to keep up with the state-of-the-art medical practice in order to renew their license every three to four years. They had no reason to doubt our credentials, other than prejudice. I told them, "It is I who is practicing, not my medical school. The medicine I practice today is not the medicine I practiced even during my US residency at the Washington Hospital Center in 1975."

At some point, deliberations became very personal, when some members went on to question my educational credentials. An AMA official repeatedly questioned the quality of the school I graduated from. I remained forceful, asking him, "Sir, are you in practice?"

He said he didn't "have to answer that question."

When I asked the chairman to compel him to answer, he answered that he was not in practice.

I told him, "Science is progressing, and I keep up with continual medical education. So judge me, not my school."

I reiterated my favorite one-liner: "A good doctor can come from a bad school, and a bad doctor can come from a good school." The point: continuing medical education and individual commitment to excellence is what makes a good doctor good.

At another hearing on the issue, I said, "We have been here for the last three decades and now, after ten, twenty, or thirty years, if you ask us how many books our libraries had, or how many PhD professors taught us in the biochemistry department, or ask us to provide the CVs of all the teachers and the heads of the departments when we were in medical schools, it is impossible for us to get this information. I personally feel this information is irrelevant, since we have taken the approved American training and are legally in practice in America."

I pointed out that this is just an easy way for state boards to eliminate IMGs from competing with USMGs in the private practice of medicine, and to inhibit or curtail IMG mobility.

In accordance with generally accepted government auditing standards, GAO's review process went on for six months, from March through August 1989. In May 1990, the agency released the report, *Requirements Different for Graduates of Foreign and US Medical Schools in Medical Licensing by Endorsement*, a significant milestone for our campaign.

The report cited the different examinations and licensing processes IMGs had to undergo before they could practice in the US. It pointed out that IMGs put in more years of training

▲ **Navin** as a student at GKHM High School in Poona Camp, 1949

▲ **Residents training** under Dr. Yashwant G. Bodhe (front center), Navin Shah (front right) Circa 1964.

▲ **Shah family** (L to R) Shefali, Navin, Amit, Sonali and Leela

▲ **Dr. Navin Shah** with father-in-law Rikhabchand Sanghvi and mother-in-law Ujiben at Bombay airport, before leaving for the US, 1971.

▲ **Chimanlal** holding Sonali, Leela with Shefali, Lilawati, Vinod, and nephew Hemant at Bombay airport.

▲ **Dr. Roshan Lal,** third AAPI president, addressing the 1987 AAPI convention in Philadelphia with Dr. Navin Shah (center) and the first president, Dr. Ujjamlal Kothari.

▲ **Dr. Navin Shah** with IAAP lobbyist Senator Vance Hartke

▲ **Dr. Shah** with HHS Secretary Tommy Thompson in early 2000s.

▲ **Executive Committee** of Doctors Community Hospital in 2003: (seated L to R) Brian Bayly, Navin Shah (medical staff president), Barlow Lynch; (standing L to R) Frank Melagrona, George Urban, and Nader Tavakoli.

▲ **Dr. Navin Shah** with Indian Prime Minister Manmohan Singh (L) at his South Block office in New Delhi, 2005.

and had to produce more documents related to their medical education than US graduates. The study cited the demands of different medical bodies on IMGs to get current documents and information about their medical education, even though these physicians had been in practice for years in the US.

The GAO observed that some of the requirements by state licensing boards were of questionable value. It supported a single exam for both IMGs and USMGs and a central repository for IMG documents. Additional medical and English language tests for IMGs, as required by some states for licensing and reciprocity, were found unnecessary. The study noted that the number of years of training should be equal for IMGs and USMGs. It pointed out that there were no uniform standards and requirements by different licensing boards. The agency upheld our arguments in substantial measure and gave further momentum for legislation to end discrimination.

The GAO stated its attempt was to figure out the differences between IMGs and USMGs in endorsement licensure and "determine the reasons for and merits of any differences." They took several steps to identify the differences between endorsement requirements for graduates of foreign medical schools and graduates of the US medical schools. The study reviewed national data on each state's requirements, as collected by AMA and FSMB. GAO representatives then visited six states (California, Florida, New York, Ohio, Texas, and Virginia) to obtain more-detailed information. They met with officials of state medical licensing boards, medical associations most closely related to licensure issues, and organizations representing IMGs in those states.

The report noted that roundtable participants did not agree on the merits of the different requirements for experience or for education documentation for IMGs. However, they agreed that a clearinghouse would be an effective way to maintain and verify documents related to licensure applicants' educational backgrounds and credentials. A clearinghouse would be particularly useful to IMGs who sought endorsement but had difficulty obtaining records from their medical schools. They believed that these physicians would benefit from their records being on a file with a centralized organization. While the GAO noted significant discrepancies in USMG and IMG licensing requirements, it did not have conclusive evidence to specifically cite "discrimination" as the reason for the situation.

Success at Last

Because of our sustained lobbying efforts, ninety-one members of Congress from both the Senate and the House lent their names to various pro-IMG bills by 1990. In addition to the support of these lawmakers, the landmark GAO study began to have an effect on the AMA. Though still reluctant to openly support our demand for federal legislation to outlaw discrimination against IMGs, the organization slowly began to adopt a more sympathetic position toward us. Notably in March 1990, the AMA stopped using the term FMG, replacing it with IMG.[2,3]

On April 25, 1990, Simon introduced a bill to end "the double standardized treatment of IMGs." The International

---

2   The AMA finally formed a special cell to serve IMGs in 1997, a decade after the AMA's House of Delegates voted to reject such a section.

3   In 2002, when the AMA publication *American Medical News* used the term FMG in an article, I wrote a letter strongly criticizing the continued use of the term, and they published my letter with a rejoinder that admitted the error.

Medical Graduates Anti-Discrimination Act (S.2515) aimed at stopping discrimination against us, especially in licensing and reciprocity. The senator said, "The lack of access to health care in our society has been well documented. International medical graduates are a valuable resource and can be part of the solution to our health care crisis. But we must end this double standard, relying heavily upon international medical graduates to provide health care by treating them as second-class citizens. The treatment of international medical graduates has been a social injustice that we can no longer ignore. The elimination of discrimination must be our number-one goal, and redressing the wrongs inflicted upon international medical graduates is one step towards the goal."

At the time, IMGs were not allowed to take the third part of the National Licensing Examination. They had to take an alternate test. Simon's bill proposed to abolish this dual examination system and put in place a single test for all medical graduates irrespective of the country where they got their degree. The bill also called for a national repository of physician records to reduce the problem IMGs face every time they applied for license. Such a repository would quicken the process of licensing, especially when moving from one state to another.

While the bill was being crafted, I was in constant touch with Floyd Fithian, Simon's chief of staff, providing our input and feedback. We met at least a half-dozen times in addition to communicating via phone continuously during the process. Fithian, a former congressman, credited me and IAAP colleagues, Virendra Bisla and Kishore Thampy, for our feedback. Later the senator wrote me a letter thanking me for our inputs.

Simon's bill was a mellowed-down version of similar legislation introduced by Lieberman and Moynihan. These bills were similar to the ones introduced in the House by Solarz and Bates. All these bills had one common provision: they would immediately end medical funds to state and hospital funding agencies that discriminated against IMGs.

Behind the scenes, Hartke, Smith, and I still worked with congressmen and their staff as they crafted pro-IMG bills. I supplied them with facts and figures that became part of the bills. Hartke and I decided that while he would help prepare the talking points and pitches, I would do all the talking. Thus the lawmakers and staff discussed the IMG issues directly with me. Hartke told me, "The emotions with which you articulate the issue, nobody can show that."

Simon was aware that it would be impossible to get the bill through Congress because some members who would otherwise support IMGs might balk at the provision. Simon tactically drafted the bill to have jurisdiction in the Labor and Human Resources committee of which he was a member.

Solarz and Dymally argued strongly for the IMGs before the House subcommittee on Health, chaired by Waxman. Introducing his bill, International Medical Graduates Equity Act of 1991, Solarz pointed out that the US healthcare system was "in critical condition and America could not afford to discriminate against IMGs." He said, "These doctors comprise 22 percent of the nation's practicing positions, serve in some of the country's most impoverished areas, and have eighteen Nobel Prizes."

The congressman said his legislation "would improve health care for Americans by alleviating some of the most blatant aspects of discrimination faced by the IMG community." The bill would also establish a national clearinghouse and an advisory board for physician credentials.

Dymally, who had introduced similar legislation, pointed out that "IMGs serve primarily in underserved urban areas (and) they are a valuable resource to the healthcare of our nation." He noted that "despite studies that have demonstrated that IMGs are comparable in medical knowledge and clinical skills to their domestically educated counterparts, and while we rely heavily on their services, they are subjected to dual medical licensing standards and discrimination in both overt and covert forms."

Dymally's bill had three major components: it sought to eliminate the differences in medical licensure and licensure by endorsement requirements between domestic and international medical graduates, which would provide equal job opportunities, hospital promotions, and other employment-related matters to IMGs. Second, it called for establishment of an advisory council under the HHS to make recommendations on the progress of AMA's national physician credentials verification. Third, it made it illegal for a residency training program to refuse slots in residency to IMGs only because of the placement of their medical school. Lastly, the bill sought to instruct the HHS secretary to collect information that was missing from the GAO report, which was information from the states on the processing of applications for residency and licensure.

In November 1990, a number of legislators who had championed pro-IMG laws were reelected with strong mandates for another term, boosting our chances. Prominent among them were Bates, Solarz, and California Democrat Mervyn Dymally in the House, and Lieberman and Moynihan in the

Senate. The IAAP could now count on the support of these members to push any potential bill it championed.

A number of provisions in the Simon and Solarz bills made further progress. However, before the Health Professions Education Amendments of 1992 were passed by Congress, some of them had to be sacrificed during final negotiations. Fortunately for us, the antidiscrimination proposals did not die.

Finally in March 1992, two years after Simon first introduced his bill, President George H.W. Bush signed into law the Health Professions Reauthorization Act of 1992 (HPRA). The new law addressed the main concerns of IMGs in a significant manner. Among other provisions, the following became law:

- A central repository for IMG credentials was put in place;
- Residency programs that discriminated based on country of medical education would lose federal funds;
- A national advisory council, which included IMGs, on medical licensure was mandated to recommend ways to make the licensure process nondiscriminatory; and
- The HHS was mandated to study licensing in ten states to determine whether IMGs were discriminated against.

The HHS and the national advisory council on medical licensure were charged with studying discrimination and report to Congress by 1994 for further action by Congress.

Postscript

Congress finally provided some justice to IMGs. After 1992, all immigrant physicians were allowed to take the same examinations that were given to USMGs. But we were still quite a distance away from our destination of total equality. The campaign for fairness and equality by IMGs was a great lesson in American democracy for all of us.

Kenneth H. Bacon, a former *Wall Street Journal* reporter who had interviewed me many times and extensively covered the discrimination of IMGs (and went on to serve as an assistant secretary of defense for public affairs), eloquently captured the essence of our struggle in his foreword to *Fight for Equality: International Medical Graduates in the United States* by Shawn McMahon in 2005. Bacon wrote: "The quest for equality for US physicians educated abroad and trained in the United States is a wonderful American story. It is a history of difficulty and determination, of discrimination and justice, of failure and success. But most of all, it is a story of how a disparate group of new citizens learned to use the American political system to win recognition and protection that their own profession refused to grant them."

Until 2012, I wrote joint letters, along with presidents of the AMA and AAPI, to all Indian American physicians to become members of the AMA and AAPI. And in 2012, I was elected as the president of the IMG section of the Maryland Medical Society.

Forty years later, AAPI remains the largest ethnic organization of physicians in the US and one of the oldest and most-influential Indian American organizations nationwide. I feel lucky and privileged to have been a founder, along with Drs. Kothari, Kakarala, and Suvas Desai, among others. Kakarala served as the fourth president of the organization, and Desai was fifth. A few participants of that meeting are still actively involved in AAPI activities.

Indian American media outlets such as *India Abroad, India West, India Tribune, India Post,* and *Overseas Tribune* covered AAPI extensively from its birth, and six Indian American news outlets carried a full-page advertisement detailing the organization's activities. Over the decades, these publications regularly reported on AAPI activities and their progress. They interviewed me dozens of times, amplifying the AAPI message and highlighting various advocacy issues.

As I look back, most of my memories of the struggle are good, even though we had more bad days than good ones in those days. In recent years, I've often tried to place my current self in the shoes of my older self. Would I do all those same things today? Would I have the courage to take on the American medical establishment, organized medicine, and its backers in Congress?

Perhaps not. But back then, as a relatively young doctor, I did not worry about consequences. We did not even expect consequences. I was an ordinary doctor who had just come from India and was thrust unexpectedly into a leadership spotlight. Of course, I gladly embraced it. My older self would have advised my younger self to focus more on my family and my medical practice. But as a practicing Jain, I am a big believer in destiny. I am happy that what I did back then made a difference.

CHAPTER 4

TAKING THE BEST OF AMERICAN HEALTHCARE TO INDIA

"What percentage of Indian American doctors would like to serve India?" Prime Minister Indira Gandhi was intrigued by my suggestion that "most" physicians of Indian origin in the US were willing and ready to help India. I had just made a fifteen-minute presentation at the Embassy of India in Washington, DC, on how US-based physicians of Indian origin could contribute to enhance the medical education and healthcare in India with American experience and expertise.

Throughout the presentation, Mrs. Gandhi, in the US capital for a summit with President Ronald Reagan, listened patiently. I asked her at one point. "Am I speaking too much?"

She replied, "No, go ahead and finish your presentation."

When Mrs. Gandhi asked the question after I finished, I told her, "Ma'am, about 75 percent of Indian physicians in the country would be willing to serve India."

Before that meeting with Mrs. Gandhi in July 1982, I had interacted with perhaps a few hundred Indian American physicians in the US. Many shared my passion to do something for India, and in India. Years later, I realized that the figure I quoted to Mrs. Gandhi was vastly overestimated; perhaps only 25 percent of Indian Americans are genuinely willing and ready to help India.

When I said, "Seventy-five percent," Mrs. Gandhi appeared surprised. She called her principal secretary, P.C. Alexander, and instructed him to connect me with Sarla Grewal, secretary of the Ministry of Health and Family Welfare.

The meeting with Mrs. Gandhi was the start of my involvement, and that of AAPI, in a series of projects to help India extending over the next four decades. The projects included continuing compulsory medical education (CME) for periodic license renewal, hospital accreditation, medical equipment donations from the US, a US-India physician exchange program, setting up trauma care centers in Maharashtra, and initiating a new infectious disease (ID) specialty.

The meeting had been arranged by K.R. Narayanan, the Indian ambassador to the US who I'd come to know well in the previous two years. Since coming to Washington as India's chief diplomat in 1980, he established a good relationship with the Indian American community. I interacted with him often in my roles as president of the local Indian Medical Association of America, Inc. (IMAAI) and the Indian Urologists Association of North America (AIUNA). He was a featured guest at our annual AIUNA convention in Boston a few months earlier.

Under the AIUNA banner, I was working on an initiative focused on India: a two-month scholarship program for an Indian urologist to come and train at US hospitals and medical schools. The scholarship was instituted in memory of Dr. Hirendra Chakrobortty. The first recipient was Dr. Satish C. Mathur, from SMS College and Hospital in Jaipur, Rajasthan, who was able to spend time in some of the finest urology centers in the US.

We organized some CME seminars and workshops in India in the early 1980s. With the Indian Urology Association, we held a seminar on prostate cancer in Patna, Bihar. The next year we organized a workshop on urodynamics, and Dr. Bhupendra Tolia and I presented a workshop on genitourinary trauma in Madras.

At an annual meeting of the American Urological Society, I collected information about all 350 urologists from India practicing in the US for a directory. By creating a platform for urologists of Indian origin, AIUNA membership grew, and the organization expanded in strength and prominence.

A big fan of the American healthcare system, Narayanan often asked me probing questions about the buildup of the US health system and reasons for its success. I explained that, apart from a huge investment in research and development and the obvious technological interventions, four key factors were behind the superb American medicine: CME and periodic renewal of licensing based on completing CME, the peer review system, maintenance of proper medical records, and hospital accreditation that assured a high standard of care across the country.

Under the peer review system, a body of doctors conducts regular reviews of hospitals, studying adverse outcomes, such as injury, complications, unplanned returns to surgery, and death. The system allows doctors and hospital staff to be transparent and accountable for their actions. If necessary, the peer review body prescribes corrective actions. Continuous monitoring renders the high-quality standard of care that is a unique aspect of US medicine.

In meetings with Narayanan and other Indian officials, I always brought up the four factors as the foundations upon which the modern US medical system was built. I urged them to consider adapting them in India, with appropriate modifications. The ambassador agreed that Indian American doctors could play a big role in improving medical education and healthcare in India.

I had also spoken to him about the possibility of donating working medical equipment (with the sales and services available in India) to government-run hospitals and medical colleges in India. US hospitals routinely upgraded their equipment and bought newer models, and the still-working equipment would help doctors in training and benefit poor patients in government hospitals.

Narayanan was interested in enlisting the help of Indian American doctors to set up a Western-style, results-oriented medical system to provide access to state-of-the-art medical treatment within India. He was keen on recruiting physicians who graduated from Indian medical schools to help improve their own alma maters.

Ambassador Narayanan had congratulated me for presenting these ideas clearly and in a compelling manner to Mrs. Gandhi. We were both happy, and I thanked him for the opportunity.

Continuing Medical Education (CME)

A few weeks after my meeting with Mrs. Gandhi, AAPI was born in Detroit with Dr. Ujmal Kothari as president, and me as vice president. For founding members like me, a primary *raison d'etre* of AAPI was to organize the Indian American physicians toward serving India. Though Kothari was more inclined philosophically to focus on activities in the US rather than in India (such as discrimination issues), some colleagues and I who wanted our group to also have a big focus on India started working on CME training and equipment donation projects, with the help of the government of India.

By July 1985, as AAPI president, my focus also included an Indian hospital accreditation project, with a CME program for Indian physicians on top of that list. In my ten-plus years in the US, I saw firsthand the enormous benefits the renewal of medical licenses every three to five years based on CME completion brought to the US healthcare system. In India, once graduating from medical school, one could be lifelong doctor with no further required education or licensure.

CME was an essential part of the US healthcare system because science develops, evolves, and advances *all the time*. Doctors must update their knowledge on a continuous basis to keep up with new developments in their fields. In addition, the US is a highly litigious society; physicians and hospitals try their best to avoid errors by updating their knowledge and practice base. Another beneficial effect of CME was that it sparked research interest. I was convinced that introducing CME to India would improve medical education, research, and healthcare practice in the country.

Most AAPI members supported launching a CME program for Indian physicians. Our sincere desire to help improve India's healthcare system was also driven by our own sense of urgency and concern for our many relatives, including parents and siblings, who lived in India. We genuinely wanted them to receive the best possible care.

Later in 1985, while I was in Delhi, Mrs. Gandhi's principal secretary put me in touch with Health Secretary Sarla Grewal. The meetings with Grewal; Medical Council of India President Dr. A.K. Sinha; and L.K. Jha, who served as advisor to Mrs. Gandhi and the current PM, Rajiv Gandhi, set the ball rolling. A CME office within the Medical Council of India (MCI) was created that December. Funded by the health ministry, the office was headed by Dr. P.S. Rugmini, who held the position of deputy secretary and worked under MCI secretary, Dr. P.S. Jain. Her job included coordinating with me as AAPI president and with the CME director in the US.

The CME program kicked off with a four-day cardiology workshop at Seth G.S. Medical College in Bombay. Dr. Navin Nanda, a cardiologist at the University of Alabama, was key speaker. A workshop on urology was held three weeks later at the S.M.S. Medical College in Jaipur with urologists as speakers: Dr. Arthur Smith and Dr. Gopal Badalani based in New York, and myself. The success of the first two workshops convinced us to scale the program.

I continued to head AAPI's CME initiative for another four years after my tenure as president ended in mid-1986. Ten seminars and workshops were held in 1986, and four were held in 1987. We expanded the program significantly in subsequent years to cover more subjects and cities. Topics and sites were chosen by MCI, and AAPI provided experts and gave participants CME course certificates upon seminar completion.

US physicians traveled to India at their own expense and did not charge for the seminars and workshops. The MCI office provided Rs.50,000 (roughly $4,000) to the host institution in India for expenses, including hotels for visiting US physicians and printed materials.

By March 1991, we had conducted thirty-two CME programs each attracting 150 to 200 Indian physicians, across India: Bombay, Delhi, Agra, Belgaum, Chandigarh, Jaipur, Jodhpur, Patna, Pondicherry, Srinagar, and Trivandrum. Host institutions included some of the best hospitals in the country: All India Institute of Medical Sciences, Safdarjang Hospital, Seth G.S. Medical College, Kasturba Hospital, Madras Medical College, and Bangalore Medical College, among others.

That summer, P.V. Narasimha Rao became India's prime minister. I had met with him a few times since 1986 when he was Health minister and briefed him about the CME proposal, and also when he was minister of External Affairs. He thought the CME program was a very constructive idea. Hearing about the success of the CME program, he readily agreed with my request to include 14,000 British Indian and 5,000 Canadian Indian physicians who were interested to join. He asked me to work with high commissioners L.M. Singhvi, in London; and Girish N. Mehra, in Ottawa. I met with both high commissioners that fall, and also engaged with Indian physicians in those countries who had also supported the CME and equipment donation programs. Singhvi launched the British program while I was there. Mehra inaugurated the Canadian program. Rao's health secretary, M.S. Dayal, told me that Sushruta, considered "the father of Indian medicine," had advocated continuing medical education for medical practitioners more than 2,700 years ago. Continued meetings with key power players in India, who gave their blessing and support to the CME program, kept our momentum going.

The younger generation of Indian doctors were enthusiastic about attending seminars. Young physicians, like sponges, absorbed everything; but older physicians resisted. Their attitude was, "Who are these people coming from America to teach us? We don't need them." Some suggested that we were a bunch of blowhards who went to America because we failed to launch careers in India.

No one was blunter than a former classmate at B.J. Medical College, who told me, "Navin, I read your interview in the *Times of India*. You said you want us to have compulsory CME and medical license renewal. Don't bring this shit to India from America, and don't tell us what to do. We read the same journals you read; we know everything you know. We don't need your advice. You went to America; stay there. Why you are telling me what to do? Who are you to tell me that I should do fifty hours of CME?"

Unfortunately, many prominent medical leaders in India shared this thinking. We were seen as outsiders. The program also faded as successive AAPI leaders in the US became more interested in promoting their own projects rather than driving the CME program.

Nonetheless during the decade that the CME program lasted, the initiative successfully helped thousands of Indian physicians update their knowledge. Roughly 100 seminars were conducted by Indian-born physicians practicing in the US, UK, and Canada. AAPI was directly involved in 60 percent of them. Many seminars were conducted by physicians in their own capacities, in their hometowns, and in the medical colleges they graduated from.

The program took off originally due to the cooperation from successive health ministers, health secretaries, and officials of Medical Council of India. MCI Secretary Jain and Deputy Secretary Rugmini, who was in charge of CME at the council, each worked hard and were committed to the success of the program.

Could the CME initiative have been saved? Perhaps, if India had institutionalized it under a central authority or a special body within MCI. I had advocated creating such a central body with subordinate state panels. Another suggestion had been to involve all 100 medical colleges recognized by MCI as CME providers. Since medical colleges have permanent teaching staff, they were ideally placed to administer CME to practicing physicians. The thirty-plus specialty associations in India could have provided compulsory CME to their members.

The CME program might have survived if the Government of India had mandated all physicians to renew their licenses every few years, making CME a requirement for renewal, as in the US. Whenever I lobbied officials to enact such a law, I always heard back that they "agreed in principle." I proposed it at a gathering of medical college deans and medical educators as well, but nothing came of it. Maintaining proper medical records and peer review systems also stayed only at the discussion level. I saw a glimmer of hope in 2000 when an MoU was signed between AAPI and the Hinduja Foundation, to fund a specific CME program, but successive AAPI presidents had no interest in following through.

Hospital Accreditation

Having worked in hospitals in both India and the US, I was convinced that a similar hospital accreditation process to JCAHO's (Joint Commission on Accreditation of Healthcare Organizations), carried out in the US every three years, would significantly improve quality of care in Indian hospitals.

In a meeting with Health Minister N.T. Shanmugam, Health Secretary J.A. Chaudhary, and Director General of Health Services Dr. S.P. Agarwal, in December 1999, I proposed a hospital accreditation system (every five years for Indian hospitals with more than 100 beds) using the services of JCAHO's international arm. Alternatively, an Indian body modeled on JCAHO could be set up with needed modifications for India. The officials "agreed in principle" with the idea, and asked me to work on it.

I met with JCAHO International director, Dr. Paul Van Ostenberg, and president, Karen Timmon, in Chicago in January 2000. They briefed me on how international accreditation works, and we discussed potential collaborations with hospitals in India. They assured me that if the government of India was ready, JCAHO International experts would visit India.

The same year, I asked a US expert on JCAHO quality review, Dr. Subhash Duggirala, to create an Indian body along the lines of JCAHO, and train Indian inspectors for accreditation. Within a few months, he prepared the program and flew to Delhi, where he had detailed discussions with Health Ministry officials.

I discussed the project with my friend, S.P. Hinduja, chair of Hinduja Foundation, to explore funding options. Back in 1996, he had asked me to help find a US partner for training hospital management personnel in India, as there was a dearth of qualified hospital administrators. I had connected Hinduja Hospital Management Institute in Hyderabad with Johns Hopkins University and helped negotiate a collaboration. Hinduja gave $2 million to Hopkins for training hospital management personnel for five years.

In a discussion of the projects with the new health minister and the health secretary in India in December

2000, the health minister said he "agreed in principle" and agreed to prepare a model. On January 8, 2001, the *Asian Age* newspaper ran a story saying the Government of India might start accreditation based on the US model. But even after the years of discussion, no concrete actions were taken.

Equipment Donation Program

US hospitals routinely replaced major equipment, such as X-ray machines, CAT scans, and other devices every few years, as new equipment with the most recent technology hit the market. Hospitals took pride in having state-of-the-art technology. But most government hospitals in India did not have the latest equipment.

Even before I was AAPI president, I had initiated talks with Indian government officials about the prospects of collecting working equipment about to be replaced by US hospitals and donating them to government hospitals in India. Officials at the Embassy of India in Washington and at the Ministry of Health and Family Welfare supported the idea. AAPI colleagues were enthusiastic about it. Many worked at large hospitals and were willing to persuade their management to donate equipment being replaced. But I soon found out that collecting the machines was the easiest part.

Transportation and delivery were not so simple, involving many logistics, costs, tax issues, crossing international boundaries, customs duty, etc. Some machines were bulky and heavy. Hospitals were ready to donate machines, but shipping costs alone would be thousands of dollars.

Logistical and administrative challenges included: who would be in charge of collecting equipment, doing required paperwork, shipping them to India, navigating the process of international shipments, and ensuring that the machines were delivered to the right hospitals?

To address each issue one by one involved several trips to Delhi to meet with Prime Minister Rajiv Gandhi, Health Minister Narasimha Rao, cabinet and health secretaries, secretaries of the aviation and transportation ministries, the MCI president, and (multiple meetings) with managers of Air India and the Shipping Corporation of India (SCI). Air India was the only Indian airline operating flights between the two countries. We explored the possibility of flying smaller equipment via Air India. For bigger and bulkier machines, the option was SCI cargo ships, which sailed between US and Indian ports, many not fully loaded. We asked Air India and SCI to carry the equipment free of cost.

Rao's support had made the project a reality in June 1986 when Prime Minister Gandhi gave the veteran politician the charge of the Ministry of Health and Family Welfare. I updated Rao about the CME initiative (launched the previous December) and sought his help on the equipment donation program, bringing to his attention the logistical difficulties we faced. I explained, "Sir, I am a practicing physician with a job that consumes most of my time. My colleagues at AAPI are similarly placed. A project like this needs someone driving it full time. Could you send someone from India to Washington, DC, to coordinate the project?"

I stressed that such equipment would prove beneficial in training doctors and treating poor patients at government hospitals.

Rao agreed to create a separate cell within the Embassy of India in Washington and send an official from Delhi to oversee the project. He added, "Navin, don't worry, I will also ensure that the consignments are not charged customs duty."

Within months, Dr. Sartaj S. Mathur, professor of physics at the Indian Institute of Technology in Delhi, and handpicked by Rao, was sent to Washington. In addition to the equipment donations initiative, he served as a liaison on the CME program, along with the deputy secretary, Dr. P.S. Rugmini, who had been coordinating efforts with me at the Medical Council of India.

I got in touch with MCI, Indian hospitals and medical schools, asking them to prepare a list of needed equipment. We urged AAPI members to contact the Indian medical schools they graduated from to learn their needs. Air India and the Shipping Corporation of India were both on board, agreeing to carry the equipment free of cost, and the Government of India waived customs duties on the equipment. With all that in place, AAPI launched a new nonprofit to administer the program: American Association of Physicians from India Charitable Foundation. Mathur negotiated terms with AAPI and donors; the donated equipment must be in working condition, be serviceable in India, and have at least five years of guaranteed working life. The initiative was launched with great enthusiasm.

More than fifty shipments of equipment were sent to India over the next few years, including X-ray machines, CT scanners, mammography units, anesthesia machines, dialysis machines, incubators, and operating microscopes. Dr. Dinesh Patel, an orthopedic surgeon based in Boston, sent orthopedic equipment worth $65,000 to Safdarjung Hospital in Delhi. Outside of the AAPI Foundation, individual physicians donated equipment, working directly with Mathur.

Sadly however, like the CME program, the equipment donations initiative could not be sustained. By the third year, AAPI's internal politics became responsible for another program's demise. *India Abroad* reported in May 1989 that "internal squabbling in the AAPI had put off some donors." Quoting sources, the paper wrote, "the recent infighting in the AAPI was 'extremely disturbing' because over the years, through sheer dedication and commitment, the group had grown to be the most powerful and credible medical group representing Indian Americans."

As AAPI grew and became more powerful, the presidency had become more coveted. Each president focused on their own pet projects, and ignored programs started by previous presidents. Continuity was lost and programs were sidelined. Successful, working initiatives, such as CME and equipment donation, which required long-term commitments from successive leaders, fell by the wayside.

The CME and equipment donation programs had demonstrated what was possible if we had a clear long-term plan and worked in unison. As a founder and former AAPI president myself, I felt somewhat responsible for not anticipating the current situation. We could not save the CME and equipment donation initiatives in spite of each taking off and succeeding as proofs of concepts.

And more tragically, we missed two great opportunities to strengthen India's healthcare and medical education system during the second wave of COVID-19 in April and May 2021. Indian Americans of all faiths and creeds were mobilizing resources to send medicines and devices such as ventilators and oxygen generators to India, but were encumbered by a lack of institutional mechanism to transport and deliver them. What if the equipment donation project had still been in place?

Speaking of COVID-19: An Infectious Disease Specialty Training Program

The devastating second wave of COVID-19 infections in April and May of 2021 overwhelmed India's healthcare system. More than 400,000 people died over a few weeks due to lack of oxygen and the inability of hospitals to treat them. Infection rates and death tolls were widely believed to be vastly undercounted. Proper last rights were not performed on many COVID victims, as crematoria and cemeteries in the northern and northwestern parts of the country struggled to handle the high volumes.

International media provided wall-to-wall coverage of the pandemic and India's inadequate response. Having watched the public health crisis unfold on TV from more than 7,500 miles away, I could only bemoan the refusal of the country's medical establishment and health ministry to put in place an initiative we tried to get implemented more than a decade before. Among the reasons and figures cited by experts for why India's healthcare system collapsed for a few days at the height of the second COVID wave, one stood apart: the insufficient number of trained infectious disease (ID) specialists in India.

Since the early 2000s, when HIV/AIDS began spreading in India, and transplant and implant surgeries became common, I was increasingly concerned about the lack of trained ID specialists in the nation. Blood infection (septicemia) had a high mortality rate. India already had the largest pool of tuberculosis patients in the world, more than a fourth of the total cases worldwide.

My biggest fear as a physician (not as a public health expert) was the lack of expertise in treating the existing and new infectious diseases, especially viral infections. A country of more than a billion people, India had only a handful of ID specialists—the crucial frontline workers in fighting any epidemic. Clearly, the government of India, as well as the country's medical education and healthcare establishment, did not adequately understand the importance of having ID specialists.

The ID specialty and ID prevention and treatment have been in existence in the US for more than sixty years. The US, with one-fourth of India's population and with far less prevalence of infectious diseases, had more than 8,500 ID physicians, and about 900 of Indian origin, whereas only about one hundred ID specialists practiced in India.

For nearly two decades, I'd been knocking on the doors of the Prime Minister's Office and Nirman Bhavan, where the Ministry of Health and Family Welfare was located, trying to convince those in charge of dispensing healthcare in India to launch initiatives with US help. None had come to full fruition. By 2004 I was convinced that India needed thousands of well-trained ID specialists.

Roughly 5 percent of the India's population (around fifty million people) had infectious diseases—the largest pool of ID patients in the world. *The Times of India* reported that 48 percent of all deaths in India in 2005 were due to communicable diseases. Every year, "2.2 million Indians get infected with TB and over a million die of diarrhea," the paper quoted the World Health Organization's *Global Burden of Disease* projections.[4] Alarmingly, TB was becoming drug-resistant due to overuse of antibiotics, and patients not completing proper courses of medication.

---

4 "India has largest pool of patients in world," Subodh Varma, *The Times of India*, Mumbai, April 2, 2007.

Since I had to start promoting my India projects from scratch with a new government administration in India after May 2004, I had decided to add the training of ID specialists to the agenda. In December, I met with the new Health and Family Welfare minister, Dr. Anbumani Ramadoss and Health Secretary J.V.R. Prasad Rao. Dr. Ramadoss, a physician, had practiced briefly in Tamil Nadu after obtaining his MBBS degree from Madras Medical College. So he was familiar with the subject matter.

I told him that considering the high prevalence of diseases and deaths due to ID, India needed at least 15,000 ID specialists to prevent and treat ID. I proposed setting up a two-year MD residency program to train ID specialists and offered a blueprint modeled on US programs with modifications for India. The program needed approval from the Ministry of Health and MCI. Indian American ID physicians and top infectious disease programs in the US would help with curriculum and training. Ramadoss immediately liked the idea.

However MCI did not climb aboard. Some officials' reactions went like this: "We don't think India needs ID specialists. We have lots of TB experts. We have diploma programs in TB and other infectious diseases. Yes, we have huge numbers of malaria and leprosy cases. But we know how to treat them. Our general practitioners and internists are trained to treat these and all other epidemics in the country. A two-year MD program will have no buyers."

Ramadoss was still positive and asked me to work with the National Board of Examinations (NBE), an agency under the Ministry of Health tasked with standardizing postgraduate medical education in India. He introduced me to NBE president, Dr. Arjunan Rajasekaran. The positive response of Ramadoss and Rajasekaran buoyed me. I was confident that an ID specialty training program would take off.

Top Indian American ID experts, including Dr. Akshay Shah and Dr. Indira Brar, offered to help establish the ID specialty training. Brar was the director of the Infectious Disease Fellowship Program and professor of Medicine at the Wayne State University in Detroit. She was also a practicing physician at Henry Ford hospital's Divisions of Infectious Disease and Internal Medicine. Shah was a clinical assistant professor at Wayne State University. Besides their expertise, the two brought the affiliation of Wayne State University and the Henry Ford Hospital & Medical Centers.

Dr. Marcus Zervos, head of the Infectious Diseases Division at Henry Ford Health System, wrote to assure me of his institute's "strongest support" for my proposal: "The US has some fifty years of experience in ID specialty. The US practice has significantly improved quality of life and decreased mortality and morbidity in ID patients. The US ID specialty has played a major role in prevention, isolation, protective procedures, and safety for patients and caregivers during ID epidemics. ID specialists have played an important role in understanding, controlling, and treating newer ID diseases—some of them spread fast with over 50 percent mortality rate. To lay a solid foundation for newly initiated ID specialty training in India, we support Dr. Navin Shah's proposal for a full partnership with the US thus benefiting from the US experience and ongoing research to prevent and treat the full spectrum of ID. The partnership will be in form of a collaboration between US and Indian institutions. This collaboration will benefit Indian and US ID training, ID prevention and treatment, ID research, and needed technology for safety of patients and health care professionals. In addition, it will create opportunities for joint projects and research."

Zervos promised to provide US CME courses to Indian physicians and facilitate the visit of one or two Indian ID teachers to visit the US "to acquaint with all facets of ID."

In a January 2006 meeting with Prime Minister Manmohan Singh and Ramadoss, both offered unqualified support for the initiative. In December 2006, I led a delegation of four US ID experts and made a presentation at the NBE headquarters in Delhi on the proposed program. ID experts Zervos, Shah, Brar, and Dr. Tom Madhavan from the US traveled with me to attend the event. From the Indian side, ten ID experts and physicians were present, including the director of the National Institute of Communicable Diseases, Dr. Shiv Lal, and three top NBE officials: President Rajasekaran, Vice President Dr. Shyam Prasad, and Executive Director A.K. Sood.

We presented details of the proposed two-year residency program, to be based on the US model with needed modifications for India. I presented letters of support for the program from Dr. Michael Saag, chairman of the ID Subspecialty Board of American Board of Internal Medicine, and Dr. Nilima Kshirsagar, president of the Infectious Disease Society of India. In a letter to me, Saag wrote, "[The] need for unique expertise in infectious diseases is a key requirement for any medical center, modern hospital, or clinic. I wholeheartedly support your efforts to establish recognition of ID specialists in India through a certification process."

At the end of the eight-hour presentation and discussions, the conference accepted the proposal. Three months later, in March 2007, members of NBE's Governing Body approved the ID specialty program.

In April, Brar, Shah, and I made a similar presentation before top officials of MCI, including the chair of its Postgraduate Committee, Dr. Ved Prakash Mishra. We offered details of the proposed program, including suggested curriculum. The officials said they would study the proposal. In a later meeting with Prime Minister Singh, Principal Secretary Nair, and Health Secretary Dayal, all three supported the initiative.

In 2008, we again made a four-and-a-half-hour presentation to Dr. Mishra, and Dr. Sneh Bhargava, a former director of the All India Institute of Medical Sciences in Delhi, and other Indian officials. Shah and Brar provided details of ID training and offered US support. Mishra and I summarized the proceedings, and by the end of the meeting, we were certain MCI would start the program.

In September, MCI approved the specialty program: MD in infectious diseases. The plan was to finalize curriculum in August 2009 and begin classes in May 2010. We submitted a syllabus for the course based on the US curriculum and modified for India in that certain diseases such as malaria that are widely prevalent in India are not found in the US, and American ID specialists do not have much experience in treating them.

We lined up a scholarship for an Indian ID teacher to come to the US and get acquainted with US programs, and made arrangements for ten American ID specialists to visit India and teach in the country's medical schools. In a major boost, we received the support of the American Board of Internal Medicine and the AMA.

Subsequent meetings and logistics entailed several trips to India, but two years passed after the ministry gave the green light to start the ID program. The ball had not moved even a yard despite all the support from major players in government and us providing everything we'd been asked to provide along the way.

Seeing no progress on ID and other projects I was working on, including emergency medical and trauma care, I wrote to Prime Minister Singh in 2013. Ever a responsive political leader, he wrote back within a few days: "I would like to place on record my appreciation for your efforts in promoting emergency medical and trauma care in India, an important requirement in this country, through India-US cooperation. I also commend you for your other initiatives such as capacity building in India for addressing the challenges of infectious diseases and connecting doctors in India with US physicians of Indian origin. I wish you all success in your endeavors."

When the Singh-led United Progressive Alliance lost the election in May 2014, I again had to deal with a different set of leaders at the Ministry of Health and Welfare and at the Prime Minister's Office. I met with the new Health Minister Harsh Vardhan, a physician, at the AAPI annual convention later in the summer and described the need for India to have 15,000 ID specialists, and that all government medical colleges across the country should start ID specialty training courses immediately to reduce mortality and morbidity in ID patients. Vardhan, a physician and a practicing surgeon himself, wrote to me, saying he was asking the secretary and the additional secretary at his ministry to "work out the feasibility of the proposals" I had suggested.

At one point that year, I was told that MD programs would be launched in three hospitals, in Pondicherry, Vellore, and Chandigarh, and six more centers would be added the following year. Again nothing happened. I learned from one of the medical colleges that had applied to start the MD program, that the Academic Council of the MCI was responsible for the delay. The college had submitted its application and fee in 2013 and was told that, though the ID program was approved years before, the norms and eligibility criteria had not been laid down. However, MCI's Board of Governors had approved the minimum standard requirement in March 2012. Somehow it seemed to have died in the cabinet of the Academic Council. With nothing further happening by 2016, I stopped pursuing ID specialty training with Indian officials.

Once again, the government and MCI missed an enormous opportunity. If the ID specialty had started in 2008, India would have had hundreds of ID specialists in place to take care of COVID-19 patients, both in prevention and treatment during the global pandemic.

Trauma Care Training and Trauma Care Centers

The US has had an advanced and well-organized trauma care system for more than a half-century. Trauma centers for civilians were introduced in 1966. Since then, mortality and disability among those injured in accidents have reduced drastically.[5]

Nationwide, the US has approximately 350 trauma centers. Through the 911 telephone call system and ambulance service, trauma patients are brought to trauma care centers within minutes. A patient is usually brought to the appropriate center within thirty minutes of the accident.

---

5 "History and Development of Trauma Care in the United States," by Donald D Trunkey, MD. *History of Orthopaedics in North America*, May 2000. https://journals.lww.com/clinorthop/fulltext/2000/05000/history_and_development_of_trauma_care_in_the.5.aspx

Before they reach the centers, patients receive treatment on the spot and during transportation. Once checked in, they are treated on priority basis by a dedicated trauma surgeon and staff. The first hour in trauma treatment is the "golden hour"; if treatment is received during this time period, the lives of most patients are saved. Because of the efficiency of the trauma care system, hundreds of thousands of American lives are saved.

India, however, lacks an orderly system to deal with trauma. As a result, hundreds of thousands of lives are lost. Nearly 10 percent of the four million-plus global deaths in accidents are in India, even though a vast majority of Indians live in villages where vehicular mishaps are relatively low. India, which accounts for only 1 percent of automobiles globally, has 6 percent of vehicle accident deaths, with someone dying on the road every six minutes. The US has two deaths for 10,000 vehicles, whereas in India that ratio is 140 for 10,000 vehicles.[6]

What if some of the best practices in the US trauma care system were introduced in India? That question had been at the back of my mind ever since I assumed the presidency of AAPI in 1985. However, I was involved so many initiatives in the US and India, I did not have the bandwidth to take it up for another decade and a half. Implementing a project like trauma care in a large and diverse nation like India would of course be challenging. After talking to colleagues in the US and India, I realized it would be best to launch such an

---

[6] *The Economic Times*, "India tops the world with 11% of global death in road accidents: World Bank Report. February 14, 2021. https://economictimes.indiatimes.com/news/politics-and-nation/india-tops-the-world-with-11-of-global-death-in-road-accidents-world-bank-report/articleshow/80906857.cms?

initiative in a single state or city as a pilot project. If it was successfully implemented in one place, other cities and states are sure to replicate it, I reckoned.

Identifying that one Indian state and city was easy. A Maharashtrian by birth, my home state was the first that came to my mind when I thought of any healthcare project. As India's most industrialized state, it has the highest accident rate in the country. The city of Mumbai and national highways within its 60-mile radius contribute to half of all road accidents in Maharashtra.

In December 2000, I approached Public Health Department Secretary S. Shahzad Hussain with an offer to help Maharashtra develop trauma care centers in the state. A veteran Indian Administrative Service officer, he quickly convened a formal meeting with Maharashtra Chief Secretary Arun Bongirwar and secretary of the Medical Education and Drugs Department, Thomas Benjamin. In the meeting, I detailed the plan for setting up full-fledged trauma care centers in three of Mumbai's largest hospitals: King Edward Memorial (KEM) Hospital, Sion Hospital, and Sir J.J. Hospital. Additionally, I proposed ten centers to be set up in some smaller hospitals in the city, and eventually in all major government and private hospitals.

Once back in Washington, I asked Dr. S. Balasubramaniam, professor of Trauma at UCLA, to do a feasibility study on the project. He traveled to Mumbai twice, both trips paid for by the Hinduja Foundation. Balasubramaniam, who served as the chairman of the Department of Emergency Medicine and director of Life Support Training at King Drew Medical Center in Los Angeles for twenty-one years, is one of the best-known experts on trauma in the country. He later served as the president of AAPI.

In July 2001, I met with Sharad Pawar, then vice chairman of the National Committee on Disaster Management, to come up with a plan to manage disasters in a better way. The meeting was facilitated by Lalit Mansingh, who had just begun his tenure as the Indian ambassador to the US. The gist of my quick presentation was this: the number of deaths and disabilities caused by road accidents in India could be reduced drastically if trauma care centers were established in the country. If Maharashtra approved my plan, four major trauma centers functioning round-the-clock could be launched fairly quickly within Mumbai's medical colleges and teaching hospitals. Pawar, a former chief minister of Maharashtra, was receptive to the idea.

Around that time, I met with a number of US officials, including Assistant Secretary of State Christina Rocca, to seek US help for setting up emergency medical service and trauma care in India. They were very supportive. In Delhi, I discussed the idea with Prime Minister Vajpayee and his principal secretary, Brajesh Mishra. Both were in favor of it.

Nothing moved in the next four years, even though I met state officials every year during my annual visit to Mumbai. In January 2005, Maharashtra Health Secretary G.S. Gill told me that the state was keen on implementing the trauma center project, but unable to come up with funding. I had two back-to-back meetings with Union Health Minister Ramadoss, in Delhi and Washington. He assured me that the central government would help Maharashtra if the project is implemented.

In July 2005, Chief Minister Vilasrao Deshmukh came to the US with a high-level delegation. In Atlanta, he addressed the annual convention of Brihan Maharashtra Mandal of North America. I flew down to Atlanta to meet Deshmukh and the officials who accompanied him, including Chief Secretary R.M. Premkumar, Principal Secretary Saurabh Lala, Health Secretary V.K. Jairath, and two influential Members of Parliament, Sanjay Raut and Mohan Rawale.

I proposed to lead a US team of ten trauma surgeons, to include Dr. Balasubramaniam, who would help set up the emergency medical services and trauma centers and train Indian surgeons and paramedics. Each US surgeon would spend up to four weeks in Mumbai. Their work would be *pro bono*. The system would be based on the US model, with some modifications to suit local needs. In my presentation, I stated that the initiative will save 35 percent more lives and result in a 50 percent improvement in preventing disabilities.

Three types of hospitals would be part of the project:

- Major medical college hospitals such as KEM, Sion, J.J., TNMC Nair Charitable, and Saint George;
- Government hospitals such as Desai, Cooper, Bhagwati, Rajwadi, Bhabha, Mulund, and Harkisan; and
- Large private hospitals, such as Hinduja, Jaslock, Lilawati, and Breech Candy.

The initial budget for the project would be 130 million Indian rupees (roughly $3 million then). Annually, $1 million would be required for maintenance.

Deshmukh agreed (in principle) to implement the project. In September, he wrote that he was instructing the secretary of the Public Health Department to "look into" the project "and inform the progress." The BBC reported on September 7, 2005, that the Medical Education and Drugs Department had prepared an internal status report on the project and was bringing all concerned agencies under one platform.

Department Secretary Gill told the news outlet that it would take three to four months to implement the project.

Meanwhile, I had discussed the project with S.P. Hinduja, chairman of the Hinduja Hospital, and explored funding and partnership opportunities. The Hinduja Hospital agreed to provide eight manned ambulances with state-of-the-art equipment, including communication devices. The hospital would also provide facilities to train Indian surgeons and paramedics. All participating hospitals would have dedicated, fully equipped emergency departments with trained trauma surgeons and staff.

On January 15, 2006, *The Times of India* reported that the emergency medical service might be unveiled within two weeks. "We have several centers of excellence, which provide in-house emergency service, be it in neuro or orthopedic surgery," the paper quoted Aziz Khan, secretary of medical education as saying. "The aim is to ensure that once a victim is picked up by an ambulance, the network will direct the driver to the nearest center that can provide best care to the victim, depending on the gravity of the situation."

In Delhi, I briefed Prime Minister Singh and Health Minister Ramadoss on the progress of the Mumbai trauma project. I requested that they consider expanding the initiative to other cities once the pilot project in Mumbai started showing results. They assured me the support of the central government for the project. I came back from India that January with a lot of optimism. Our plan was to kick-start the first phase of the program by spring. But the government missed the spring deadline for reasons not known to me.

In early March 2007, I met with Dr. J. Wayne Meredith, medical director of Trauma Programs at the American College of Surgeons, which has a membership of more than

82,000 surgeons. He offered support of the college, the largest organization of surgeons in the world, for the program in Mumbai. He wrote the following week, "I believe [the program] has the potential to save hundreds of thousands of, if not millions, of lives over time by improving the accessibility, the expertise, and the coordination in emergency and trauma care in such a large populous region in the world."

Meredith and I kept in touch over the next few years. He became one of the cheerleaders of the project. I kept him abreast of the progress, or lack thereof, of the project. Later he agreed to invite one participating surgeon from Mumbai to spend a week in the US and get acquainted with US practice, saying, "We will be glad to provide airfare as well as a national model for India which other metros of India can replicate."

More than a year later, on April 3, 2007, I chaired a meeting held at the Hinduja Hospital, and once again detailed the plan and its benefits. Attendees included officials from Mumbai's twelve major private hospitals, top Maharashtra government officials, and US Consul General Michael Owen. At the meeting, it was announced that the first phase of the project would begin June 1. Aziz Khan, now principal health secretary, announced a new helpline number: 1298. But nothing took off in June.

While waiting for the launch of the initiative, we kept improving the blueprint. Our initial plan for the first phase was to provide services in available facilities and later develop it to a full-fledged initiative based on the US model with needed modifications. Per the plan, Mumbai's four medical colleges and ten large private hospitals would be part of the emergency medical services and trauma centers system, along with twelve government and municipal hospitals, burn and rehab centers, and children's hospitals. All would be brought under a single command structure, with a dedicated telephone and ambulance dispatch center.

The participating hospitals would be divided into four categories from Level 1 to Level 4, based on the services and facilities available. The Level 1 hospitals, such as medical colleges and large private hospitals, would have general surgeons, anesthesiologists, emergency room physicians, operating room staff, and a respiratory therapist around the clock. They would be able to make available thoracic, cardiac, neurosurgery, and other subspecialty experts within twenty minutes to half an hour. They would have priority CT scans, MRI and laboratory facilities, as well as operation rooms and ICU facilities. Additionally these hospitals would have trauma education and research facilities. Level 1 to 3 would take care of patients depending on specialty need to treat trauma patients. Level 4 centers would have only resuscitation and stabilization facilities.

In December 2007, I chaired another meeting at Hinduja Hospital, attended by top medical and police officials and municipal commissioners. Once again, it was decided that trauma care training and trauma centers would launch.

When Chief Minister Deshmukh was succeeded by Ashokrao Chavan, in 2009, I met Chavan and Jayant Kumar Banthia, secretary at the Public Health Department, and briefed them about the work we had done until then. Later on, Banthia convened a meeting with all participants, and once again I detailed the EMS and TC project.

Ashokrao Chavan's tenure as chief minister lasted less than two years. Prithviraj Chavan became chief minister in November 2010. The following month, I wrote to Chavan, stating that we were in a position to start the service immediately "with present expertise and facilities available in Mumbai."

Within two weeks, he responded, saying that he was "having the proposal examined." Nothing further.

The next year, in August, Health Secretary Bhushan Gagrani informed me that the state government had floated a bid for Emergency Medical Services, and he was hoping to finalize it by September 2011. "The bid intends to appoint a service provider cum turnkey operator to operationalize Emergency Medical Services in the entire State of Maharashtra, with a universal three-digit call number," he wrote. He added that the state was planning to procure 950 ambulances within two years.

"Once we know the service provider, we would like to work out the training strategy with all the help of [the] American College of Surgeons," he wrote. "I appreciate your initialing in this regard. We are all grateful to you for your constant follow-up and valuable suggestions to make this program happen."

In May 2013, I received a letter from Additional Chief Secretary of Health T.C. Benjamin, stating that the initiative had received the green light and inviting me to travel to Mumbai for a seminar on "Emergency Medical Services and Trauma Care," as part of a series of capacity-building activities for public and private hospitals in emergency and trauma care. "My department has embarked on the Maharashtra Emergency Medical Services Project," he wrote, "I am expecting the first ambulance to be on road by the third week of July 2013."

Four weeks later, I was in Mumbai, leading a delegation of topnotch trauma surgeons from the US for the two-day interactive training for roughly 100 government surgeons from all over Maharashtra. The physicians who traveled with me included Dr. Thomas Scalea, a professor at Shock Trauma Center at the University of Maryland Medical System, one of the best-known trauma surgeons in the country. Dr. Scalea, Dr. Amy Hildreth, a professor at Wake Forest University School of Medicine, Dr. Manjari Joshi, an ID specialist at the University of Maryland School of Medicine, and I gave presentations.

During the two-day seminar, US specialists spoke about multi-organ trauma and management of complicated injuries, and shared information on the US model and services. Over the next three days, we met with several government officials and surgeons, visited trauma centers, and had detailed discussions on launching trauma care centers.

One of the highlights of our visit was a MoU signed between University of Maryland's RAC Shock Trauma Center and the Government of Maharashtra. The MoU included interactions between UMD and various trauma centers in Maharashtra, and the state would get assistance from the university in the areas of research and CME. It could also potentially lead to NIH funding for joint trauma research,

At a press conference held in Mumbai on June 20, state Health Minister Suresh Shetty announced, in the presence of visiting US surgeons, that the services would begin in August. It would be a more ambitious project than we envisaged more than a decade earlier. With a budget of $200 million, there would be forty-seven trauma centers. The minister said that the government had purchased 927 ambulances, three-fourths of them equipped with basic life support, and a fourth equipped with advanced life-support. Each ambulance would have a physician.

I told reporters that two major US hospitals would be offering fully paid scholarships to Maharashtra surgeons to visit the US for a week: the RAC Shock Trauma Center and the Wake Forest Trauma Center, in Winston-Salem, North Carolina. Shetty and Benjamin praised me profusely for my years of persistence with the project. The next day, I met with Banthia and Benjamin and presented a three-year plan for the program and services.

Within a year of the announcing the initiative, the government led by Chavan fell, following differences between his party, the Indian National Congress, and its coalition partner, the Nationalist Congress Party. In a subsequent election, in October 2014, the Bharatiya Janata Party and Shiv Sena won the majority and Devendra Fadnavis became the chief minister of the state. As with every government change, many initiatives started or being planned by the predecessor, went to the back burner, which unfortunately happened in the case of this initiative as well. I continued to stay in touch with the health ministry officials, but there was no progress.

Sadly, the government never followed up on the MoU signed with the University of Maryland, essentially ending a collaboration that would have improved the potential to change the treatment of trauma victims in Maharashtra and possibly across India. The Maharashtra government missed a golden opportunity to set up world-class EMS and trauma centers. The services we envisioned would have provided quick treatment to Mumbai residents.

Looking back, I can only say that my colleagues and I tried our best. The project would have drastically improved the outcome of trauma victims and kickstarted joint research and expert exchanges.

Selling Ayurveda to Americans

Aap ko karana hei! was a request from the Prime Minister Atal Behari Vajpayee in 1999, during a meeting with him at this official residence. On my way to 7 Race Course Road, I had brushed up my talking points about the need to set up trauma care centers and establish an infectious disease specialty in India. But after exchanging pleasantries, the prime minister wanted to discuss something else.

"Navin *bhai*, you have to promote Ayurveda in America," he said in his measured Vajpayee-esque tone.

Surprised, I said, "Sir, I am an allopathic doctor, a urologist. I have no knowledge of Ayurveda. So I may not be the right person to do that."

I was familiar with some herbal medicines, oils, and herbs used in Arurveda. The natural system of medicine had been practiced in India for several thousand years. Certainly, home remedies were important in my childhood. We were too poor to avail the services of doctors or hospitals except in the most serious situations.

But Vajpayee would not take no for an answer. "*Aap ko karana hei!*" Meaning, "You have to do it!"

Vajpayee wanted my help in finding avenues to properly introduce Ayurveda in the US.

I had always wanted to know more about Arurveda. Perhaps the practice could be helpful in US healthcare treatment. India had something to offer the US. Feeling compelled to agree to the prime minister's wishes, I said, "I will try my best, sir."

I agreed to work with the health minister, secretary of the Department of Ayurveda, Yoga and naturopathy, Unani, Siddha, and Homeopathy (AYUSH), and report to him any progress made.

I returned to Washington with a new task: to promote Ayurveda in the US and to advance the knowledge and information about the ancient Indian medical science and lifestyle system. I spent the next few months, researching how to do that.

Holistic health and complementary and alternative medicine (CAM) had seen a growing interest for a couple of decades in America. The National Institutes of Health had created a new center, the National Center for Complementary and Integrative Health (NCCIH) in 1992 to study medical care that is not part of "conventional medical care, or that may have origins outside of usual Western practice." CAM was already a big business in the US.

Acupuncture and herbal medicine were beginning to be popular. Homeopathy was gaining market. Yoga was increasingly popular, but Ayurveda, in general, did not yet get as much attention.

As I studied and explored the subject further, a few truths dawned on me. American medicine is evidence-based with a well-spelled out standard of care. Ayurveda, the ancient philosophy and practice of maintaining wellness of mind, body, and soul, has benefited hundreds of millions in South Asia. In the modern world, it was being used for ageing, rejuvenation, and repair remedies. But for it to gain acceptance and achieve legitimacy in medical education and patient care in the US, it had to be rebranded as an evidence-based science.

In January 2000, I presented a plan in Delhi to Health Minister Dr. C.P Thakur, Health Secretary Shailaja Chandra, and her colleagues, which contained two initiatives. The first was to offer Ayurveda courses in medical schools under the "complementary and alternative medicine" category. I had met with officials of the Association of American Medical Colleges and contacted some top medical schools. Close to a dozen medical schools showed some interest in making Ayurveda part of their curriculum. They wanted well-known teachers from India to come and teach their students, which was not going to be a difficult task, as there were four Ayurvedic universities in India conducting scientific studies on Ayurvedic medicines at that time. In addition, India had about 150 Ayurveda medical colleges and fifty postgraduate Ayurveda institutions.

A second initiative I proposed was to create a joint US-India research project on Ayurvedic medicines, oil massage treatment, yoga, and meditation. A half-dozen US researchers had expressed interest in working on collaborative projects with Indian counterparts.

Health Minister Thakur and Secretary Chandra and other officials in the ministry liked both ideas and readily agreed to help implement them. I was delighted to see that, for a change, the initiation of a project was moving fast. In September 2000, during his New York visit to address the annual UN General Assembly meeting, Vajpayee attended an Ayurveda conference hosted by the Bharatiya Vidya Bhavan at the State University of New York.

Describing Ayurveda as a "way of life," the prime minister said Indians in India and the US must make use of the rising interest in herbal and other alternative medicines in this country to popularize Ayurveda and other ancient Indian medicines. Americans were already spending roughly $15 billion a year on herbal medicines.

Vajpayee sounded alarmed at the practice of Western companies patenting Indian herbal medicines, which he said would deprive India of knowledge. Citing the example of China, the country's northern neighbor, the prime minister said India could also earn useful foreign exchange by marketing Ayurveda.[7]

After the UN address, I met with Vajpayee in New York City and briefed him of the Ayurveda initiative in the US. A few days later, on September 17, we spoke again at a state dinner in his honor hosted by President Clinton at the White House.

Two months later, in November, Secretary Chandra and I met with Joanna Rosario, NIH director of the National Center for Complementary and Alternative Medicines, to discuss the possibility of including Ayurveda as an academic subject in medical schools funded by the center. Rosario told us that US medical schools would be interested in having accredited programs in Ayurveda under CAM.

Chandra and I had similar meetings with officials from Johns Hopkins University in Baltimore, and the University of Maryland in College Park, just outside of Washington, DC. Both schools agreed in theory to offer brief courses in Ayurveda by visiting Indian faculty. Chandra told Aziz Haniffa of the *India Abroad* newspaper before returning to India, "Once the details are worked out, students and practitioners would come to India to look at Ayurveda being practiced or to get educated in it."[8]

During Chandra's meetings with American officials, it was decided that Indian Ayurveda teachers would visit the US in early 2001 and present models of accredited courses in Ayurveda to NCCIH and medical schools it funds. At the

---

7   "India must remain strong and vigilant." PM, Amberish K Diwanji in New York, *Rediff.com*, September 9, 2000. https://www.rediff.com/news/2000/sep/09pmus3.htm

8   "US may learn a lesson of two on Ayurveda by next year." Aziz Haniffa, *India Abroad*, December 7, 2001.

time, NCCIH was funding CAM courses at forty-seven medical schools, and NIH had a total budget of $300 million for research in CAM. Chandra and Rosario agreed that collaborative research, under proper ethical guidelines, could be conducted. Rosario also accepted an invitation by Chandra to visit India in April 2002.

In the interview with Haniffa, Chandra said I'd been "helpful for many years and instrumental in trying to motivate us to really start talking to the US medical schools and the NIH, rather than simply talking to the general public."

In subsequent months, I worked with George Washington University in DC, to develop an Ayurveda course for practicing physicians. By 2004, news articles began appearing in Indian and Indian American news media, stating that Ayurveda was likely to be part of the curriculum in US medical schools.

This initiative also suffered a setback when the Vajpayee-led coalition lost the parliamentary elections in 2004, and Manmohan Singh, an economist who served as the finance minister during the Rao tenure, became PM. I had discussed various India projects with Singh when he visited Washington as finance minister in 1996.

Ayurveda Workshops

At a meeting with Prime Minister Singh in New Delhi in March 2007, we discussed all the initiatives I was working on, including the promotion of Ayurveda in the US. I was frustrated that despite trying for seven years, there was no progress on the Ayurveda project. Singh was in favor of implementing all the projects. Pointing out the benefits of

Ayurveda, he said a joint India-US Ayurveda research initiative under the NIH would be beneficial.

I asked the prime minister to send two professors to teach a short Ayurveda course, which would go a long way toward the popularity of the discipline. Singh listened to me patiently and told me that it would be done.[9] He called principal secretary to the PM, T.K.A. Nair, and instructed him to implement the project.

A few days later, I paid a visit to Vajpayee at his residence, and reported to him that Prime Minister Singh had agreed to go ahead with the project, and hopefully Ayurveda would be introduced to the US medical education and medical practice. The former prime minister was very happy to hear that.

"Operation Escalation" worked. Within days, the Ministry of Health decided to send two Ayurveda experts to conduct workshops at US medical schools: Dr. H.S. Palep, director of Palep's Medical Research Center in Mumbai; and Dr. Tanuja Nesari, an Ayurveda specialist at Tilak Mahavidyalaya in Pune. Both were deputed by AYUSH. Palep, an OBGYN, was trained in both allopathy and Ayurveda. He authored the 2004 book, *The Scientific Foundation of Ayurveda*.

With help from a number of Indian American doctors, I arranged workshops in multiple medical colleges, mainly on the East Coast. The first workshop was held at the Howard University College of Medicine in Washington in May 2007, less than two months after my meeting with the PM. Besides Howard physicians, it was attended by faculties of three major medical schools in the area, Georgetown University, George Washington University, and the Uniformed Services University of the Health Sciences.

---

9 "American Medical Schools Offer Ayurveda Course," *India-West*, May 4, 2007.

Palep used 250 PowerPoint slides on Ayurveda philosophy, Ayurvedic anatomy, physiology, pathology, pharmacology, clinical exams, treatment, yoga, and detoxification and rejuvenation therapies. In subsequent weeks, five more workshops were held at Johns Hopkins University, Harvard University, Rutgers University, and a few other medical schools on the East Coast.[10]

Unfortunately, the workshops did not bring about intended results. While those present at workshops participated in the interactive sessions and asked probing questions, they were not excited enough to go back and make a passionate case to their respective schools for introducing Ayurveda as part of their curriculum.

One of our objectives with the workshop was to highlight the evidence-based aspects of Ayurveda. In certain diseases and conditions such as a diabetes, arthritis, obesity, hypertension, depression, menopause, colitis, and psoriasis, studies done in the previous decade had shown some evidences of Ayurvedic treatment being effective.[11] But a big part of Palep's presentation had focused on history, philosophy, and practice of Ayurveda in India for 5,000 years. Mostly anecdotal evidence was presented, which lacked scientific evidence and data on follow-up with a series of patients.

For American schools to accept Ayurveda, they had to see the evidence that a disease could be cured completely, or its symptoms could be ameliorated, or in the case of some chronic diseases and cancer, show that their progress

---

10 "Ayurveda Goes Mainstream in Several US Universities," *India Abroad*, May 4, 2007.
11 Ibid.

was arrested.[12] Clinical benefits of Ayurveda could not be adequately substantiated at the workshops.

Despite the poor response to the workshops from the US side, I was not ready to give up. Workshops were only one part of the puzzle. Another aspect I saw as critical was collaborations between US and Indian scientists on various research projects, potentially funded by NIH. With the NIH already funding a number of projects in complementary and alternative medicines, if compelling proposals were identified, I hoped NIH would provide grants. Prior to my India visit, I met with Jack Killen, director of International Research at NIH's National Center for Complementary and Alternative Medicine (NCCAM). He was willing to work with me to explore funding for joint ayurvedic research.

The US Delegation

The most effective way to midwife the collaboration was by taking directors of CAM programs in some of the best US medical schools to India and give them a firsthand experience of Ayurveda as practiced in India. I started coordinating with officials of the Health Ministry, especially AYUSH Secretary S. Jalaja, Joint Secretary Dr. Rakesh Sarwal, and Health Secretary Sujata Rao, as well as officials at the Embassy in Washington. In fall 2009, we finalized the plan to take a delegation of CAM and integrative medicine faculty leaders in early 2010 to India. I would lead the delegation comprising heads of CAM programs in six of the most elite medical schools in the US:

---

12 "American Medical Schools Offer Ayurveda Course," *India-West*, May 4, 2007.

- Dr. Annstsia Rowlands-Seymour, assistant professor of Integrative Medicine, Dept of Medicine, Johns Hopkins,
- Dr. David Eisenberg, director, Harvard University Osher Research Center,
- Dr. Aviad Haramati, chair, Committee on Complementary and Integrative Medicine Curriculum at Georgetown University School of Medicine,
- Dr. Benjamin Kligler, vice chair of Beth Israel Integrative Medicine Dept at Mount Sinai in New York,
- Dr. Victoria Maizes, executive director, Integrative Medicine at University of Arizona College of Medicine, and
- Dr. Anne Nedrow, director, Center for Women's Health, OHSU School of Medicine in Portland, Oregon.

The mission of the trip was to expand the knowledge of Ayurveda within US medical schools, identify aspects of Ayurveda to be taught to US medical students, and review top research proposals selected by the Health Ministry for collaboration between US and India.

Prior to our India visit, I had multiple discussions with the delegates and with AYUSH officials to provide the delegates the best Ayurveda experience and objective evidence. The delegates were all pro-Ayurveda and enthusiastic to learn and participate in the Ayurveda program and joint research. Dr. Haramati, who would be coordinator of the delegation, wrote to me in November 2010, accepting my invitation to be part of the delegation. "I hope my participation in this delegation and my exposure to best evidence available in this field will help me and my colleagues determine what aspects of Ayurvedic medicine should be taught to US medical students at Georgetown and throughout the US."

We arrived in Delhi on January 27, 2010, and over the next few days, interacted with more than sixty Indian Ayurveda experts and top government officials (Minister of Health and Family Welfare Ghulam Nabi Azad; his deputy, S. Gandhiselvan; principal secretary to PM, T.K.A. Nair; Health Secretary Sujata Rao; AYUSH Secretary S. Jalaja; AYUSH Joint Secretary B. Anand; and Foreign Secretary Nirupama Rao, among others.)

On February 1, an interactive meeting was held where several proposals for NIH-funded Indo-US joint research were presented. Delegates listened to evidence-based presentations on various diseases and drugs. Experts who attended the session included researchers and academics from some of India's premier institutions: National Institute of Mental Health & Neuroscience (NIMHANS) in Bangalore, Indian Institute of Science in Bangalore, Kasturba Health Society in Mumbai, and the Banaras Hindu University.

Delegates visited some of the top Ayurveda institutions in Delhi: National Institute of Yoga, Maharishi Ayurveda Pharma Factory, Arya Vaidya Sala, and the National Institution of Ayurveda in Jaipur. The purpose of the visits was to inform and educate delegates about various facets of Ayurveda, such as yoga, meditation, and oil massage treatments, as well as teaching, training, practice, patient care, and drug manufacturing.

The delegates, including myself, were impressed by the hospitality, but not by the presentations. A report submitted to AYUSH Secretary Jalaja bluntly spelled out the deficiencies. Although "the presentations on potential research were interesting, with only a few exceptions, the proposals were not well-developed enough to be considered for possible NIH grant application." Most of the ten proposals selected by AYUSH for joint Indo-US research "were not of sufficient quality for submission as NIH grant applications in their current form, and also did not have strong objective data to entice collaboration with the US partners... More pilot research is needed, which most likely will necessitate internal funding by AYUSH before these proposals can be moved forward as part of any Indo-US collaborations. Furthermore, the joint projects must address relevant pathology and common diseases in the US, and the treatment plans should be acceptable to US patients. To be specific, it may be unreasonable to expect patients in the US to adhere to a complete Ayurvedic treatment regimen."

Regarding yoga, the report said that though yoga demonstrations "were exceptionally good," the "claims made of its beneficial effects on kidney, pancreas, etc., need to be better substantiated in order to be convincing." Similarly, the successes claimed by the Arya Vaidya Sala "for treating [various] neurological conditions were not documented, nor published." Some other deficiencies cited:

- The pharma industry "has not participated or funded educational, research, or US exchange programs."
- At presentations "on evidence-based Ayurveda, yoga, meditation, and oil massage treatment, the delegation members were disappointed that the specific topics chosen were not of sufficiently high significance or the data compelling to either complement or replace the current allopathic treatment."
- The delegation "did not come away with enough evidence-based information" during the visit to the National Ayurveda Institute. "The delegates were delighted to learn that the undergraduate students were

also taught allopathic anatomy, physiology, pathology, pharmacology, etc. However, it became apparent that the subjects were taught by Ayurveda-trained teachers (who did not have the qualifications of comparable allopathic teachers). There was little engagement from the NIA faculty to the delegates. Further, the delegation was not provided with any significant scholarly papers published in known scientific journals in India or the US."

- Members of the US delegation were also not happy that, "in spite of repeated requests, the presentations and research proposals were not sent to them a month in advance so as to provide enough time for in-depth review and preconference interactions."

The delegation made several recommendations and suggested future actions to "establish a roadmap for further understanding and utilization of evidence-based Ayurveda in the US. Among them were providing funding and collecting preliminary data to develop viable research proposals to NIH, disseminating best-available data on the efficacy of Ayurveda treatments in international scientific literature, and presenting them at top global conferences. It also recommended forming a "standing committee" to oversee the already initiated Indo-US activities. A project to develop a partnership with Harvard University School of Medicine, similar to the one that Harvard had with the Chinese government to study Chinese medicinal plants was also recommended. In addition to the general report, each member of the delegation also submitted individual observations for the record.

Unfortunately, the report seemed to have had an adverse effect: it dampened the enthusiasm on the Indian side.

AYUSH officials appeared to be taken aback by the bluntness of the delegation's opinion. A critical news article in *The Times of India*, which quoted some members of the delegation, including me, sealed the fate of future cooperation between the two sides. "There is a lot of data, but the level of evidence is in its infancy, perhaps too low right now to meet FDA [Food and Drug Administration] standard," the paper quoted one of the members as saying. Months later, I learned that AYUSH officials were unhappy about the report and the *Times* article.

Members of the delegation continued to brainstorm for a few months on how the cooperation could be taken to the next level. Haramati, coordinator of the delegation, and I continued our conversations till October of 2010. We had clearly stated that our visit (and the report) was "the first step in a long journey toward utilization of evidence-based Ayurveda." However, by the end of the year, the vibe I was getting from Delhi was that the project was as good as dead.

Regrettably, such a promising initiative, which had the potential to change the healthcare in both countries, like the other initiatives mentioned in this chapter, never got off the ground. It was the dream of Prime Minister Vajpayee to promote Ayurveda in the US. Later his successor, Prime Minister Singh tried his best to make it a reality. Both leaders were keen to popularize Ayurveda in the US in medical education, as well as in practice. A joint India-US Ayurveda research project, as Singh told me, would have benefited not just India and the US, but the whole world. Azad, the health minister, shared the same opinion. To this day, I believe it was a missed opportunity for India.

US/India Physicians Exchange Program

Nearly two decades after the CME initiative came to an end, I started working on another idea that is conceptually similar and also had some of its missions. The basic goal of the CME project was to keep Indian physicians up to date with the latest developments in medical education and medical practice. Hundreds of mainly Indian American physicians conducted a series of CME courses in different specialties in various medical schools and teaching hospitals across India. While a few Indian physicians were offered fellowships to come to the US and spend time in US hospitals getting acquainted with the hospital system and patient care here, most of the education and trainings were to be done in India by visiting Indian American doctors. In essence, it was a one-way street.

Exchange programs between professionals in different countries are common in many professions, and several governments promote them. The US Department of State administers many such exchange programs, which mainly bring professionals from other countries to the US. Several US universities have exchanges programs that allow their students to spend a semester or two at colleges in other countries.

In 2003, the Indian government launched the Pravasi Bharatiya Divas (PBD), or the "Non-Resident Indian Day." The idea was to celebrate the diaspora's contributions to the development of the country. In the first PBD, I was asked to chair a medical seminar.

The thought of bringing Indian physicians as observers to US hospitals as part of a physicians' exchange program had been brewing in my mind ever since the CME initiative ended. Unlike its predecessor, the new program would have two-way traffic. More or less the same number of physicians would travel in each direction. While visiting US doctors would conduct CME and training courses in India, physicians coming to the US would observe the practice in hospitals, education in medical schools, and participate in US CME programs. In the US, only licensed physicians can legally participate in patients care, but visiting doctors are allowed to observe. By being in US hospitals, Indian physicians would get firsthand knowledge and experience of how patient care and hospitals work in this country. Even though the program would not be a substitute for a well-structured CME and training course, it would be the next-best avenue. If we were able to bring interested Indian doctors here, and a same number of US colleagues could travel to India, it had the potential to make a significant difference to India's healthcare system, medical education, and research.

By now I had also analyzed the reasons for the initial success of the CME project and failures of my other India initiatives. In each case, I realized that the basic reason they did not survive was because of the dependence on the government and lack of institutional support. Governments change all the time. Since my tenure as AAPI vice president, when I first started working on India initiatives, the country has had nine prime ministers, and even more health ministers, not to mention the number of health secretaries.

So I decided I needed to find a strong institutional partner if I were to make the physicians exchange program a success. Luckily, I found one without having to search for too long. The US-India Business Council (USIBC) is a trade group representing hundreds of major businesses having presence in both the countries. As part of the influential US Chamber of Commerce, and located within the Chamber's office in Washington, DC, two blocks away from the White House, the USIBC had been an influential player in the US-India bilateral relations over the decades. It facilitated closer business and economic ties between the two countries like no other organization. Furthermore, most of the major US pharmaceutical and healthcare giants are members of the trade body. For all these reasons, USIBC was the right fit to anchor the physicians exchange program.

I approached Ron Somers, the organization's president, with the plan in 2009. Prior to assuming the presidency of the organization, Somers had spent several years in India, working as a US business executive. Having traveled widely across India, he was even familiar with some Indian languages. I proposed the physicians' exchange program, and Somers loved the idea. He straightaway assigned the USIBC in-house healthcare expert to work with me.

In the next several months, I worked with the USIBC, perfecting the contours of the program. The basic idea was plain: In 2009, more than 60,000 physicians born in India had graduated from the country's medical schools and were practicing in the US. A significant number were in faculty positions.

Thousands of Indian American physicians visit their hometowns in India annually to see their parents, other family members, and friends. Our projection was at the time was that at least 10 percent of Indian American physicians were willing to volunteer their expertise and services in India. Since they came from nearly every Indian state, the program would benefit all regions of the country. Similarly, at the other end of the spectrum, in India, there were 70,000 specialists in various fields. Many of them would like to visit the US to acquaint themselves with the medical education, health care, and research in the country. Also the US has many alumni groups that helped their medical colleges and hospitals from time to time. Many of these colleges and hospitals, run by state governments, are underfunded.

Our plan was to connect doctors from both countries on the web. When the CME program was launched in the late 1980s, email was almost nonexistent. But by 2009, the internet was a big part of everyone's life. We decided to leverage the new technology. It would work like this: Indian physicians interested in visiting US hospitals, and Indian American doctors wanting to go to India to augment healthcare and medical education, would apply on a website, which would match their specialties and pair them. No fee was involved. Each would travel at their own cost, but the host would provide free lodging and professional expertise. An additional upshot: it was expected to lead to multiple joint projects in various medical fields, business and philanthropic, and result in joint research by Indian and US institutions, with potential NIH funding. As an ongoing program, India would be continually benefited by the program.

In 2000, Dr. N.R. Karve and I collected $100,000 from fifty-seven members of the US-based alumni group of B.J. Medical College. The money was spent to extend its library and buy more computers. Initially, the library was built for 360 students. But by 2000, the college had more than 1,000 students. We hoped the exchange program would allow more alumnus groups like ours to support their alma mater.

As the first step, I created a nonprofit, the American Professional eXchange Association (APXA) in 2009. Initially APXA had a counsel, an IT employee, and a board. My friend and former *Wall Street Journal* reporter and former assistant secretary of defense, Kenneth Bacon, then president of the nonprofit organization Refugees International, was an honorary advisor. Within a few months, we created a sophisticated website for the organization. The next task was securing funding and support for the program.

I was elated that USIBC was on board. As expected, it opened doors for me. The trade group connected me to pharmaceutical companies with a presence in India. I made two presentations for them in Washington, DC, and another at a Columbia University conference on India in New York in 2010. In theory, USIBC was willing to launch the project, provided the government of India approved and funded it. I hesitantly agreed to USIBC's proposal, as once again it would involve the government of India.

Around the same time, I sought the support of the AMA. The AMA called me for a meeting, during which its officials asked about the structure of the organization that would oversee the program and other aspects of it. After I presented the details, we received the AMA stamp of approval. I also received the backing of the World Health Organization's Global Health Workforce Alliance, and of course, AAPI. Indian Ambassador to the US Meera Shankar, Assistant Secretary of State Robert Blake, and Deputy Assistant Secretary of State Michael Owen also supported the program.

With USIBC's help, I approached the US Department of State for its support. We projected the education exchange of physicians as a way of building more goodwill for the US and improve India's healthcare infrastructure. The response was positive. The department wanted the program to include other countries as well. Apart from India, the second-largest immigrant physician population is Filipino American. So the Philippines was an obvious choice. Other nations the

State Department wanted included were Egypt, Nigeria, South Africa, and Turkey. It also recommended an exchange program for other professions such as engineering. The State Department lauded the APXA effort in reaching out to these nations and mobilizing voluntary services of American professionals. However, APXA would focus mainly on an India-US physicians program.

The next big challenge was convincing the Indian government to be a partner, which was critical to securing funds from US pharmaceutical companies. Simultaneously, we explored direct funding from the government of India. The project would require about $360,000 annually for operational expenses. That included salary for staff in the US and India, expenses for the maintenance of a state-of-the-art website, and limited travel expenses. In order to reduce the cost, we decided that the program would be run out of the USIBC offices in Washington and Delhi.

During my visits to Delhi in 2010, I briefed Prime Minister Singh and Health Minister Gulam Nabhi Azad about the project. During my next two visits, in 2011 and 2012, I discussed the initiative with Azad, Health Secretary Keshav Desiraju, MCI President K.K. Talwar, and the prime minister's advisor, T.K.A. Nair.

At my request, Azad designated Dr. Damodar Bachani, a deputy commissioner at the Health Ministry, as a liaison for the India projects, including the physicians exchange program. He suggested we launch the project at the All India Institute of Medical Sciences, in Delhi, with a focus on five areas: oncology, cardiology, endocrinology, pulmonary, and infectious diseases.

In 2014, the USIBC sent a detailed proposal with bylaws regulating the program and specifying how it would be run.

A new avenue for funding opened up when India began implementing a new Corporate Social Responsibility law (CSR) in April 2014. Under the law, businesses that had a net worth of 500 crore rupees (5 billion rupees) or a turnover of 1,000 crore (10 billion rupees) were required to spend at least 2 percent of their profits on philanthropic activities. Many pharmaceutical companies fell within the gambit of the law, and we were confident that they could be tapped to fund the program.

When the Bharatiya Janata Party, under the leadership of Narendra Modi, came to power after the May 2014 election, I presented India projects to the new government. Two months prior to the election, I had met Modi, then chief minister of Gujarat, and briefed him about various India initiative, including the physicians exchange program. After the election, I wrote a letter to the new PM, asking him to launch the projects. In the meantime, I met Health Minister Vardhan and later wrote to him about the exchange program and other India initiatives. Vardhan wrote to me saying that he had asked the health secretary to look into it. As I did not hear from Vardhan after that, I wrote to the new health minister, J.P. Nadda, and health secretary, Lov Verma. I did not hear from them either.

Earlier, Bachani connected us to Ali Rizvi, a joint secretary at the ministry, under whose purview the project would fall. On January 20, 2015, Rizvi emailed Amy Hariani, the number-two USIBC official who would be in charge of the project, that the Government of India (GOI) has in "in principle" agreed "to Dr. Navin Shah's proposal for a limited US-India Physician Exchange Program." He wrote, "We were to further explore means of financing the initial cost of $360,000. Our proposal to Dr. Shah was to explore if USIBC or any other international funding agency could join hands with GOI to fund the initiative. In such a case, the program could be scaled up and many more physicians could be part of it."

I was delighted that finally the India government had given the green light for the project. The following week, I met with Hariani to revise the proposal per Rizvi's recommendations. She sent the new proposal to the Indian official. We had revised the annual budget to a little over $200,000. Raising even that amount was a challenge for us. Our efforts to find partners in both the US and India were not successful. Though initially we thought we could solicit contributions from pharmaceutical firms under the CSR regulation, we soon realized that the new law had some provisions that would make USIBC and APXA ineligible to receive funding. I spent almost $300,000 in creating and maintaining the APXA website until 2017. Though the site was functional for several years, not a single visit occurred.

As described throughout this chapter, I tried my best to help augment medical education, medical research, and healthcare in India based on decades of the proven success of US practices. After four decades, 1981 to 2017, and more than thirty-five India visits, I could not bring about the needed change. I had some limited successes on three initiatives: CME, medical equipment donation, and trauma care projects. On the infectious disease specialty, hospital accreditation, compulsory CME for renewal of medical licenses, US-India physician exchange program, and promoting Ayurveda in the US, I was not successful. I saw what was possible but I was just one doctor, and my own sense of urgency about these issues was not enough to convert the Indian government's mindset.

In 2022 in the US, we have 80,000 US doctors of Indian origin (like me); and 20,000 second-generation Indian Americans, like my son Amit. I still envision the potential of the vast pool of Indian American doctors to augment medical education and healthcare in all parts of India.

At age eighty-seven, I am sharing my experiences here, hoping that others will learn from my mistakes and undertake furthering some of these initiatives. A significant number of the Indian American physicians are willing to help India in many capacities. If properly utilized, they could be a great resource for India. Sadly, the Government of India has so far not been able to leverage the experience and expertise of the Indian American physicians willing to improve medical education and healthcare in India, which would benefit all Indians, especially the poor.

CHAPTER 5

FIGHT FOR PROSTATE CANCER PATIENTS

After the enactment of the equality legislation in the early 1990s, most of my energy was focused on my urology practice, involvement in Doctor's Community Hospital in the Washington, DC, metro area, Maryland State Medical Society, and the healthcare projects I was promoting in India.

My practice grew nicely. I had several opportunities to serve in various leadership roles of the Doctor's Community Hospital where I practiced, and in a number of professional organizations. I was elected president of the Maryland Medical Society's International Medical Graduates section in 1998, where I later served as a trustee. At the hospital, I was elected chief of urology and the chair of the Department of Surgery in 1990s. I served as the president of the medical staff from 2003 to 2005. Since 2010, I've served as medical education director of Mid-Atlantic Urology Associates.

Being a practicing urologist and medical education director, I followed closely the new studies and breakthroughs in the field. The *Journal of American Medical Association* (JAMA) appointed me as a urology book reviewer from 2008 to 2012.

I moderated two seminars in urologic cancer with the NIH Cancer Institute faculty in Washington, DC. Within general urology, an area I specialized in over the years, was prostate cancer, a common type of cancer in men, especially above age sixty. Prostate cancer is the second-leading cause of cancer mortality in men in the US.

For two decades (1992–2012), a prostate-specific antigen (PSA) blood test was used along with digital rectal exam (DRE) as an effective tool for detecting early prostate cancer. A high level of PSA in the blood and/or abnormal DRE often indicated the presence of prostate cancer.

Prostate cancer screenings helped urologists detect early prostate cancer in patients before it spread out of the prostate gland. Treatment at that point was usually successful. If cancer got out of the prostate gland, it spread fast, leading to death in a few years. However, complaints emerged that PSA screenings triggered a lot of "false-positive" and "false-negative" results. Some patients with a high level of PSA did not have prostate cancer. Similarly, normal level of PSA did not always mean the absence of prostate cancer. Yet on the whole, I have found PSA and DRE-based annual screening a useful and reliable tool for early detection. Prostate cancer screenings and treatment have helped save and prolong millions of lives. As of 2022, there are 3.1 million prostate cancer survivors in the US.

In 2012, the US Preventive Services Task Force (USPSTF) recommended that PSA-based screening was not necessary.

USPSTF, an independent body of experts that recommends best practices in disease prevention based on evidence, usually assigns four grades (A to D) to its recommendations, i.e., "Grade A" means that the benefit from a specific service or procedure is substantial and is therefore highly recommended. The Task Force gave a "Grade D" recommendation on prostate cancer screening. It concluded that "there is moderate or high certainty that the service has no net benefit or that the harms outweigh the benefits."

The Task Force report stated: "Such results cause worry and anxiety and can result in follow-up tests and procedures, such as biopsies, that aren't needed. Biopsies can cause harms such as fever, infection, bleeding, urinary problems, and pain. A small number of men will be hospitalized because of these complications. Because there is so much uncertainty about which cancers need to be treated, almost all men with prostate cancer found by the PSA test now get treatment with surgery, radiation, or hormone therapy. Many of these men do not need treatment because their cancer would not have grown or caused health problems even without treatment. This is called 'overtreatment'... Until we have a better test and better treatment options, based on a comprehensive review of the science, the USPSTF recommends that men not get the PSA test to screen for prostate cancer." [13]

The USPSTF recommendation did however contain a caveat: "Whether or not to be screened is a decision each

---

[13] "Prostate Cancer Screening." The U.S. Preventive Services Task Force (USPSTF) recommends against prostate-specific antigen (PSA)-based screening for prostate cancer. May 15, 2012. (Out of date and archived) https://www.uspreventiveservicestaskforce.org/uspstf/recommendation/prostate-cancer-screening-2012

man should make once he understands the facts and based on his own values and preferences."

But the recommendation baffled urologists like me who had relied on PSA tests as a cost-effective way of diagnosing cancer in the early stages. The moment I browsed through the details of the report, I realized that the recommendation was based on an unreal and flawed study, the Prostate, Lung, Colorectal and Ovarian Cancer Screening Trial (PLCO study). The randomized trial, upon which the study was based, contained only 4 percent African American men, a high-risk group, and some patients left studies for treatment of prostate cancer.

Black men are at greater risk of having prostate cancer due to genetic factors. According to a study, African American men are nearly 2.5 times more likely die of prostate cancer compared to non-Hispanic white men."[14] In general, African Americans represent more than 14 percent of the US population. In some of the nation's largest cities, they represent more than 30 percent.

The underrepresentation of Black men in the study jolted me for another more personal reason. The region I practice urology, Prince George's County, Maryland, is an African American-majority county. About 70 percent of the nearly million-strong population of the county, located in the Washington, DC, metro area, are Black. A significant share of our patients have always been Black men. I had no doubt in my mind that the group that would suffer most because of the recommendation was this demographic group.

---

14 See https://jamanetwork.com/journals/jamaoncology/fullarticle/2734259 Association of Black Race With Prostate Cancer–Specific and Other-Cause Mortality

Frustratingly, in many studies, African American men were not adequately represented; while in others, the race of the patients was not characterized. This is despite the fact that African American men, men older than seventy, and men with a family history of prostate cancer, are at a higher risk for harboring high-grade prostate cancer. Black men not only have earlier onset of prostate cancer, they also have more aggressive type of cancer.

Secondly, the USPSTF recommendation totally ignored studies that found that prostate cancer screenings had decreased prostate cancer death by about 40 percent from 1991 to 2012. It incensed me that the Task Force ignored the benefits of PSA and DRE tests.

The USPSTF recommendations are usually followed by federal agencies such as Medicare and Centers for Medicare & Medicaid Services, as well as frontline primary care physicians. Following the 2012 recommendation, roughly half of primary care physicians nationwide did not offer annual prostate cancer screening, especially to men seventy years and older. Many influential trade groups like the American Urological Association (AUA) and AARP, which represents the interests of Americans over the age of fifty, follow USPSTF recommendations.

AUA, the most influential organization within the urology specialty, released a guideline in April 2013 that more or less followed the USPSTF recommendation on prostate cancer screening. According to the guideline, routine PSA screening is not recommended for men seventy years and older, or for men "with a life expectancy less than ten to fifteen years."

In 2013, I conveyed my disagreement with the AUA policy in a call with the then-AUA president who told me that an AUA committee had studied the issue, and they stand by the new guideline. "The committee made the decision and I am not authorized to change it," he told me.

In January 2014, I wrote a letter published in the *Journal of Urology*, the official peer-reviewed publication of the AUA, disagreeing with the guideline. In April, the *Canadian Journal of Urology* published my paper, written in collaboration with Dr. Vladmir Ioffe, a radiation oncologist and my long-term coauthor, based on our study of 402 biopsy-proven prostate cancer patients between the ages of forty-four and seventy-seven years. Approximately 60 percent of the individuals had high-grade cancer, while 40 percent had low-grade cancer. After the publication of the paper, I called the president of the AUA to alert him to the study, but he stuck to his previous position.

The Task Force recommendation and its adoption by Medicare and AUA were immediate. Since 2012, prostate biopsies have decreased nationwide and positive diagnoses for prostate cancer have increased with higher rates of high-grade cancers. According to our studies and patient data gathered by other US researchers, there is an increased incidence and higher grades of prostate cancer among all three vulnerable groups: African American men, men above age seventy, and men with a family history of prostate cancer.

Data showed that, as a result of the 2012 recommendation, the prostate cancer screening decreased. Since then, the number of patients with prostate cancer, prostate cancer metastasis, and mortality due to prostate cancer have been increasing in the US. According to the American Cancer Society, new prostate cancer cases increased from 161,360 in 2017 to 248,530 in 2021. The prostate cancer deaths for the corresponding years were 26,730 and 34,130. Our own studies, from 2014 onward, published in the *Reviews of*

Urology, showed that the number of prostate biopsies has decreased by 41 percent since 2012, while the diagnosis of prostate cancer has increased by 100 percent.

There has also been monetary impact. The Medicare spending on prostate cancer treatment went up from $11.8 billion in 2010 to $13.4 billion in 2014 and $15.2 billion in 2016. The increase has been largely due to an increase in treatment of metastatic prostate cancer. Once prostate cancer is metastasized, treatment is extremely costly, and death is almost certain. An injection, which prolongs death by a few months, costs roughly $40,000. Three injections are administered to each patient. An annual PSA test, on the other hand, costs about $25.

If prostate cancer is treated in early stages (while still confined to the prostate) there is a 99 percent chance for a five-year survival. Once it spreads outside of prostate, the survival chance drops to 28 percent. Based on data from various studies, including our own research, I believe that annual prostate cancer screening, including a PSA test and digital rectal exam, should be offered to all men fifty years and older.

Since 2014 I have been strongly urging policymakers to increase early prostate cancer detection based on PSA and digital rectal exams. Dr. Ioffe and I have published six papers and twelve letters to the editor on the topic in various reputed US urology journals and other publications. Like me, Ioffe believes that prostate cancer screening significantly decreases prostate cancer morbidity and mortality. Our research has been highlighted by prominent newspapers and publications such as *The Washington Post, The Wall Street Journal, Urology Times,* and *India Abroad.* In all our writings, the crux of the argument has been: annual

PSA- and DRE-based screening will help increase the number of early diagnosis cases and cure of prostate cancer, which will reduce prostate cancer morbidity, mortality, and the cost associated with late-stage treatment.

One of the main rationales behind the USPSTF recommendation to discourage PSA screening was that it leads to over-diagnosis and over-treatment. Ioffe and I have argued that both over-diagnosis and over-treatment have been drastically reduced because of improved risk assessment tools, such as parametric MRI, PSMA PET/CT scan, genetic and other tests, and active surveillance in low-grade prostate cancer patients.

Legislative Route

Based on my experience in getting the law changed to guarantee equality for international medical graduates more than two decades ago, I decided to go through the legislative route to reverse the USPSTF recommendation. One of the important lessons I learned during the fight for equality for IMGs was that America has a democratic process to make a change. By mobilizing elected representatives, one can bring about changes.

In the fall 2014, a friend told me that Senator Jeff Sessions, a Republican, was familiar with the prostate cancer issue, and he suggested that I lobby him. Immediately, I called the Alabama senator's office and sought an appointment with him. Despite the senator's busy schedule, I was able to meet with him at his office in the Russell building on Capitol Hill.

During the meeting, I learned that Sessions had introduced a bill on prostate cancer, the "National Prostate Cancer Council Act," in September 2014, along with California

Senator Barbara Boxer, a Democrat. I found Sessions sympathetic to the plight of prostate cancer patients. He listened patiently while I explained the harms caused by the USPSTF recommendation. I urged the senator to make PSA and DRE screening available to men seventy years and older.

At that point, he intervened. "Dr. Shah, what I would do is not focus only on men seventy years and older. I would focus on the whole concept of the USPS Task Force recommendation and rectify and restudy, and come up with a new recommendation. We cannot just legislate for a segment of the population, seventy years older; let the experts decide on that."

After meeting with Sessions, I decided to enlist three different groups of lawmakers. The first was the influential Congressional Black Caucus. Since African American men were one of the worst-affected groups, having the support of the powerful caucus was crucial. Since I am from Maryland, the state's elected representatives were the second obvious choice. The third group I approached were physicians serving in US Congress.

The chair of the Congressional Black Caucus in 114th Congress was Representative George Kenneth Butterfield, better known as G.K., who represents the first congressional district of North Carolina. A few weeks after my meeting with Sessions, I received an appointment to meet with Butterfield. Like the Alabama Republican, the North Carolina Democrat was also approachable and friendly. He agreed with me that the USPSTF recommendations are not only not beneficial, but also dangerous.

I reached out to all eight members of the Maryland congressional delegation (six from the House and two from the Senate) through the Maryland State Medical Society, and they all supported my position. In 2015, sixteen members of the Republican Doctors' Caucus, chaired by Representative David P. Roe and Senator John Boozman, wrote a letter to Medicare, expressing their opposition to the USPSTF recommendations. This was in response to Medicare's policy against prostate cancer screening and designating those physicians performing prostate cancer screening as "low-quality providers." Every member and staffer I met knew a family member or friend who had prostate cancer, so they were all sympathetic to the issue. After the letter from the sixteen lawmakers who were all physicians, Medicare suspended its policy in April 2016.

In January 2015, Sessions and Boxer introduced the "National Prostate Cancer Plan Act" (S.222), which calls for establishing a National Prostate Cancer Council within the Department of Health and Human Services (HHS) for screening, early detection, assessment, and monitoring of prostate cancer to:

1. develop and implement a strategic plan for the accelerated development of diagnostic tools for prostate cancer,
2. review the effectiveness of diagnostic tools for prostate cancer,
3. coordinate prostate cancer research and services across federal agencies,
4. evaluate all active federal prostate cancer programs, and
5. ensure the inclusion of men at high risk for prostate cancer in clinical, research, and service efforts.

Interestingly, the AUA strongly supported the legislation. In a letter addressed to Sessions and Boxer, dated January

20, 2015, AUA president, Dr. William W. Bohnert, wrote: "The AUA strongly supports your legislation, which is aimed at developing and implementing a national strategy for the accelerated creation, advancement, and testing of diagnostic tools through the National Prostate Cancer Council. The bill is well aligned with the AUA's goals of improving prostate cancer screening and early detection."

In June 2015, Butterfield introduced the House companion bill to the National Prostate Cancer Plan Act, H.R. 2730. Like the Sessions-Boxer bill, its House version was also a bipartisan effort, cosponsored by twelve lawmakers.

In a letter to Representative Joe Pitts, chairman of the House Subcommittee on Health, Butterfield wrote: "Prostate cancer is an epidemic in our country, and it is incumbent upon Congress to bring federal agencies, medical experts, and patients together to facilitate improvements in care for those living with disease."[15]

In an interview with Aziz Haniffa of *India Abroad*, Butterfield graciously acknowledged my role. "No question, Dr. Shah's leadership on this issue is really appreciated."[16]

I had an excellent relationship with the congressman, who admired the work I do with African American patients. He once called me "Gandhi" for it.

Both the Senate and House bills never came out of the committee. But they created awareness about the issue on the Hill and outside of it.

In June 2016, Sessions introduced a resolution designating September 2016 as "National Prostate Cancer Awareness Month." Its aim was to educate Americans "including

---

[15] "Dr. Navin Shah's fight to save lives from prostate cancer gets Senate boost," Aziz Haniffa, *India Abroad*, July 1, 2016.
[16] Ibid.

healthcare providers, about prostate cancer." The resolution said, "early detection strategies [are] crucial to saving the lives of men and preserving and protecting families." Cosponsored by twelve senators, it was passed without any amendment. A companion resolution expressing support for designation of September as Prostate Cancer Awareness Month was passed by the House of Representatives two months later.

Since the bills and resolution were introduced, a number of influential groups changed their positions on the PSA screening. The Centers for Medicare & Medicaid Services, an agency within the HHS that administers Medicare and Medicaid, changed its policy in April 2016. Medicare now allows annual PSA screening for men above age sixty-five, while Medicaid offers annual tests for men fifty and older.

One of the most-influential institutions to openly campaign against the USPSTF recommendation was the Duke University School of Medicine. Ignoring the Task Force's recommendation, Duke started offering prostate cancer screening for free in 2016. The school even put up billboards inviting men over seventy to avail the free prostate cancer screening opportunity.

In 2018, USPSTF itself changed the PSA screening recommendation from "Grade D" to "Grade C," which allowed screening to be done selectively to individual patients based on judgment of the physician and preferences of the patient, especially for men within the 55–65 age group. In other words, it believes the benefit is small, and screening can be done depending on individual circumstances.

Since 2018, I have focused on Medicare to encourage primary care physicians to offer an annual prostate cancer screening. Roughly half of primary care physicians in the US do not offer annual prostate cancer screening, especially to men seventy years and older, a consequence of the USPSTF recommendation.

In our 2020 paper, "A Trend Toward Aggressive Prostate," published in *Reviews in Urology*, Ioffe and I have shown that, as compared to 2012, more prostate cancer cases, more metastasis and more prostate cancer deaths occurred in 2020 due to fewer annual prostate cancer screening. I requested the director of Medicare & Medicaid Services, Dr. Meena Seshamani, to write to all participating primary care physicians that an annual prostate cancer screening is covered by Medicare. My seven-year (so far) struggle for prostate cancer screening continues, but now I have more support; and hopefully soon US men age fifty and older will be offered annual prostate cancer screenings.

CHAPTER 6

A LIFELONG LOVE AFFAIR WITH INDIAN COINS

As a child, my parents and teachers told me India was very ancient and was ruled by many foreigners, and I saw British rule and British soldiers. When I got 1905 British coin, I found out that Britishers reigned in India for 200 years. That inspired me to read the history of India and learn about its heritage and culture.

As a twelve-year-old in 1947, I sensed that Diwali had a special resonance. Roughly two-and-a-half months after the British left India, the Festival of Lights was celebrated with great joy and loud music across my neighborhood in the Poona Cantonment. The streets were bustling with activity. Men and women in colorful new clothes were doing last-minute shopping. Every home in the area was illuminated with *diyas*, decorative lamps that represented the victory of light over darkness. The skies above were resplendent with fireworks. Diwali follows New Year's and gifts from the elders was a practice. My siblings and I received customary gifts from our mom: a four *anna* coin.

Anna was the denomination of the pre-Independence British India. A rupee consisted of 16 annas. Each anna was four *paisas*. The coins were in circulation till India adopted the metric system in 1957, when the Indian rupee was divided into 100 *naya* paisas. (naya means new.) A paisa has no value now, as the Indian rupee devalued precipitously decade after decade. However, in the 1940s, a rupee could buy a lot. In fact, it was almost equal to the US dollar in value. So the British copper paisa meant a lot for a poor kid like me.

At school, most children my age rushed to *gaadi walas* (food vendors on carts) during lunch breaks to buy sweets and snacks. Since I almost never had any money, I studiously avoided the vendors during my school life. Diwali was an honorable exception. When school reopened after the festival, I (now a proud owner of four annas) was eager to splurge at least a couple of them on my favorite snack. *Chikky*, a peanut bar made with nuts and jaggery, or unrefined sugar, cost one paisa. I gave the vendor one *anna* and he handed me a small bar of chikki and three paisas.

One of the three paisa coins triggered a curiosity in my preteen brain that no other material possession until then had. That particular coin was much older than the other three. It was a British coin minted in 1900. I had no idea why I wanted to keep that coin, but eventually it cultivated in me a love for old coins. Thus at the age of twelve, I unknowingly became a coin collector and amateur numismatist.

A whole year later I was able to add to my "coin collection." My second coin was acquired in the same manner as the first—from a vendor. Nearly all coins I collected in the first few years came to me as change given to me by street vendors when I bought a snack, or by a store clerk when I purchased groceries for the family.

Each time I received an old coin, I saved it as a prized possession, a treasure. I kept them stuffed in a small four-by-five-inch postal envelope. The envelope was tucked in a pocket of the school bag that I carried to school every day—a waterproof haversack I bought from a vendor selling used goods on the street. Being a cantonment town, plenty of secondhand military merchandises were available in Poona Camp.

I soon realized that what started as a fascination for an old brown copper paisa was not just a passing fad or a childhood craze. Collecting Indian coins from different eras, dynasties, and kingdoms would become my lifelong mission and passion. Over the next six decades, it took me to dozens of cities in India and other countries.

In Search of Coins

As I grew older, my family shopping activities increased. By the time I completed high school, I had about eighty coins, nearly all collected without spending much money.

Most numismatists add to their collection by purchasing coins from the market. But being a teenager from a poor family, buying them from the market was out of the question. But that changed when I started pre-medicine at Nowrosjee Wadia College. I began doing odd jobs. Every time I was paid, I almost always handed over the cash to my mother. With my father not earning enough to take care of our family of five, and being the eldest son, I needed to contribute whatever I could. However, at least once a month, she asked me to keep a few rupees for myself.

I purchased old coins from mainly two sources. First were local jewelers. People normally sold their old silver and gold coins to jewelers, unless they were collectors. Jewelers melted the metal to make ornaments. Coin collectors often visited jewelers and purchased coins, paying a higher price than their value. The first coin I purchased was from a neighborhood jeweler: an Indo-Scythian silver coin from around 10 AD.

The second place for buying old coins in the city was the market where old goods were sold. Most big Indian cities have such flea markets that sell all kinds of goods, from old car tires and cycle parts, to utensils, used clothing, and books. Big cities such as Mumbai have permanent flea markets, meaning open seven days a week. Vendors from all over Poona (now Pune) and neighboring regions descended on the street to sell all sorts of preowned goods.

Pune's popular flea market, Juna Bazaar (Old Bazaar in Hindi) was located in an older part of the city, known as Kasba Peth, on the western banks of the Mutha River. The first time I went to Juna Bazaar was during my Wadia College days when someone told me that old coins were also sold there. My first purchase from the Bazaar was a coin minted in the era of Chatrapati Shivaji, a Maratha icon who ruled much of present-day Maharashtra and neighboring regions from 1664 to 1680. After that first visit, I went many times, often early in the morning. My usual budget was a few rupees. Once you identify the coins, you bargain. Nobody ever bought anything from Juna Bazaar without bargaining.

Medical College

My financial health improved considerably after starting at B.J. Medical College in 1955 for two reasons. I received a long-term interest-free loan from the foundation of philanthropist C.M. Patel, father of my school classmate and friend Arun. The loan covered my 600-rupee annual tuition for all five years I was in medical college. Providing my family with a huge lifeline, it also enabled me to focus on studies.

The second reason I was in a better space financially was because of the part-time jobs I was able to land: tutoring Mr. Patel's grandchild, reading a Parsi newspaper to a lady, reading the *British Medical Journal* to a retired surgeon, and selling soap crumps collected from a soap factory. The most lucrative job was serving as a ticket collector at the Pune Race Course on Saturdays. Though the job was seasonal, it fetched me fourteen rupees a day, a decent amount back in the days. For the first time in my life, I had some money I could spend on items other than essential goods such as food, clothes, and books. By then, coin collecting had become an important part of my life, and I was willing and able to spend some money on it.

I started going to Juna Bazaar every Saturday to buy old coins. The Bazaar was close to B.J. Medical College, just a mile and a half away. I also expanded my sourcing locations beyond the Juna Bazaar and the jewelers. One time I met a Marathi gentleman who had a number of good coins he was looking to sell. I bought a few coins from him. Later I dealt with several old coin sellers.

I started attending a coin exhibition that took place in Pune annually in a large hall, with vendors from all over Maharashtra. Like at Juna Bazaar, I could bargain for coins at the exhibition. I visited the exhibition every one of the five years I was at BJ Medical College.

So my medical school years were productive from the standpoint of the numismatist in me. My stockpile ballooned to nearly 400 coins by the time I became a doctor. I had coins from 600 BCE to 400 BCE. I had Maratha coins from the age of Shivaji through the eighteenth century. Most of the coins were paisas, and some were punch-marked and silver coins.

Doctor's Salary

In 1960 I completed my bachelor of medicine and bachelor of surgery (MBBS) and enrolled for the four-year residency almost immediately. As a house surgeon, I was provided with a free room and a stipend of 80 rupees a month—not a huge amount by any means. But for a man of my spending habits, it was not a small paycheck either, as I hardly spent any money on food. My mother sent meals from home once a day. On some weekends, I went home. That allowed me to spend a small part of the salary on coins, which made me busy and happy.

After my wedding in 1965, Leela and I moved into a new apartment and soon set up a new private practice with the help of my father-in-law Rikhabchand Sanghvi and C.M. Patel. Once I started earning a little bit more, I began buying ancient coins, which were more expensive. Each coin cost anywhere from 5 to 15 rupees. Between 1965 and '70, I accumulated a nice collection of ancient coins.

I also started buying coins from the Chor Bazaar in Mumbai. The Chor Bazaar, in South Mumbai, is much bigger than Pune's Juna Bazaar. My father-in-law was based in Mumbai at the time, looking after the Sanghvi family business there, and I visited him occasionally. I had a couple of friends and classmates from school days working in the city: Devendra Shah and Navnit Shah. I mostly traveled to Mumbai by local trains, which offered lower fares.

I knew some private collectors and dealers by now. Once I met one dealer, he introduced me to others. Dealers charged more for the coins. I could only afford copper and silver coins. I never purchased gold coins as they were beyond my budget. By the time, I came to the US, I had some 1,500 coins. They were mainly ancient coins, mostly silver, copper, lead, punch-marked coins, and British coins.

Coming to the United States

While packing bags for the US trip, one item I stuffed inside my check-in luggage was a cotton *theli,* a handbag. That bag contained three small, thick, yellow, discolored bags. Tucked inside them were all the coins I had collected over nearly a quarter century. I had no idea what I was going to do with them in the US. I was excited about coming to the US, but at the back of my mind was a realization that I wouldn't be able to collect coins in the foreseeable future. No Juna Bazaars, exhibitions, dealers, or anything to do with Indian coin collection for a while.

During my surgery residency in Ohio and urology residency later in Washington Hospital Center, the cotton theli remained in the big bag. Only when I moved to a new house in Potomac, MD, in 1977, did the coins find a safe house. I rented a bank vault at a bank near my home.

As a numismatist, my first six years in the US were quiet. I was busy training, settling in, and building a career. I could not visit India during residency. My first US job was in 1976 with a base salary of roughly $35,000, which would top $100,000 in a few years. Once I could afford a trip to India with the family, I could resume my coin collection. During the first trip to Pune, in December 1977, I visited a coin exhibition after a gap of six years.

I could now buy coins that previously were not affordable. During each India visit, I budgeted $1,000 to $2,000 for coins. Each dollar was worth more than 8.5 rupees. With more purchasing power, I also made friends with some coin dealers.

India visits were part of my winter calendar as noted in previous chapters. Between 1977 and 2018, I made thirty-five visits. During every trip, my nephew Hemant Shah, son of my sister Aruna, scheduled meetings with the dealers ahead of my visit. When some of those dealers visited me at home, my father learned about my collection for the first time. Another supportive person in Pune was businessman and coin collector V.B. Agarwal.

During every trip, I visited multiple cities in search of coins. Cities I visited for coins over the years included Udaipur, Jaipur, Jaisalmer, Mount Abu, Agra, Ahmadabad, Baroda, Chandigarh, Patna, Madras, and Manipal. In Maharashtra, I also bought coins from Kolhapur and Sangli, where I had relatives. Delhi, Pune, and Bombay were part of the itinerary of every trip.

Bombay was a gateway to my hometown of Pune. Besides the Chor Bazaar, I also bought coins from a company in the city, run by a Parsi. The Delhi stop was primarily for meetings with government officials as part of my various health initiatives in India. Taj Mansingh Hotel on Mansingh Road, New Delhi, was my home in Delhi; I stayed there every time I visited the city. It is close to the prime minister's house and South and North blocks, the citadel of the Government of India. The hotel was also close to my contacts in Delhi's numismatics world. On my annual visits, I got to know many dealers, as one led to another. I dealt with half a dozen individuals who bought and sold coins. Once dealers knew that I was from the US and staying at Taj Mansingh, they charged much more, but they sold good coins.

When I came to the US, I didn't have coins from the Mughal period, or the preceding Delhi Sultanate era. The two Muslim empires had ruled much of India for more than 650 years, beginning in 1206. At the back of my mind, I knew it was a notable lacuna that had to be addressed, so I made buying those coins a priority.

Overseas Trips

The US is not a big market for Indian coins. However, I purchased a few coins from New York and Chicago. Overall, I purchased more coins from Europe and North Africa than the US. I visited cities such as London, Rome, Athens, and Cairo in search of coins. During the early years, I had a stopover in London during every visit to India. In the mid-1970s, my uncle (my father's younger brother) Shantilal Shah had moved to London for a job. I visited him on my way to India or on my way back.

In London, I always made sure to check out the local coin market. One place I did not want to miss while in London was the British Museum. My first tour of the museum and its Department of Coins and Medals was in 1977. In addition to British and Indian coins, I saw ancient Greek, Roman, and Egyptian coins. Britain, being a Colonial power that ruled several countries in different parts of the world, its museum had coins from many nations and great collection of Mughal and Maurya gold coins. Shops near the museum sold coins and artifacts. I bought several coins from these vendors over multiple visits.

A particular visit in the early 2000s was quite memorable. Thanks to my friend, Dr. Richard Doty, then curator of Numismatics at Smithsonian's Museum of American History, I had a chance to see some of the more precious coins at the museum. Richard wrote a letter to a British Museum official, introducing me and requesting that he arrange a tour for me. The museum opened the vault, which contained many ancient coins. This was the best collection of ancient Indian coins, as well as British coins I have come across anywhere.

Richard provided similar introductory letters to Silvana de Caro, coordinator, del Museo Nazionale Romano, and Despina Evgenidou, director of Numismatic Museum of Athens. Like the British Museum official, de Caro gave me a tour of her museum when I visited in the summer 2002. Rome is full of ancient monuments like the layered coliseum, and history is well preserved there. Coins are similarly showcased in Rome. Most Roman coins have good portraits of kings.

I had a good and lively discussion on Indian coins with de Caro. Before I left, she gifted me with a book on the Roman coinage. I was so fascinated by del Museo Nazionale Romano that I made another trip to the city two years later. I was received in a similar manner at the Athens museum by Evgenidou, who showed me ancient coins, especially gold coins.

During my visits to various cities in India and Europe, I purchased several books related to Indian coins. One of my favorite locations for books is in the Daryaganj area of Old Delhi, a popular flea market in the Indian capital. I picked up a number of wonderful books there, including rare books, such as Major-General Alexander Cunningham's seminal work, *Coins of Ancient India: From the Earliest Times Down to the Seventh Century A.D.*, first published in 1891; *The*

Coins of India by Brown C.T. (1922); and *Coinage of Ancient India*, by Satya Prakash and Rajendra Singh (1968).

I bought some great books on Indian coins at bookstores near the British Museum in London. And I received some books as gifts from museums in Athens and Rome. I have fifty-five Indian coin books in my library.

Cataloguing the Collection

I have known the Hinduja brothers since the mid-1980s, especially the eldest brother S.P. Hinduja, known as SPH. I have served as an advisor to Hinduja Hospital in Mumbai, run by the brothers, helping in its collaboration with Johns Hopkins University and AAPI. Our paths crossed in the numismatic area as well. In December 2015, prior to an India visit, Ashok Hinduja, the youngest of the Hinduja brothers, known among friends as AP, called me. "Navin, you're a coin collector and an expert," he said. "This British colonel gave us his collection of coins before he died. Why don't you come and see the coins while in Mumbai?"

A few weeks later, I visited AP at his home in Mumbai near JW Marriott, where I usually stayed during my visits to the city. After lunch, he took me to the Hinduja Foundation Antiquity Collection office. The Antiquity Collection also has paintings, sculptures, photographs, and other artifacts. Not surprisingly, the coin collection captivated me the most. I spent the rest of the afternoon with Manish Verma, a curator and numismatist at the foundation.

The collection has more than 26,000 coins from 600 BCE to 600 AD. By my reckoning, it is the finest collection of Indian coins outside of the National Museum in Delhi and the British Museum in London. Verma and his staff of six experts manage the Antiquity Collection. Impressed by their meticulous cataloguing of the coins, I asked AP whether the foundation could help me catalogue my collection, which is roughly a tenth of the size of theirs. Ever gracious, he readily offered to send Verma to Washington, DC, to help me.

Verma worked at the Indian Institute of Research in Numismatic Studies in Nasik, Maharashtra, for several years before joining the Hinduja Foundation. In 2017, Verma flew into Washington to catalogue my collection. Over eight days, he painstakingly went through more than 3,000 coins collected over a span of seven decades. He measured, weighed, and studied every coin, and photographed every coin of the entire collection. I was impressed with his knowledge of the coins. Verma reminded me of Rita Sharma, who served as the numismatic head of National Museum for several years. Both recognized the coins quickly, and instantly cited the dates and dynasties during which they were minted.

For the first time since I started collecting coins as a hobby, I had a complete sense of the range, depth, and scale of my collection. According to Verma, the collection, which mainly consists of silver, lead, copper, zinc, and billon coins, is among the best individual collections he has seen. It would be "nearly impossible" for an individual from a different profession to acquire "such a wide variety of coins," he said. He divided the coins into the following seven categories:

1. Ancient Indian coins, which include punch-marked coins; early uninscribed cast copper; post-Mauryan-Ujjayini and Narmada Valley coins; Pre-Satavahana, Satavahana and contemporary coins; Western Kshatrapas, Taikutaka coins; coins from South Indian Sangam period. Pallava, Chera, and Pandya dynasties;

2. Indian coins of foreign origin, such as Indo-Greek, Indo-Scythian, Indo-Parthian, Parthians, Constantine and Roman, and Roman imitation coins;
3. Early Medieval coins, such as coins from Sasanian and Indo-Sasanian, Gadhaiya kingdoms; later Pandyas; Imperial Cholas; those of Hindu kings of Kashmir and Ceylon rulers.
4. Sultanate coins of the Amir of Sind, Mamluk, Khalji, Lodhi and Suri dynasties;
5. Coins from the Mughal era, including Vijayanagar Empire, Maratha, Rajputana, Scindia, Gaekwad, Bhonsle, Holkars, Nayakas, Mysore, East India Compan,y and Indo-French coins;
6. British Indian coins; and
7. Post-independent coins, including annas, paisas, and rupees (1947–2020).

Of the two immediate outcomes to Verma's cataloguing, one was positive and the other not-so-positive. Impressed with my collection, which he termed "PhD material," Verma suggested that it warrants a book. If that is the case, I told him, he is the best person to write it, being the first expert to study and catalogue it. Verma agreed to write the book himself. *Coins of India*, based on my collection(scheduled to be published in 2022). In the book, he writes that the collection comprises "a complete series of significant coins from 600 BC onwards," and it "presents a glimpse of the Indian coin tradition."

The other outcome of the cataloguing was the realization that nearly 10 percent of my coins were not authentic. Fake coins, a bane of collectors, come with the territory. I have to depend on my eyes and instincts to find counterfeits. From time to time, I depended on Dr. Rita Sharma during my visits to Delhi, and the good folks at the American Numismatic Society in New York to weed out fake coins.

Two of a Kind

In the first few decades of my life as a coin collector, I had only elementary knowledge about coins and their history. Two people who helped me expand my numismatic horizon were Dr. Rita Sharma and Dr. Richard Doty. Sharma was the chief numismatist at the National Museum of India's Coin Gallery in New Delhi. Richard was the senior numismatic curator at the Smithsonian's National Museum of American History in Washington, DC.

It would be hard to find two more-different personalities than Richard and Rita. But both shared some fine qualities that made them exceptional human beings and public servants. They were civil servants who were wedded to their jobs, committed to public service, and ethical to the core. Professionally, both were giants in their field.

I met Rita in the mid-1980s via an introduction by Narasimha Rao, then the minister of Health and Family Welfare, in the government of Prime Minister Rajiv Gandhi. At his office one evening, after discussing my health projects, he casually asked me what I was doing in town. I told him I was collecting coins and planned to explore the city's coin market. He told me that the National Museum of India has one of the best coin collections in the country and suggested that I visit its Coins Gallery. He specifically asked me to meet Dr. Rita Sharma, a numismatist there.

When I visited the museum the next day, Rita greeted me warmly. During that first visit, she offered me a cup of tea and biscuits, and assigned an assistant to accompany me to the Coins Gallery. I was overawed by the depth and breadth of the collection. truly breathtaking. I had not seen such a vast collection of Indian coins before then. The Gallery also had educational models of coin-making in different eras.

I remained in touch with Rita after I came back from India. Next December, before I left for India, I wrote her a letter informing her about my Delhi visit and expressing an interest in visiting the museum again. On that visit, she accompanied me to the vault, opened it, and explained some of the rare coins in great detail. She gave me a CD containing photos of some of the coins in the collection. After that trip, every time I was in Delhi, I visited Rita. She almost always showed me around the museum and discussed her projects with me. And every time, she welcomed me with a cup of tea and biscuits in her office.

Rita also wrote a book on punch-marked coins, which were the oldest Indian monetary objects dating back to sixth century BCE. Punch-marked coins contained hundreds of different marks, which distinguish each coin. Some marks were in the shape of flowers and trees.

At the National Museum, Rita's official title was keeper (numismatics and epigraphy). A PhD holder and great academic, she was one of the topmost experts on ancient Indian coins. Rita was a passionate history enthusiast whose interest in coins was unparalleled. Every Wednesday, she held forte on the ground floor of the museum to examine coins of visitors who wanted them examined by her to see if they were real or fake, and to know their history. Sitting behind a table, she met people who lined up to show her the coins. After authenticating the coins, she provided details about them.

During my visits, I showed her my coins and had them examined. In fact, I made it a point to be in Delhi on a

Wednesday, to avail of her free coin examination service. Of course, I stood in line, waiting for my turn.

Overtime, Rita and I developed a close personal connection. Once, she invited me to her home, not far from Hotel Taj Mansingh. She shared a small two or three-bedroom apartment with her husband and son. she and her family lived a simple life. Rita, who always wore a sari, was an honest official.

During my visits, we talked about different coins. She knew so much that it only took a half minute to describe details about a particular coin. She was also good at telling coin stories. Her stories would transport me from the twenty-first century to 600 BCE in a matter of minutes.

Besides our usual meetings at her office during my Delhi visits, Rita and I used to speak on the phone multiple times a year. Sometimes I called her excitedly to share information about coins I acquired during recent travel. I invited her to visit Washington to see my collections, as well as vaults of the American Numismatic Society, and the Smithsonian. She said she would come whenever she got two weeks of vacation. But the visit never happened.

Dr. Richard Doty

I had been curious about Smithsonian's coin collection ever since moving to Washington, DC. My first visit to Smithsonian was in 1976, when it hosted a mega exhibition to celebrate the bicentennial anniversary of American independence. Nearly a decade later, I spent more time there when the National Museum of American History hosted an exhibition titled "Aditi: The Monies of India" in 1986. It featured 300 numismatic objects. A book by the same title was published on the side lines of the exhibition. I was lucky to get a copy of it from a Smithsonian official, Dr. Raymond J. Herbert, in 1988. That year, Hebert, a senior official at the National Museum of American History, and I had multiple conversations about coins of India. A resident of Potomac, Maryland, he visited my house to see my collection. He was impressed with the collection and gave me a copy of *Aditi*.

Later I learned that the National Numismatic Collection (NNC) had more than a million monetary objects covering three millennia. As I didn't have gold coins in my collection, I was especially interested in seeing Indian gold coins. So one afternoon in 1997, I went to the National Museum of American History. I was led to an official who was in charge of the gold collection. The lady told me that she didn't know much about Indian coins and advised me to meet Dr. Richard Doty, who was not in office that day.

The next week, I made another trip to Smithsonian to meet Richard. My first impression was that he was a friendly and knowledgeable person. When I told him about my collection, he asked pointed questions about the coins. I figured that he knew a lot about Indian coins. He led me to the NNC vault, where all the coins are stored, and showed me all the Indian gold coins. He was rather apologetic about the small storage space.

That was the beginning of my nearly fifteen-year friendship with Richard. We talked about Indian coins and about coins from other countries. I had Greek and Roman coins as well. Romans never conquered India, but they were doing business with India. Greeks ruled the northern part of the country through governors. Richard was very much interested in Greek coins.

In November 2001, on a Saturday afternoon, he came to my home in Potomac to see my collection. I took him to the bank nearby where the coins are stored. He was impressed by the variety of my collection. The following week, he wrote, "Your collection is truly encyclopaedic in scope and distinctly superior to our cabinet with respect to the earliest coinage of your country. It was obviously assembled by someone with a passion for the subject, as well as persistence and good judgment."

In addition to expanding my knowledge of coins, Richard facilitated my visit to some of the finest museums in Europe. Prior to my visits, he wrote letters introducing me to top museum officials and requesting them to show their vaults to me. Because of these letters, which praised my collection, I was well received at museums in Athens, Rome, and the British Museum in London.

I discussed the idea of an exhibition with the Smithsonian and the American Numismatics Society, as well as officials of the Government of India in both Washington and New Delhi. ANS curator, Dr. Robert William Hoge, wrote a letter in support of the exhibition. I also explored the possibility of organizing an exhibition with museums and organizations such as the Metropolitan Museum of Art in New York and the National Geographic Society in Washington.

A Dream

For four-and-a-half decades, my coins have been safely stored in a bank vault near my home. Only a few friends, fellow numismatic enthusiasts, and collectors have had a chance to see them. Some of those individuals who have seen the collection often asked me to consider hosting an exhibition of the coins. Since there aren't many collectors of Indian coins in the US, American numismatists seldom get to see ancient Indian coins. Such an exhibition, either in Washington or New York could showcase the Indian culture and history through the medium of coins and give a glimpse of the country's monetary history.

I would very much like to show the history, culture, and changing boundaries of India to Americans through the medium of coins. India is one of the first melting pots of the world as various local and foreign rulers ruled it over millenniums. India kept its culture, while adding rich elements of other cultures. For the same reason, the country has a rich and diverse collection of coins.

CHAPTER 7

FAMILY

Luckily I was able to surround myself with wonderful and wise people, who have been huge blessings in my life. Whatever little I have accomplished is mainly due to sustained and unrelenting support of a great many individuals. I could count on these people, no matter what the situation was. They always had my back. It is hard to imagine if I could have overcome the poverty of early years and pursued my dream profession without the support of my father Chimanlal and mother Lilawati. Despite their hardships, my parents gave me a decent education to succeed in life and inculcated in me the right values and principles.

Similarly, I could not have completed the medical education without the financial assistance and love of C.M. Patel (Papaji) and Chandanben Patel (Momiji), parents of my classmate and friend Arun Patel. Arun and his wife, Yasuben, also encouraged me to pursue my dream and supported me a great deal.

After our marriage in 1965, Leela came with a stellar support system, from which I benefited immensely. The Sanghvis, especially my father-in-law Rikhabchand Sanghvi, was as invested in my success as I was. Rikhabchand's brothers, Soorajmal, Bhabhutmal, and Phoolchand, all considered me as their own son-in-law, and helped me in my practice in Pune. All four Sanghvi brothers argued loudly when they had differences, but their wives stood in unison to calm them down. The wives kept the tradition of joint family.

My mother-in-law Ujiben was a loving person. She was down-to-earth and respected everyone, including domestic help. Even though she studied only up to middle school, she insisted that her children have college education. Ujiben was a pillar of strength for the family, and Leela's temperament was in part a reflection of her mother. The Sanghvi children became my friends, and I felt that I was a part of the Sanghvi family.

The entry of Leela into my life was perhaps my greatest good fortune. In my adult life, no one played a bigger role in my success than my wife. Almost instantly, Leela became my anchor, friend, partner, and manager of my life. The thirty-some years she was physically present in my life and the twenty-five years since her death, Leela continues to remain my Rock of Gibraltar. Ours was an unlikely marriage; the sort of which are common in Bollywood films, but not in real life. It was not a story of a rich girl falling in love with a poor boy and marrying him by overcoming all odds. On the other hand, it was an instance of a rich girl marrying a poor boy in a so-called arranged marriage setup. She wanted an educated partner, and she willingly overlooked my family's financial status and struggles.

To this day, I am amazed that Leela Rikhabchand Sanghvi chose to marry me. We were from diametrically different social and economic backgrounds. The Sanghvis were rich and famous beyond my imagination. They lived in a huge bungalow in one of the most affluent areas of town. For every need and every chore, they had helpers. On the other hand, my family had been living in a one-room chawl since my childhood, living barely above subsistence level. Bhai was a salesman in a clothing store, and Bun was a housewife who took care of my younger brother Vinod, our sister Aruna (the youngest of the three Shah children), and me.

I had met Leela only a few times prior to our marriage. It was during our honeymoon in Mahabaleshwar, a hill station on the western coast of Maharashtra, a few hours to the southwest of Pune, which was arranged by my father-in-law, we got to know each other well. In those four days, I knew that she was as authentic and loyal as one could get. She never talked of her wealth or my family's poverty.

Leela's standard of living actually fell after our marriage. When we moved into our small apartment, she did not have the luxury of having the kind of helpers she had at her parents' house. But Leela never complained. She became part of our family and seamlessly fit in with my parents. Whenever we visited Bhai and Bun, Leela would head straight to the kitchen to help my mother. This continued during our annual visits to Pune, till her last visit 1992.

When I decided to come to the US for training in Akron, Ohio, Leela fully backed me, even though she knew that my parents, especially my father, did not want me to leave town, not to mention the country. Leela also knew that she and our two daughters would not be able to join me for a few years, while I completed the training. She believed that, with US training, I would scale greater heights in my profession. With a smile, she frequently reminded me that the difficult period will pass. It was her optimism and wholehearted backing that strengthened my resolve to travel to the United States.

During my first year in the US, in 1971, I badly missed Leela and our two daughters, Shefali (Tony) and Sonali. Finally, when the three of them came to the US in 1972, my sorrow vanished and was replaced with joy and fulfillment. I was surprised how quickly Leela adjusted to the American way of life once she was in the country.

In fact, it would not be an exaggeration to say that Leela pretty much ran our household. Initially, as a junior resident and later as a practicing urologist, I was working hard to build a career in this new country. Then circumstances made me an activist, spending long hours and practically all weekends on the various causes I inherited and espoused.

While I was focusing on my professional career and pursuing other activities, Leela managed the household, did all the chores, and paid the bills without any help from me. She took care of children's school and after-school activities, driving them to various classes and events, weekend after weekend. Because she was short (4 feet 10 inches) and thin, her large Chevrolet station wagon had a seat extender and an additional pillow that allowed her to have a clear view of the road. The joke in our household was that cops never stopped Leela because they could not see who was driving the car.

But the joke apart, Leela was a good driver, having cut her driver's teeth on the chaotic roads of Pune. Her road sense was impressive. GPS was not available in cars till the mid-1990s. In those days, motorists routinely carried maps, but Leela did not need one. You just tell her where to go, and she would reach there without any trouble.

Though she was short in stature, Leela was tall in courage, heart, and spirit. To me, two of her most-admirable qualities were humility and compassion. She never discussed her family's wealth with me, the children, or her friends. She managed the household and children within my income.

Leela had several great attributes that made her a noble human being. Her ability to empathize with people, love and care for the family, and her tolerance for different viewpoints were exemplary. Once she went to India for almost two months to take care of her sister-in-law (her elder brothers' wife) who was injured in a fall. When her father came to the US for heart surgery, she took great care of her both parents and her brother Nandu. Leela took care of visitors, her eight cousins, sister Sharda and her husband Niranjan, my aunt and her family, and other relatives and friends from India, be it in our small apartment in Hyattsville, Maryland, or in our house in Potomac, Maryland.

Philanthropist

Leela always believed in helping the needy. Growing up, she had seen firsthand much of the charitable work her extended family did. The Sanghvis used to sponsor one of the largest *jatra* (pilgrimage) groups to Rajasthan, India, sending hundreds of devotees to various sacred Jain religious centers. However, in the first dozen or so years of our married life, I hardly had the resources to share with anyone. Leela knew that my primary responsibility was to our immediate family and my parents. She helped me save enough money to buy Bhai and Bun a brand-new apartment in Poona Camp.

Once our financial situation improved, we began sending money to India to help poor people, mostly in the Poona area. These donations coincided with the Mahavir Jayanti, the birthday of Lord Mahavir, the last of the twenty-four Jain Thirthankaras (gods). Our advantage was that dollar increased in value against the Indian rupee, year after year, allowing us to help more people.

Leela suggested that we also feed the poor and hungry in our own backyard in the Washington, DC, area. Our hometown was the political capital of the world, but it was also home to thousands of poor people. The plight of the city's poor was thrust to the center in the mid-1980s when activist Mitch Snyder fasted for forty days to highlight the condition of Washington's destitute.

The New York-born and Harvard-trained Snyder had a rough childhood before becoming a lifelong campaigner for homeless people. An admirer of Mahatma Gandhi, he ran a nonprofit, Community for Creative Non-Violence (CCNV) in Washington, DC, which provided food and shelter to the homeless. In 1986, a biopic of the activist, *Samaritan: The Mitch Snyder Story*, in which Martin Sheen starred as Snyder, was aired on CBS. The film was nominated for Oscar that year.

Leela and I got in touch with Snyder to see if we could help, and he liked the idea of serving lunch for homeless people at CCNV on the occasion of Mahavir Jayanti. At the first lunch, held on April 27, 1986, we provided food for 400 homeless people. The vegetarian food was prepared by the local Siddharth Restaurant, owned by an Indian American, Saurabh Ponda. Impressed with our effort, in an interview with the *Overseas Tribune* newspaper, Snyder urged more Indian Americans to come forward and help poor people.

The next year, on Mahavir's 2,513[th] birth anniversary, we served lunch and donated clothes and undergarments to some 900 CCNV residents. Leela, Tony, and Sonali served lunch to women, while Amit and I served men. The family participated with respect to all occupants of the shelter. Our annual lunch and donation drive continued till 1991. It came to a halt when Leela was diagnosed with ovarian cancer and only had a few more years to live. Leela taught me and our children the joy of helping poor with dignity and love.

Children

Looking back, one of my profound regrets in life is that I could not spend enough time with Leela and my children when they were growing up. As a family, we have had numerous vacations together, as well as our annual India trips. But the feeling that I could have spent more time with my family hounds me, and that sentiment has remained since Leela's death a quarter century ago. But I take solace in the fact that she has given me three wonderful children, who have succeeded in life in their respective fields.

All parents want their children to do well in life. Leela and I have been lucky in that respect. I give credit to Leela for that.

"For Mom, the most important thing was to raise children that were educated, hardworking, and kind people," says Sonali. "My siblings and I have embraced this belief as we raise our own children."

When I left for the US in 1971, Tony and Sonali were young. In my absence, Leela raised the girls, with the help of her parents. When they came here roughly fourteen months later, I was thrilled beyond words.

Public schools in Prince George's County, where we initially lived, were not as good as the ones in the neighboring

Montgomery County. So we moved to Potomac, in Montgomery County in 1977, to enroll our children in a better school system. Tony and Sonali attended the Lake Normandy Elementary School and Churchill High School in Potomac. Both schools were not far from our home. Our son Amit (born in 1975) followed his two sisters through school.

We decided to raise our children with roots in both the US and Indian culture. We taught them the Jain religious values, especially vegetarian food and nonviolence, and taught them Gujarati and Hindi languages. Both girls trained in bharatanatyam, the classical dance form originated in southern India, and painting for several years. They used to perform bharatanatyam at the local Gujarati association and IMAAI annual events. Amit's passion is tabla, the percussion instrument popular in South Asia, which he learned for almost eight years. He won several prizes in tabla competitions.

Unlike now, there were fewer Indian immigrants in the Washington, DC, area in the 1970s. So it was not easy teaching children Indian art and imbibing them the Indian culture. For each activity, one has to either take the kids to the teachers' house or bring them to our home. So to teach the children the Gujarati language, we had a teacher come to our home on weekends. For bharatanatyam, painting, and tabla classes, Leela drove the kids to the teachers' home, which she did for many years. Leela was a good swimmer, and she trained all our children to swim.

Of our three kids, Tony was probably the one most attuned to the Indian culture. A good artist and painter, she is also well-versed in Indian music and poetry. I introduced her to qawwali and many other Indian classical musical genres. She learned the Urdu language in college to better appreciate the music and literature of the subcontinent.

After completing her high school at Winston Churchill in 1986, Tony attended University of Maryland at College Park, from where she earned a bachelor's degree in English. She lived at home during undergrad years and commuted daily. Later she earned a law degree from the George Washington University Law School in 1993.

While in law school, Tony met Prakash Mehta, a friend of Sonali who was enrolled for the JD program at Georgetown University. After a whirlwind romance, the two got married in Pune in 1992. The wedding was a fabulous affair, and our families had a great time. After the marriage, Tony and Prakash moved into a small apartment in Roslyn, Virginia, right across the Potomac River, a thirty-minute drive from our home. Soon both landed jobs with different Washington law firms. However, Tony had to leave her job during pregnancy.

Today Prakash is an accomplished attorney and senior partner at the powerhouse law firm, Akin Gump Strauss Hauer & Feld LLP. They shuttle between their Manhattan apartment in New York and their home in Washington, DC. Prakash is a world traveler and a fitness enthusiast. Tony and Prakash have two children, daughter Sahana and son Raz. After graduation, Sahana moved back to New York City to teach in a school. Raz attends the University of Southern California in Los Angeles.

Sonali displayed leadership skills from an early age, serving as a patrol during the middle school days. She was good in both studies and after-school activities. During her final year at the Winston Churchill High School, in 1987, she was the valedictorian. She completed her bachelor's degree in economics from Georgetown University in 1991. During undergrad days, Sonali went to London for a year as part of a study abroad program. Leela spent a month with her in London at the time. Having fallen in love with London, Sonali went back to do her master's in economics at the London School of Economics. After her graduation in 1994, she worked for a few years before going back to school to do an MBA at the Wharton School of the University of Pennsylvania, which she completed in 2000.

At Wharton, she met Praveen Tipirneni, a medical doctor who was doing an MBA there. They got married in Washington, DC. The absence of Leela was felt throughout the three-day wedding. However, Tony stepped up to the plate and made sure that everything went smoothly. Our neighbors and friends, Manubhai and Kirtben Dhokai, helped us in a big way during the wedding. After the wedding, Praveen and Sonali moved to San Francisco for a while, where they worked for different companies. Praveen now serves as the president and CEO of Morphic Therapeutic, a biomedical company that develops new generation drugs. Praveen loves sports and adventures. Recently, he spent several days cycling in Italy. Sonali now serves as the chief product officer at Invicti Security, a cybersecurity firm. Sonali and Praveen live in Boston with their two boys, Armaan and Ishaan.

Like his sisters, Amit graduated from Winston Churchill High School. While in high school, he worked with my parents to create a family tree, so I have the names of my grandfathers going back five generations: Navin, Chimanlal, Chunilal, Hakamchand, Manekchand, and Devchand.

Leela passed away while Amit was in his fourth year of college at the University of Maryland in College Park. The youngest, he was the one most affected by her death. However, he did well to recover and was valedictorian when he graduated from UMD with his BS degree.

Amit wanted to follow in my footsteps and become a physician from early childhood. As a senior at Churchill High, he had volunteered at a nearby hospital. While in college he worked at the National Institutes of Health and participated in a medical research program. I was delighted when he was admitted to Duke University School of Medicine in 1997. He earned the medical doctorate in 2002. Initially, he enrolled for residency in orthopedics before switching to ER medicine. After completing residency from University of California, Los Angeles, he came back to Washington, DC, to work as ER physician at the Washington Hospital Center. It was destiny that decided Amit to serve at the Washington Hospital Center, where he was born in 1975, when I was the chief urology resident there. Amit also runs a medical device company.

In 2013, Amit met Helma, who was then working as a nurse practitioner at the George Washington University Hospital. A year later, the two were married. The couple, who live not far from my home in Montgomery County, have three children: seven-year-old son Sahaan, and five-year-old twins, Cyrus and Sabrina. Their company is always fun. Amit and children visit me and I visit them almost every weekend. Since Leela's death, Tony, Sonali, and Amit, and their children, have been at the core of my support system and happiness.

In March 2020, when COVID-19 devastated New York City, Tony and Prakash moved back to Washington, DC, with their two children. Their move was comforting for me. Since then, Tony has been taking care of every small need of mine, including ordering groceries online for me. Once she even gave me a haircut. Sahana, like her mom, has also been a great help. She sends me sweet nutty desserts, which

I relish on a regular basis. Sahana is one family member who has followed in the footsteps of Leela. Sahana, whom we call Gussy, is making a career of helping people through her work with nonprofits. Gender equality is of particular interest to Gussy. During the pandemic, Raz was busy with online classes and college admission applications. He is now at the University of Southern California in Los Angeles.

Sonali calls me often and briefs me on progress of Armaan and Ishaan. Armaan, eighteen, is a good student who loves math. He got early admission to Harvard. In the summer of 2021, he received 100 percent (1,600) in his SAT exam. A great debater, he has participated in many competitions. Recently, his team finished fifth in a national debating contest. Both Armaan and Ishaan play baseball. Ishaan, sixteen, amazes me with his knowledge of sports, especially football and baseball teams. He is both playful and studious.

Several years ago, I traveled to Egypt and South Africa along with Sonali and the two boys—a memorable and joyous experience for all of us. We learned about ancient history and saw wildlife in its natural environment.

I am fortunate to have several members of my extended family in my life. Most notably, Hemant, son of my sister Aruna, has been part of my life ever since he came to stay with my parents in Poona as a three-year-old. He was brought to Pune mainly for schooling, since the city had good educational institutions, especially English medium schools (all classes taught in English). He stayed with Bhai and Bun and attended Dastoor School, an English medium school. Vinod and I treated Hemant more like a younger brother than a nephew.

Yash, the brilliant son of Hemant and his wife Manasi, received his PhD from University of Waterloo, in Canada, in

October 2021. He moved to Canada after graduating from the Indian Institute of Technology (BHU) Varanasi. Bharat, son of my brother Vinod, is another second-generation Shah who has gone on to do well in life. Bharat and his wife Hema are both chartered accountants (equivalent of CPA in the US). Bharat owns a large accounting firm in Pune. Bharat and Hema take good care of Vinod and his wife Mangala. During our annual visits to India, we enjoyed the love and hospitality of all our kith and kin in the Shah and Sanghvi families. Vinod took leave from his work to be with us. It was annual family get-together.

My father retired from his job as a salesman in 1980. Bhai died in 1996, and Bun passed away in 2002. Till their death, Hemant, Vinod, and Aruna looked after our parents. My mother's death made me feel lonely and abandoned. She sacrificed a great deal in raising the three of us.

Loss of Leela

Leela and I used to go for walks in our neighborhood during evenings and weekends. During one such stroll, in March 1991, I noticed that she was struggling to keep pace with me. She also looked tired. She had an annual checkup scheduled at her gynecologist the following week. During the checkup, a mass was found in her ovary, suspiciously cancerous. In two days, she had an operation at the Leland Hospital. To my family's horror, in the frozen biopsy, done on the spot during the surgery, it was found that she had an ovarian cancer, which had spread in her abdomen.

Leela underwent aggressive chemotherapy at Johns Hopkins University Hospital. For a while there was remission, which gave us some hope. Eventually as the cancer spread, more surgeries were done. Sadly, it was a losing battle.

It was during the remission we had the wedding of Tony in Pune. Even as she fought for her life, Leela was fully involved in planning the wedding. She participated in all functions, and enjoyed the wedding, probably knowing that she might not live to attend another wedding in the family.

The four years my wife battled cancer were the most difficult period of my life. My children and I were heartbroken. For more than three decades in the medical profession, I had operated upon at least a thousand patients and seen people die. But I was not prepared to see my partner and the mother of my children suffer and slowly embrace death. This one was different.

Even while she suffered, Leela was a pillar of strength for me. She would constantly tell me: "Everything will be alright with the children, and everything will be alright with you." She always kept a little smile all the time, and never complained. I could not fathom how she could be so strong and optimistic even when she knew that the disease had already spread, and death was near.

In 1996, my father passed away when Leela was at Johns Hopkins, where plates were inserted to strengthen her spines, which were affected by cancer. She was in tremendous pain after the surgery. But having noticed my melancholic face, she asked me, "Why do you look so sad?"

Having lived together for thirty years, she knew me well. I told her that my father had just died.

Leela's mother had visited her and stayed with us for almost two months, and she left a few weeks prior to Leela's death. My mother-in-law grieved for her daughter till her death in 2011. Leela's father had died in 1983,

As Leela's end neared, we went to our attorney to write her will. I told her that I would not want to accompany her for the meeting with the attorney, and she was free to do whatever she wanted to do. In the will, she left all future family decisions to me. She distributed her jewelry and properties to the three children.

In the last few months of her life, Leela was so sick that she could not walk up the stairs. So we moved her bed to the ground floor of our home. She could barely breathe, as her lungs were full of metastasis. She had an oxygen cylinder with her. When she went to the bathroom, she never bothered us, even though we told her that she should call any one of us. The only thing she would ask for was some chocolates or sweets to keep in her mouth. She could not eat well. In her final days, we took her to the nearby Suburban Hospital. Leela left us on September 25, 1996. She was fifty-four.

Just before Leela's death, I had called a prominent Jain priest, Gurudev Chitrabhanuji, who was close to my father-in-law. He lived mostly in Mumbai, where he had a big following, but would come to the US a couple of times a year. During visits to the Washington area, he stayed at our home a few times. I asked the priest what I should do, as she was going to die soon. He said, "Navin, I never advised this to anybody, but I am telling you. She is a great soul and a loving person. So let her die in a peaceful way. You don't have to do any last-minute mantras (prayers or chants)."

Leela was a pure and clean soul. So we didn't do anything, except for a memorial event at the NIH building just outside of Washington, DC, which was a solemn occasion. All family members and friends who were there were silent with teary eyes.

Condolences from friends and family members poured in from all corners of the world, and Indian American newspapers wrote glowing obituaries. Aziz Haniffa, who had known Leela for more than a decade, wrote in the *India Abroad*:

> A diminutive lady whose unassuming charm and ever-pleasant demeanor belied the painful struggle she underwent fighting the cancer that in the past had all but consumed both her lungs. Leela Shah always shunned limelight but was always there for the underdog, the poor and the homeless...
>
> She was also indefatigable in her efforts to alleviate the lot of India's villagers and was also instrumental in convincing her husband for the past two years to conduct a free prostate cancer screening clinic in Maryland.
>
> Consequently, she touched many lives and bearing ample testimony to this were the several hundred people from all walks of life who packed the Assembly Hall of the National Institutes of Health on September 29 for her memorial service.

Aziz quoted a family friend, Daksha Patel, as saying: "Leela Shah's legacy will be that of a strong family who has lived the last thirty years under the guidance of her firm, steady, and always loving hand. Throughout her fight with cancer, that had never wavered."

I could not have said it any better or more eloquently than Aziz and Daksha.

In a way, I was a little relieved that Leela died because that meant all her suffering came to an end. In fact, I used to pray to God to take her as she could hardly breathe. But I was devastated. Initially I thought that she was around at home. But it took me three to four years to realize that she was no more. After her death, during my annual visits to Pune, I would remember her activities in my home and her reverence for my parents.

In 2020, in the aftermath the COVID-19 onset, and twenty-four years after Leela's death, my daughter Sonali and her husband Praveen launched a philanthropic drive to honor Leela. The Leela Fund was created to donate to various charitable organizations. Sonali told me, "I decided to name the fund after my mother because she played a big role in shaping my view of what is important."

Sonali recalls her mother's passion for helping others: "She was a very giving person, not just to her family and friends, but also to people she did not know. I remember her throwing a *mehndi* party for a Pakistani girl who was getting married but had no family in the US. She opened her home to this girl, who we had only recently met, and her friends for a pre-wedding party with henna artists, food, and music. Mom also wanted to help those that she had never met, in the US and India. I remember visiting an orphanage in Poona, the city where we lived before coming to the US, a few times to donate clothes and education materials. In the US, she regularly donated clothes to homeless shelters. I especially remember one day sitting with her when she was sick, both of us reading. She saw an article in a newspaper about a free eye surgery by a nonprofit foundation ran by Jain nuns in Rajgiri, in Bihar, for curing blindness in India, and she immediately asked my father to make a donation to this organization, which he did. While mom donated to various causes, the one I think she most believed in was girls' education. In Poona, she was one of the few women of her time who drove [a car]. She had a college education. Although she never worked outside the home and the Sanghvi factory, she was the reason behind my dad's success. She handled all of the household bills and repairs, mine and my siblings' education, and later helped out in my dad's office."

Leela and I had been married for thirty years. And it is almost twenty-five years since Leela's death, and still my children and I feel that her blessings are with us on a continual basis. Since her death, many friends have told me to consider remarrying. But I've never been attracted to anyone else.

CHAPTER 8

A SPIRITUAL ODYSSEY

Jainism has always been a part of my identity. As a toddler, I watched my parents pray in our small single room in a chawl every morning and evening. Born into a family of devout Jains, I naturally adopted the Jain way of life. It started with following what Bhai and Bun did and listening to stories about Lord Mahavir and other spiritual guides of Jainism from my parents. My formal introduction to the Jain *dharma* occurred around the age of four, when I started going with Bhai and Bun to the neighborhood temple in Poona Camp.

The temple, two blocks from home, was one of the first social spaces in the Camp that captured my imagination. The serenity and the tranquility of the temple was in stark contrast to the world outside, which was always busy and bustling. If I could pinpoint one place where my lifelong spiritual quest began, it was that temple.

Two-thirds of the year, the temple was manned by a single *pujari* (temple keeper), a Gujarati. He performed daily *pujas* (worship rituals) and took care of the *murtis* (marble and metal statues of gods), washing them with milk and water, applying saffron and sandalwood paste, and adorning them with flowers. During monsoon season, lasting roughly four months, two or more priests were present. Each priest, known as *maharaj*, preached sermons on Jainism at the temple and stayed in a building near the temple called *Upashray*.

At age eight, I began attending the Jain school, the *pathshala*, across from the temple. Classes were from 7:00 to 8:00 p.m. The teacher, affiliated with the temple, was well-versed in scriptures. At the pathshala, I learned the basic Jain scriptures.

Even before enrolling at the pathshala, I started observing some main tenets of Jainism. Around age ten, I began fasting on the eighth or the fourteenth days of the lunar month. On those days, I could not eat anything, even vegetables. Harming any living organism is against Jainism. We never ate onion or potatoes, as they were grown underground, and believed to be containing more living organisms.

Once a year, I observed *Paryushana*, during which Jains fast for eight days. I fasted on the first and eighth days. On the eighth day, I sat in prayers, along with other Jains, from three to four hours, asking for pardon for all wrongs and sins I committed in the previous twelve months. As is the tradition, I verbally sought forgiveness from all family members and friends, saying, "Please forgive me if I have hurt you by my mind, speech, or action."

Like every Jain kid, I celebrated Diwali with my family. The Festival of Lights is sacred for Jains, considered the night Mahavir, the twenty-fourth Tirthankara, achieved nirvana (liberation of the soul). Tirthankaras, the "liberated souls," are spiritual guides of Jains, and Mahavir was the last. Diwali was the biggest festival in the neighborhood, dominated by Jains and Hindus who celebrated it. At home, we lit *diyas* (earthen oil lamps) and distributed and ate sweets. Everyone wore new clothes and exchanged gifts. Since school was closed, I had no pressure to study or do homework during the Diwali and New Year holidays.

In the eight-and-a-half+ decades of my life (five spent in the US), I have followed my faith. I cannot remember a day when I did not pray. Daily, I seek blessings and ask for success and good health for myself and my family, and I pray that no harm is done by me to my patients. I pray for success and guidance prior to all surgery procedures.

In the first two decades of my life, my religion was uncomplicated. I followed Jainism in letter and spirit, just as my parents and generations of forefathers had. For me, Jainism was about right knowledge, right faith, right conduct; about death, rebirth, *karma* (actions), and *moksha* (liberation). I did not ask myself why I was doing what I was doing; did not reflect on whether mine was the *only* right path, or if there were any *other* faiths that could also lead to the right path. Jains respect all faiths and opinions.

Later in life, I began grappling with many questions related to my existence, death, and afterlife. I pondered, *Does God exist? If He does, is He an all-powerful God? Who controls our life? Why is there so much suffering and poverty around in this world? Why do some people live comfortably while others have a miserable existence?*

As a result, in recent decades, my attitude toward spirituality and belief in God evolved considerably. I now feel that each life is affected by one's past and present behaviors (karma), and not controlled by God. I may be right, wrong, or both.

Core of Jainism

Jainism is considered the oldest religion in the world. Jain followers believe that the Jain *dharma*, faith, is as old as eternity, having no beginning or end, and was originally established by its first *Tirthankara* (liberated soul who conquered the cycle of life, death, and rebirth), Adinath. In its present form, Jainism dates back to Lord Mahavir, the last Tirthankara. Mahavir was born in 599 BCE, thirty-six years before the birth of Lord Buddha. At the age of thirty, after the death of his parents, Lord Mahavir (similar to Lord Buddha) abandoned his princely privileges to meditate and live life as an ascetic. Though insulted and sometimes physically assaulted, Mahavir bore everything patiently.

Twelve years later, on the banks of the Rijuwalika River, under a sail tree, in the midst of deep meditation, he became enlightened. Mahavir knew what he had come to earth to seek. He preached Jainism and traveled through most of the country. At age seventy-two, he attained *nirvana*.

Jainism teaches that worldly and bodily sorrows and happiness in this life are determined by one's actions of past lives (karma), and it offers an escape from a continuing cycle of life, death, and rebirth. At the core of Jainism are principles of *ahimsa, anakantavada, aparigraha,* and asceticism. Ahimsa is the state of absolute nonviolence (against all forms of violence). Physical violence and violence of the mind and words must be renounced. *Anakantavada,* which roughly means "many-sidedness," is tolerance of and respect for other faiths and opinions. *Aparigraha,* or non-possession, means not having an attachment to worldly possessions or sensual pleasures. By living a moral life based on the principles mentioned above, one can be rid of all karma and attain *moksha* (liberation).

Jains are encouraged to seek enlightenment—a greater level of awareness that detaches one from selfish love of anyone, including parents, spouse, and children (love all unselfishly). Of course, this is difficult to achieve.

Taken together, Jain tenets are plain: lead a simple life, do not harm others, be truthful, and do not be obsessed with the accumulation of wealth and worldly possessions, which doesn't mean that you give up all the money or embrace poverty and destitution.

A Pep Talk from a Niece

From 1977 to 2018, I regularly visited Pune at least once a year to meet members of my family and the Sanghvi family. Relatives from the city and neighboring regions, including six nephews and nieces as well as friends, routinely came to see me during my stays there. My sister Aruna stayed at our apartment during my visits. In February 2010, after visiting Delhi and Mumbai, I flew into Pune.

One of the relatives who came to see me was Aruna's daughter Supriya, a religious person in her early forties. She and I had engaging conversations on Jainism on a few occasions. She was familiar with the various medical education and health care projects that I was promoting in India.

On this visit, the moment she I arrived, I figured Supriya had an important matter to discuss with me. She began, "*Mama* (maternal uncle), you are in your seventies now, and you are still working hard. You routinely meet the prime minister, the health minister, and other high-ranking officials. These are all very good initiatives."

Then she threw a question at me, "But have you thought about doing something on your salvation?"

Supriya suggested that I had been paying more attention to worldly matters than my soul, spirit, and salvation. Considering my age (seventy-five), she said I might want to undertake some important *jatras*, or pilgrimages, to ancient Jain shrines to worship, pray, and meditate. I did not argue with Supriya. She was making a genuine point out of concern for me. I simply told her that I would carry out her wishes soon. My niece's words struck me, and stuck with me. On the flight back to Washington, I thought more about her pep talk. *Did I move away from my religious roots? Is my social and voluntary work, mostly in the medical field, causing me to disregard my faith?*

Many observant Jains go to jatras almost every year. During my childhood, I had gone on a few pilgrimages. I remember my visit to an historic Jain holy site near Vadnagar, in Gujarat, where my Uncle Rajaram, a cousin of my mother and an Ayurvedic doctor, had a house. He took me to a nearby hill temple of Taranga.

I now realized that I had not been to jatras since coming to the US. I had visited local Jain temples in Pune and other cities during more than thirty trips to India, but I had not gone for any jatra for nearly forty years.

Once back home, I spoke to my son Amit and asked him to spend a couple of weeks accompanying me on a few jatras. As an emergency physician, Amit had a busy schedule, but he agreed to travel with me to India in October. In the next few months, my nephews, Hemant (son of Aruna) and Bharat (my brother Vinod's son), both based in Pune, who would join us on the journey, went to work, choosing the places to visit and finalizing the itinerary. We would visit Jain temples in Gujarat and Rajasthan. We would begin our jatra at Palitana, in the Saurashtra Peninsula, and end at Ranakpur in Rajasthan—a roughly 315-mile journey—and also cover Hastagiri, Mahudi, and Abuji. This route allowed us to visit five important temples in less than a week. The roads in the region were also relatively good.

Most jatras are physically demanding, as they require climbing mountains since many Jain pilgrimage centers are on mountaintops. The more you walk and climb, you forget yourself and think of God. You leave it to God to help you reach the temple. So prior to the trip, for several weeks, I prepared spiritually and physically (spending more time in the gym).

When I reached Pune, Supriya and other members of the family were overjoyed. It was the first time I was visiting India for jatras. The four of us set off on our journey on October 25, 2010, via Mumbai. The newly built Pune-Mumbai Highway made the first leg of the trip swift and comfortable. By noon we were at the Mumbai airport to catch a 2:00 p.m. flight to Bhavnagar, Gujarat.

The Mumbai airport looked like a massive bazaar with hordes of passengers zigzagging in every direction with only a few gates for multiple flights. From jam-packed and chaotic gates, passengers were bused to the waiting aircraft. The flight was full. We reached Bhavnagar two hours later.

A Pilgrimage After Four Decades

At the Bhavnagar airport, our local host, Jasiben Jobalia, had arranged a driver who welcomed us with bottles of cold water. Our first destination was Kanji Swami Jain Center in Songhad, an hour away. There we met a Jain scholar who made a brief presentation about the center, followed by discussions on Jainism at my request. I wanted us to familiarize ourselves with basic philosophy, principles, and practices of the religion before embarking on the jatras.

The next morning, we headed to the Shatrunjaya Hills in Palitana. Some 1,300 beautifully carved marble temples are located on these hills. More than 3,700 steps over three miles led to the shrines. Before the climb, we prayed at the base temple, where we were mobbed by a horde of helpers, male and female, who offered to hold our bags (containing clothes worn during worship) and carry us from the base to the top in chairs (*dolly*), each lifted by two men. Laborers have been serving pilgrims and earning their livelihood for generations in this manner.

We were not keen to be carried to the top of the hill, but we were unable to short circuit this mob. We ended up hiring an eighteen-year-old woman named Kanchan. Her father and an uncle carried people to the hilltop in dolly for a living. She said they had not had a single customer in five days. She told us she had three small brothers and sisters, and the family would starve if we did not help them. Kanchan asked for 100 rupees (roughly $2.20) for carrying our small bag to the top and back.

We had been advised by our host to climb slowly and steadily without taking breaks. By starting early, we covered the distance to the top in an hour and fifteen minutes, as heat makes the climb more difficult after 9:00 a.m. Puja at the main temple in Palitana involved cleaning and worshipping the *murthi,* the marble and metal statue of one of the twenty-four Tirthankaras.

While chatting with Kanchan during the climb, I learned that she had never been to school and could not read or write. She could count money, but that was all she knew. For six years, she had followed the same routine: arriving every day at the base of the Shatrunjaya Hills at 5:00 a.m. to find a customer to help up the hill and be done for the day by 4:00 p.m. Kanchan was a good guide and a strong climber.

Each time I felt a little tired, I asked her how far the temple was. She always replied, "It's very near now."

Kanchan told me about her family. Her father and uncle had been carrying pilgrims (usually the old, disabled, or obese) for thirty years. She felt sorry for her father as he was getting old, and it was difficult for him. They worked hard eight months of the year. The temple was closed during the four-month monsoon season.

I advised Kanchan to learn to read and write from her younger brother and sister, who were attending school. She promised she would try to learn some basic reading and writing during the next monsoon season.

Upon reaching the top, before heading to the main temple, another 100 steps away, we bathed with hot water and changed in anticipation of the puja and *aarti*. Aarti, performed after puja and prayers, involved singing hymns, accompanied by the ringing of bells. The most auspicious hymn, "Namo Arihantanam," is sung by Jains daily to offer reverence to souls already liberated and those pursuing the path of liberation.

Clad in worship clothes, *dhoti* (bottom) and *khes* (top), we reached the ancient temple of Adinath where he preached his first sermon and later attained nirvana. His son Bharat built the first temple in his father's honor there. Adinath's statue sits in the lotus position. Exquisitely carved pillars, domes, arches, doors, and statues of Tirthankaras and deities adorn the massive temple. I found it difficult to imagine how such a colossal marble temple was built on top of a mountain so long ago, how laborers carried such massive marble stones from quarries hundreds of miles away. The delicate, intricate, and elaborate carvings depicted excellence of human imagination and craftsmanship.

The dates we visited Palitana worked in our favor, as it was off season. Rather than just a few minutes for aarti and puja, we had the place to ourselves for two hours. But the heat made descending from the hilltop at 1:00 p.m. tiring. We consumed water generously. As we came down, Kanchan told me she would start learning to read and write from her brother and sister right away. Her eyes lit up when I gave her Rs. 400, four times the amount she had asked for.

She said with a big smile: *"Aawjo!"* (Goodbye and come back!)

After Palitana, we headed to the Hastagiri temple on the banks of the Shatrunjaya river, about 24 miles away, along a narrow winding mountain road. This temple was also built by Bharat to commemorate his father's nirvana. A paved road led from the base to the top. Near the ancient temple, a magnificent new marble shrine spread across more than a hundred thousand square feet was under construction.

On day three of our pilgrimage, we headed north to the Ghantakarn temple in Mahudi. The six-hour drive was comfortable as our car was air-conditioned and had plenty of leg room. On the way, we stopped for lunch at a restaurant in Ahmedabad, the state capital. A fixed four-course meal (*thali*) was served in sequence by multiple servers. We enjoyed a gastronomic treat with fast service and a variety of dishes for $4 each.

When we arrived in Mahudi, we prayed to Ghantakarn, one of fifty-two protector deities in Jainism. Jains flock to this temple with the belief that wishes will come true if you offer prayers to Ghantakarn. After prayers, we were served with freshly made sweets.

Our last stop in Gujarat was two hours away, a temple dedicated to Ambamataji, also where prayers make wishes come true. More than 2,000 people were waiting in a single line with barricades on both sides. I felt a little uncomfortable at first in such a large crowd, nonetheless I waited patiently for my moment before Ambamataji. At aarti time, bells rang, singers chanted prayers, and a band played religious music. Overall, an exhilarating experience.

In Rajasthan

The next destination was Mount Abu, in Rajasthan, 30 miles away. The journey, via a mountainous road known in India as *ghat*, was frightening. The road was narrow, steep, and curvaceous. Large trucks passed both ways. But our experienced driver, Ahmad, masterfully negotiated the way to the top. I prayed silently and frequently during the harrowing ride. I wondered whether these rough, scary journeys to holy sites are a way to make us God-fearing! We reached our hotel at 10:00 p.m.

The renowned, exquisitely carved Dilwara temples outside Mount Abu, a hill town in Rajasthan along the state's border with Gujarat, was our plan for day four. The five temples were each constructed during different periods with stunning and flawless designs. It is difficult to realize how human hands could have created such magnificently sculptured beauties in marble. Truly a miracle!

We performed a puja and prayed in a tranquil atmosphere that really felt divinely blessed. While visiting sacred shrines, Jains have to take a hot shower before a puja, and they do not eat while at a temple of God. You don't think about yourself, but about the soul.

We visited the magnificent Achalghad temple, two-and-a-half miles from the Dilwara temples, and built 2,100 years ago in a walled fort. The 1,404-foot climb was tiring in the afternoon sun, and we took an hour to reach the top. The temple had four statues of Adinath made of amalgamated metals (gold, silver, brass, and copper), each weighing twenty-six tons. Eighteen other metal idols of Tirthankaras are in the temple. Again I wondered how such massive statues were made and installed at that height so long ago. Only with heavenly help could mere mortals achieve such a remarkable feat!

After lunch we left Abu for Ranakpur on a one-lane road with heavy traffic: camel carts, colorful camel riders, and many three-wheeled auto-rickshaws. Each vehicle had about eight passengers. It looked unsafe to me, but the passengers looked at ease. We arrived at the Ranakpur temple before evening aarti worship time. The temple was lit with oil lamps. Bells were ringing, and prayers were being chanted by pilgrims. With peace and happiness, we left the temple for our hotel, to return the following morning.

The next morning, we were greeted by hordes of monkeys at the temple, which has a beautiful story behind it. The temple had appeared in the dreams of a nobleman called Dharanasha, as a celestial spaceship called *Nalinigulum Dev Viman*. After sharing his dream with a priest, he contacted many architects. Most laughed at the idea of building a temple from a dream. But he found an architect who created the dream temple on paper with 1,444 pillars, covering 80,000 square feet area. The center of the main temple has four six-foot-tall idols of Adinath, facing four different directions. An amazing aspect of the architecture was that one can look at Adinath's statue from any place in the temple without obstruction by any of the pillars. The priest who gave us a detailed tour was an eighteenth-generation descendent of the first temple priest!

Ranakpur was the last temple we visited during the jatra. We flew back to Mumbai from Udaipur, three hours away. In Mumbai, we stayed at JW Marriott on the beach in Juhu, a northern suburb, and spent the next day meeting with friends and relatives.

The last call I made, just before departure home to Washington, was to Supriya. I thanked her for encouraging me to go on the pilgrimage.

She said, "It was in your destiny. I was simply a reason."

On the flight home, I felt jubilant and happy. Before we left for India, in spite of all the homework and preparations, I was quite apprehensive and not sure of what to expect. But now at the end of the trip, I had a feeling of fulfilment. In the journey of life, we are all pilgrims.

A Pilgrimage to Bihar

My first pilgrimage in more than four decades brought an unusual calmness to my life and made me aware of the final destination of my present life. It may be death and nothing beyond, or a rebirth based on the karma collected over multiple past lives. Thoughts of that final destination of the present sojourn stimulated me to undertake another pilgrimage. Now I wanted to visit Bihar and Jharkhand, home to some of the most sacred temples in Jainism. Two millenniums ago, the region (then known as Magadha) was one of the richest and most-religious kingdoms in the entire Indian subcontinent.

In mid-November 2011, I reached Delhi. As usual, I had scheduled meetings with several health ministry officials to discuss the health-related initiatives I was promoting in India. Then I headed to Patna, a ninety-minute plane ride. Bihar is the birthplace and site of the nirvana of two of the most renowned religious leaders who lived in the fifth and sixth century BCE, Mahavir and Buddha. Both of these enlightened masters concurrently preached and meditated more or less in the same region of Bihar (the Rajgir and Nalanda areas) for many years.

Mahavir taught the ancient Jainism, which had been followed by Parshvanath, the twenty-third Tirthankara, some 250 years earlier. Buddha initiated his dharma for the first time, which was known after his death as Buddhism. Though many principles, philosophies, and practices of Jainism and Buddhism have similarities, each is a distinct faith. During the same time of Mahavir and Buddha, philosophers like Plato (in Greece) and Confucius (in China) also lived and taught and delivered spiritual messages.

Present-day Patna is a large and densely populated city. Congested roads and roundabouts slow traffic to a snail's pace. But more than 2,500 years ago, Patna (then Pataliputra) was the crown jewel among the cities of India.

From Patna, I took a taxi to Rajgir. The 55-mile ride on the national highway took three hours. The road had only two lanes, so only one vehicle could travel in one direction. Fortunately, most drivers on the road had remarkable driving skills and judgment. Large, heavy cargo trucks moved within a few inches from other vehicles. Many stranded and stationary vehicles, bullock carts, three wheelers, animals, and horse buggies, not to mention human beings, shared the road. Unmistakable signs of absolute poverty lined both sides of the road, with mounds of rotting garbage, stagnated dirty water cesspools, and huts where families dwelled.

In Rajgir, I visited Veerayatan, a large Jain institution. Spread across 60 acres, it has ninety-room living facilities; a museum, temple, hospital, and an outpatient clinic; and well-kept green grounds, administered by the *sadhvis* (nuns). The center's property and activities appeared efficiently managed. The center had been providing medical help at no cost or at minimal cost for forty years. The eye department, with seven ophthalmologists on staff, had carried out a quarter million eye surgeries. In addition, the institution provided Jain education, spiritual development, and modern education to poor students of Bihar by constructing and operating schools and colleges.

We visited an ancient Jain temple, where Munisuvrath, the twentieth Tirthankara, attained enlightenment. Nearby a Buddhist temple on the top of a hill had cable car access provided by a Japanese Buddhist group. Thousands of Jains and Buddhists travel to this area from all over the world for annual pilgrimages but sadly, at the moment, Rajgir is a small, congested city with negligible facilities for pilgrims and tourists.

I was lucky to have Sadhvi Shubhamji of Veerayatan accompanying me in my travels in the region. She taught me a lot about local history and geography, Jainism, and Buddhism. Having studied Jain scriptures for decades, she has preached and traveled around the world, spreading the teachings of Mahavir, in addition to humanitarian work for the region's downtrodden folks at Veerayatan's health facilities. Her calm, rational, and eloquent answers to my multiple queries about Jainism and Buddhism helped me understand the preaching and practices of Mahavir and Buddha and their relevance in the contemporary world.

On the way back to Veerayatan, I visited a *mela* (village fair). People in colorful garments were arriving on overcrowded trains, buses, three wheelers, and horse buggies. The trains, buses, and jeeps had passengers all over—inside, outside, and on the roof. No safety precautions. I found it rather scary to watch.

The next day, we traveled by car to Nalanda, less than 10 kilometers from Rajgir. Mahavir spent three monsoons preaching Jainism and in meditation at Nalanda. Buddha had an even a longer presence there, establishing a monastery where he meditated and preached for years. After Buddha's death, educational and monastery activities continued for centuries.

Later we traveled by car to Pavapuri, roughly 20 kilometers to where Mahavir delivered his first and, later, his last sermon. He breathed his last while delivering the sermon, which lasted twenty-four hours. A prince by birth, Mahavir lived a royal life for thirty years, then spent twelve years in the forest and mountains meditating and performing penance. He attained enlightenment at age forty-two on the bank of the Rijubalika River. For the next thirty years, he traveled on foot all over the subcontinent, including Sindh, Kandahar, and Taxila to preach Jainism, before attaining *nirvana* at age seventy-two. Jains believe Mahavir had twenty-six previous lives. He left his physical body on a dark, moonless night. His followers celebrated his *nirvana* by lighting lamps. According to Jain tradition, this was the origin of Diwali, the Festival of Lights.

After we had a night's rest at Veerayatan and enjoying a fresh hot breakfast, we left for Sametshikhar, also known as

Shikharji and Mount Parshvanath, in the neighboring state of Jharkhand. The five-hour bumpy car ride included 26 miles on mountain roads. Shikharji is located in Madhuban, a small, crowded, and congested town with *dharamsalas* (inns), temples, and shops. Traffic on the narrow roads is a nightmare with large tourist buses, cars, bullock carts, horse buggies, and people carrying dolly. We saw many pilgrims including, one *sangh* (a group sponsored by a wealthy person providing travel and food for invitees) of 960 persons who arrived by train from Mumbai, and another from Jaipur with 263 persons.

We stayed at a hotel with air-conditioning, but there was an outage of electricity. At 3:00 a.m., I took a quick cold-water bath and reached the base temple of Bhomiyaji for prayers for a successful trip. With twenty of twenty-four Tirthankaras cremated on these mountains, it is considered the most auspicious and pious place of pilgrimage for Jains. The mountain, at 4,479 feet above sea level, is steep, nearly six miles long, with twenty-four gods on top.

I started the climb at 4:30 a.m. by flashlight. Most of the 100+ climbers carried long canes for support. Some elderly and obese pilgrims were being carried on a dolly. After the first mile, I felt tired, but kept on. Around 6:00 a.m., the sun rose. Slowly and steadily, I kept climbing. At the halfway point, I just stood for about five minutes and had some water. I was told not to sit and rest as it would make the climb more difficult to resume. The dolly carriers kept asking me to allow them to carry me. With extreme poverty in the area, these carriers' livelihoods depended on the pilgrims. I felt bad and had tears when I saw four malnourished men, with large varicose veins in their skinny legs, carrying a 250-pound lady who was happily conversing on a cellphone. On the way up were multiple stalls selling foods, fruits, and drinks. I prayed and climbed slowly and steadily. I was sweating and tired. After two hours and thirty minutes, I reached the top.

Sadhvi Shubhamji guided me to all twenty shrines. After praying in the main temple of Jal Mandir, we had some food and water. The climb was exhausting, but on top of the mountain, the atmosphere was serene and infused me with a feeling of calm and happiness—a spiritually gratifying experience. Once again, just as I did after the previous pilgrimage in Gujarat and Rajasthan, I thought deeply about life, living practices, and life's final destination. I felt extremely fortunate to be standing on the sacred soil where twenty enlightened Jain masters attained their nirvana. I headed toward the base with this unique sense of fulfillment. On the way I saw leftover food, paper and plastic bags, water bottles, and other kinds of trash all around the holy site. This special place had no restroom facilities—no organized or structured facilities available for the pilgrims. I wondered why no one cared to keep such an auspicious site clean and welcoming.

I descended by crisscrossing to slow my speed. Heat made the descent difficult. Profuse sweating and thirst made me drink almost two bottles of water. The joy of descent increased as the distance to the base decreased. Finally, at 2:30 p.m., I reached the base. Almost ten hours of arduous journey! Sadhvi Shubhamji accompanied me to Bhomiyaji temple for prayers for a successful journey. I prayed with tremendous gratitude.

Back to the hotel by 4:00 p.m., I was lucky to have a hot bath, which almost rejuvenated me. Another five-hour journey took us back to Rajgir. I enjoyed a full night's sleep in an air-conditioned room at Veerayatan. During the entire stay and travel, communication was efficient as almost all involved (drivers, servants, and others) had personal cellphones.

The next day I met with Acharya Chandanaji for discussion on Jainism and ask her opinions on Jain shrines and the pilgrimage. A scholar and authority on Jainism, she made it simple for me to understand the meaning of the present life and its destination. Her forty years of service for the poor in all aspects (social, educational, medical, and spiritual) reminded me of Mother Teresa. In spite of meritorious achievements and superb expertise on Jainism, she was humble and pragmatic. Her message, simply put, is that our sacred duty (*dharma*) is to live and work happily and help those in need with love and respect, without any expectations and rewards. According to her, physical and mental work and meditation are needed for all, including priests and nuns, to live a holy life.

Her enthusiasm to modernize the present hospital, especially the eye department, impressed me a lot. I met with seven staff ophthalmologists to discuss their needs to upgrade the services. They decided they would like to have some prominent US ophthalmologists visit Veerayatan for a short period of time to augment the expertise, facilities, and services. I offered them my help in locating interested US ophthalmologists. I also made a modest contribution to the eye department. Just a few months prior to her death, Leela had read in a newspaper that these nuns were providing medical help for poor blind people. She asked me to send a donation to Veerayatan. And I did.

After the doctors' meeting, it was time to go back to Patna to catch a flight to New Delhi, and home to Washington, DC. This was the fastest and most-valuable five days of my life. I gained knowledge of Jainism and Buddhism from both

Chandanaji and Shubhamji. Feeling overwhelmed I would require some time to comprehend it all. With gratitude to all on staff, I bid a loving farewell to Veerayatan.

Varanasi Beckons

The next city on my list was Varanasi, also known as Kashi since time immemorial, and home to some of the holiest places for Hindus, Jains, and Buddhist. A divine habitat of many gods, the city is also known as the religious capital of India.

In 2014, while planning my annual trip to India, I contacted my great-nephew Yash Shah, son of Hemant, then a student at the Indian Institute of Technology Varanasi, part of the Banaras Hindu University (BHU). He made all arrangements for my visit, including hiring guides in the city. Yash scheduled meetings with BHU professors of history, religion, and archaeology, as well as experts in culture and commerce.

After staying in Delhi for a few days for my health projects, I took the hour-long flight to Varanasi on December 6. Since my activities and meetings were around BHU, I stayed at a hotel near the university. The next day by 6:00 a.m., we set out on a boat ride on the Ganga River (Ganges), along the renowned Ghats, a five-mile-long stretch where stone steps descend to the waters from the street at several locations. The panoramic view of some eighty-four temples, from the river, is a greatly uplifting experience.

According to legend, Varanasi dates back to the god Shiva's life on Earth, many thousands of years ago. Archaeology experts have evidence of human habitation in the area since 1800 BCE. Varanasi was the capital of Kashi. Both names are used interchangeably, referring to the city. Hinduism, Buddhism, and Jainism prospered in unison in Kashi. Some locals believe Jesus Christ had visited Kashi.

The Ganga is revered as a mother in India. The sacred river originates in the Himalayas, passes through four major states and finally flows into the Bay of Bengal, touching the lives of some 200 million people on its journey. During a 6:00 a.m. boat ride, we saw a spectacular bright-red sunrise in the cloudless blue sky. The river water was full of dirt, plastic bags, wooden pieces, food, fruits, flowers, small oil lamps, and more. On the banks, many were bathing, washing clothes and praying. Boat operators negotiated with pilgrims for a ride. The ghats, built by various kings and religious heads over the last 3,000 years, are stairsteps from the street level to the riverbank. I walked on different ghats as the guide detailed the history of dozens of Hindu, Buddhist, and Jain temples. The architectures of ghats and temples create a magnificent façade on the long riverbank.

Over the next two days, I met with a number of experts, including BHU professors and learned a lot about Varanasi, its past and present. In the evening, during sunset, we went back to the ghats for a Ganga aarti (worship of Mother Ganga) with drums, lamps, music, and priests chanting mantras. Hundreds of people were participating on the steps of the ghats, and hundreds more joined in boats. We sat on the top deck of a large boat to get a clear view of the vigorous, hour-long ceremony.

On the following day, we visited temples of four Jain Tirthankaras who were born in the Varanasi area and Sarnath, all within a two-hour car ride from the city. In Sarnath, we saw an ancient stupa built in 300 BCE by Emperor Ashoka, a devout Buddhist. The Sarnath area temples, stupas, and monasteries are quite clean compared to many other Indian cities. During the entire visit, I found local people to be happy and friendly. Most of them had a good knowledge of Varanasi's history, philosophy, and religion, and felt fortunate to live in the holy city.

Mount Girnar

In January 2014, I was scheduled to lead a US delegation to a conference on Emergency Medical Services and Trauma Care in Ahmadabad, Gujarat. While planning the first jatra in 2010, Amit and I had considered visiting Girnar Mount to pray at the temple of Neminath, the twenty-second Tirthankara. Girnar is in the Saurashtra region, where we kicked off that pilgrimage. We had only a week to travel to as far north as Ranakpur in Rajasthan, so we decided to skip it. But Girnar was in my mind. So when the Ahmadabad conference was scheduled, I decided to make use of the opportunity and visit Girnar. The two nephews who accompanied me in 2010, Hemant and Bharat, traveled with me to Girnar.

I had a meeting with then-Gujarat Chief Minister Narendra Modi related to my India health projects on the last day of the conference. After the meeting, he casually asked me about the rest of my schedule in Gujarat. I told him that I was planning to leave for Girnar the next day to visit Jain temples. Modi suggested that, since I was in the area, I should also visit Sasan, the Gir National Park and Wildlife Sanctuary, a two-hour car ride from Girnar. So after consulting with Hemant and Bharat, I decided to add that to our itinerary.

The next day, the three of us left Ahmadabad for Junagadh, the nearest town from Girnar. After an almost eight-hour drive, we reached Junagadh just before dinner. The next day, we set out at 5:00 a.m. Mount Girnar, with many Jain and Hindu temples, has a volcanic origin and five peaks that are at least 3,600 feet above sea level. We started on a two-mile long, steep climb of 9,000 steps to reach various temples on the mountains. After two hours of climbing, covering 4,000 steps, we reached the main Jain temple dedicated to Neminath, the twenty-second Thirthankara. Hundreds of pilgrims were there.

The magnificent main Jain temple of black granite stone was built between 1128 and 1159 C.E. The carvings and architecture are awesome—a massive structure with intricate sculptures built on such a steep mountain and at such a height!

Neminath, born as Arishtanemi, was a prince in the Gujarat region. On his wedding day, he saw a large number of wailing animals in a fenced area. On enquiry, he learned that the animals were going to be slaughtered for his wedding feast. Pained with the planned killings of the animals, Arishtanemi liberated the caged animals and abandoned his wedding. Later, he left his kingdom and traveled to Mount Girnar to become a Jain monk. He attained enlightenment after praying and meditating for fifty-four days on Mount Girnar.

He traveled all over India for many years, preaching Jainism. He taught the practice of nonviolence, truth, detachment from worldly possessions and bodily pleasures, equanimity, respect for all religions and views, charity, and compassion. After many years of travel and teaching, he returned to Mount Girnar where he attained nirvana.

After the climb, we had a traditional hot bath and changed into worship attire. Jain worship is done by touching the idol of Tirthankara with saffron and sandalwood paste and offering flowers. When I touched the ancient statue of Neminath for puja, I felt content and tranquil. After the worship, we prayed and meditated in the temple for blessings. Later on, we climbed further to reach other temples for puja and prayers. Amazingly after so much steep climbing in the hot sun, I had minimal feelings of tiredness or exhaustion.

While descending, I again contemplated life, living, and its final destination. With the sense of divinity, elation, and accomplishment, we reached the base and enjoyed a delicious freshly prepared late lunch.

Lion Safari

The next day, we left Junagadh at 6:00 a.m. and reached the Sasan Gir safari area by 8:00 a.m. Sasan is an entry point of the national park and sanctuary. The forest covers 7,488 square miles. The terrain of mountains and forests is mainly of volcanic origin. The large Shetrunji River runs in its midst. The forest, which has some 300 water points, is home to thirty-six species of mammals, 300 species of birds and thirty-seven species of reptiles—the only place in India where one can see lions in their natural habitats. There are also leopards, deer, crocodiles, lizards, cobras, and many varieties of small and large birds like eagles, woodpeckers, peacocks, and parakeets.

The safari started at 9:00 a.m., with eight jeeps, each with its own guide. An adventurous ride lasted four hours. We saw two large male lions, one resting and the other yawning with a wide, open mouth. Within a few feet of the lions, we stopped the vehicles to take photographs. The lions didn't bother to look at us at all. Nobody in any of the jeeps had any arms for protection. We saw a number of beautiful spotted deer moving in groups in the vicinity of the lions. Further down, we saw antelopes, sambar deer, peacocks, and other rare birds and animals up close.

Animals in their natural habitat looked comfortable despite the presence of the jeeps and tourists. In the jungle, we saw many settlements of a tribe called Maldharis, who have been living in the region for centuries, raising livestock. This fearless group lives and moves around the forest with ease and carries just a long stick for their protection.

The Mount Girnar area showed us a completely peaceful coexistence of trees, birds, animals, humans, and gods too! The philosophy of "live and let live" is very much alive and flourishing in these mountains and forests. The Gujarat government must be complimented for making available multiple tourist facilities to worship gods, enjoy the flora and fauna, and see animals in their natural habitat. This visit was a reminder of an elementary fact that we often forget that humans are part of nature.

The Gir visit inspired me to undertake another safari, in another corner of the world. Once back home, I shared my experiences with my children. My daughter Sonali, who has two boys, was especially interested in hearing the stories. I suggested that we plan a South African safari, along with the boys: Armaan (eleven) and Ishaan (nine). The next year during their summer break, we traveled to Johannesburg for a seven-day safari to the Kruger National Park, a sanctuary named after Paul Kruger, a former South African president who created the park in 1889 to protect wildlife.

Almost fourteen times the size of Gir National Park with much better infrastructure, in terms of access roads and hotels Kruger had the "big five" animals (lion, leopard, elephant, buffalo and rhino), as well as cheetah, giraffe, zebra, antelope, kudu, hyena, jackal, baboons, monkeys, waterbuck, impala, and nyala. Many mammals, birds, and reptiles lived there. Both grandsons enjoyed the safari. They learned to spot animals and named them correctly. Sonali photographed as many animals as she could.

If you may wonder why I am writing about a pleasure trip with grandchildren while discussing my spiritual journey, here is why: The safari was witnessing life in its rawest form and we were absorbing some of the lessons of the animal world. In the forest, life is challenging and survival of the fittest is the norm. From the birth only about 50 percent of cubs of lions, leopards, and cheetahs survive. The cubs are killed by other large males or other animals. The lions and leopards are territorial and control their territory ferociously. Many times, fights between males result in injuries and death. The zebras, rhinos, elephants, impalas, wild beasts, buffalos, and hippos have to move and eat vegetation and grass to survive from the same area. The food resource is the same.

I noticed a remarkable difference between humans and wild animals. I saw lions and leopards sleeping in bushes near rocks. I saw no different standards of living; there is equality in that the animals eat, live, and sleep in the same area and same surroundings. Humans and wild animals are similar in some ways, as power, strength, and tactics decide their survival; but living for humans and wildlife differs drastically.

For thousands of years the wildlife has survived, but humans have been continuously encroaching their space. We kill them for sport and for meat, skin, horns, tusks, or other body parts to sell and make money. It is shameful that wildlife poachers are still in abundance.

The Ganga and the Nile: A Tale of Two Rivers

Thousands of years ago, two ancient civilizations existed, one on the banks of the Ganga in India, and the other on the banks of the Nile in Egypt. These two mighty rivers nestled human habitation along their banks mainly by providing water and facilitating agriculture and transportation. Both civilizations flourished in different manners, but they also had spiritual dimensions, with God, soul, life, death, and afterlife at the center.

Two trips I made within a three-month period revealed to me great truths about people who lived some 4,000 to 7,000 years ago in two different cultures and continents. The first was in December 2014, to Varanasi on the banks of Ganga, and the second was in February 2015 to Cairo, Alexandria, and Luxor on the Nile, with my daughter Sonali and her two sons, Armaan and Ishaan.

For millenniums, both these societies shared the way they saw life and God; they invoked natural elements, in the form of a multitudes of gods and goddesses and deities who symbolized all these aspects of life. Ganga and the Nile were worshipped as goddesses and mothers.

Even their rituals of worship had many similarities despite the geographical and cultural differences. People of the Nile and the Ganga bowed down to the Supreme Power to gain favor as well as to seek forgiveness for wrongs done. Their mythologies are varied and rich in their scope and content, reflecting the importance they gave to nature and environment, human values, and truths.

Temples in both civilizations contained one main deity and several other deities, each honored in ceremonial rituals that invoked their powers and blessings. The statues installed in temples were "brought to life" with a consecration ritual. The priest in charge of the temple cleaned and decorated the deities daily and performed multiple rituals. The priest's religious authority was sovereign as a messenger of God.

Devotees made offerings of food, fruit, and other items. They similarly celebrated many festivals by feasting, singing, and dancing in praise of God. Rulers, who projected themselves as specially sent by God, had special temples and rituals. Sometimes kings portrayed themselves as small gods. Kings and queens prayed to God for enrichment and pleasure in the present life and sought a straight passage to heaven. All this was common in both cultures some 3,000 years ago, when travel to distant lands was rather impossible.

However, when it came to philosophy of life, death, and afterlife, the two peoples could not have been more different. Indians believed in phases of life: education and apprenticeship, followed by family and worldly life, then partial detachment to focus on the soul, God and religion, and the last years of life to achieve nirvana or a better rebirth in the next life. The cycle of birth, life, death, and rebirth is based on karma. Once all karma is done, the soul receives freedom from the cycle and achieves a status of pure soul. At death, the physical body is cremated to ashes. The Indic practice and philosophy of detachment from worldly, material life and bodily pleasures to attain a better life after death were completely different from the Egyptian pleasurable and royal lifestyle before and after death.

God

Over the decades, I was fortunate to visit many countries, including places where sophisticated civilizations existed for millenniums. While many trips were for professional reasons or in pursuit of hobbies, some were spiritual journeys. I went to Jerusalem where I visited the Western Wall, and the Al-Aqsa Mosque. In Rome, I visited the Vatican. During these trips, I had opportunities to interact with religious and spiritual leaders from different faiths, in addition to visiting their holy places.

I am fascinated by the religious sites, whether it is Jain, or Hindu, Christian, Muslim, or Jew, and I like to study other faiths in an academic manner. During previous India trips, I took short courses on Jainism at the University of Pune where I learned most of what I know about my religion. After that course, I studied other religions, mainly Hinduism, Buddhism, Christianity, Islam, and Judaism, in lesser detail. I grew up in a neighborhood where all these faiths coexisted and was surrounded with a lot of friends from different religions. We did not just tolerate each other's religion, we respected it.

One of my closest friends was Bashir Shaikh, a Muslim. Whenever I went to his house, Bashir's mom cooked vegetarian food for me. She knew I did not eat meat. Another friend, Jerri, a talented soccer player, went on to become a priest after he found his calling from Christ. My classmate Abid, a Bora Muslim; and Datta Dhamdhere, a Brahmin; and others of different religions supported me. My biggest supporter to date has been my friend Arun, a Hindu, and his parents, C.M. Patel and Chandanben. Growing up in such a milieu, it was impossible not to respect other faiths.

I undertook these journeys because I wanted to explore the meaning of life, afterlife, and other faiths. The other reason I visited various religious centers is to try and find answer to some of the questions that have troubled me, in fact, troubled much of humanity for a long time. Among them, "Does God exist?" "What is the meaning of life?" "What happens after death?" Minds more brilliant than mine have tried to decipher the mystery of life and death. To us, life and death are understood, but God, the afterlife situation, and living life are still a mystery to me. So are heaven and hell. Though I met with leading religious scholars, including priests and rabbis, to better understand the religious philosophies and practices of their respective faiths, I still do not have satisfactory answers to the questions that I set out to answer.

Does God exist? Do we believe in God because we fear pain, failure, sorrow, and death? Do we worship God because we think that faith in God will consequently bring blessings, which can alleviate pain and fears? Why does God seem to be so unfair—or indifferent—to the enormous numbers of humans throughout the world who are poor and suffering? Perhaps the truth will remain unknown to each of us till we leave this earth.

I know that I am grateful to be a Jain, to have followed a gentle faith that supports efforts to help others, do good, be kind, do no harm, remain nonviolent, and respect all others and their faith. And I like the idea of being fully liberated from the cycles of birth, death, and rebirth in a world that is so full of pain and suffering.

~

About the Author

Navin C. Shah, MD, MS, FACS, FICS, FACIP, is board certified in Urology and Quality Assurance and Utilization Review Physicians. He is medical education director at Mid Atlantic Urology Associates, and CEO of the American Professional Exchange Association.

Born in Maharashtra, India, he received his MBBS and Master of Surgery at the University of Poona (now Pune). He served as Assistant Professor of Surgery at B.J. Medical College and Sassoon General Hospital, Poona. He came to the US in 1971 and completed urology residency at Washington Hospital Center in DC.

As a founder of American Association of Physicians of Indian origin (AAPI) and the International Association of American Physicians (IAAP), he fought for justice for international medical graduates and initiated multiple health projects, with the help of Indian American physicians, to improve medical education and healthcare in India. He served in leadership roles at Doctors Community Hospital and the Maryland State Medical Society, published twenty papers in medical journals, and was a book reviewer for *JAMA* (*Journal of American Medical Association*).

Dr. Shah's was awarded *India Abroad*'s Person of the Year, *India Tribune's* Gandhi Award, AAPI and American College of International Physicians awards, among many others. His lifelong efforts to help others and promote justice are informed by his Jain faith.

For over forty-five years, Dr. Shah has been in urology practice in the Washington, DC, area. His current focus is on early detection and treatment of prostate cancer. He lives in Potomac, Maryland.